YOU,
TOO,
CAN
CANOE

YOU, TOO, CAN CANOE

THE COMPLETE BOOK OF RIVER CANOEING

By John H. Foshee

THE STRODE PUBLISHERS, INC.
HUNTSVILLE, ALABAMA 35802

Preface

Learning to canoe is a cumulative experience. You see a paddler do something here, you watch another one there, you ask questions and read books, but mostly you paddle and practice and persist.

If you're like me, then somewhere along the way you'll realize that there's really no one paddle stroke or maneuver or idea or technique or way that makes the difference between the dubber and the paddler who knows what he's doing! It's putting your experience and knowledge together into cohesive and useful practice. And just as much, it's all the little odds and ends of esoteric information that you have gradually assimilated, the time-saving and labor-saving ways of doing things that do so much to make a better, smoother canoe trip, the things that might well be called the practical mechanics of river canoeing.

And that's the reason for this book, to assemble into one handy and truly useful volume not only the basic techniques and maneuvers and paddle strokes of river canoeing but also many of those other 1,001 things that prove to be often important and always useful to know.

This book is *not* a magic carpet to the world of professional-level whitewater running. No canoeing book is. It is not intended to equip you to try out for the Olympics; to run the Colorado River backwards (or forwards); or to win friends, fame, or trophies through a masterful display of canoeing skills that brings you into the fore at every wildwater race you enter. What it *is* intended to do is give you the practical aspects of basic river running as performed by that vast throng of canoeists whose basic goal is to get safely down a stretch of river containing shoals and rapids without smashing up a valuable canoe and to have fun while they're doing it.

These skills, of course, will not be *given* to you by this book. But, if you study and practice its preaching, if you go out often enough, get wet enough and fall out of your boat enough, you will absorb something other than water if only you profit by your mistakes.

Like any other sport, canoeing looks simple when it's being done by a skillful paddler. Yet, like any sport, canoeing demands instruction and training and many hours of practice before you can really enjoy it to its fullest. Remember, there is no substitute for a good teacher. Although this book will help you immensely, you'll learn faster if, in conjunction with it, you affiliate yourself with some local river-running canoe club that offers training, take that training, and then get out and conscientiously practice what you've been taught. What you'll find in this book is the way things are really done out on the river—possibly not always the way they *should* be done, but the way a lot of the real world does them a lot of the time. Other canoeists may have their own methods and techniques and may not always agree with everything I say. Nevertheless, I think that basically we'll still be striving for the same goals of better, more skillful, and safer canoeing.

If you're already a lake canoeist, then remember some of what you know but also try to forget a lot of it. Don't say "Well, that's not the way we did it up at Camp Tishi-wishi-washi." The old camp's lake techniques were probably great for their intended purpose, but you're about to enter another world where many things are done differently—so expect it.

Above all, don't get grim about all this: learn and practice, yes; and never be complacent or overconfident of your abilities, but don't attack the process of river canoeing with a do-or-die attitude. As far as I'm concerned the whole idea of recreational canoeing is just that—recreation. To have your skills challenged perhaps; to get tired, wet, and muddy quite possibly; but to *have fun* doing it all *is* the heart of the sport of canoeing.

And now—good paddling and happy river trails to all of you!

Introduction

Probably the hardest part of writing an "instruction" book on canoeing is trying to organize it. The goal is to present information so that it's clear and understandable and so that each bit of "how to" builds on the one preceding it. Unfortunately, many of the various aspects of canoeing are so totally inter-related that I was often hard pressed to decide what preceded what and where some things most aptly fit! So, whether I have accomplished my goal or not is an answer only *you* can give.

I have divided this handbook into four basic sections in what I fondly hope is an orderly, logical, and useful form.

Part I is general stuff intended to get you started on your way to the river. Some of it is concerned with transporting your canoe and understanding "canoe talk," but most of it is the all-important equipment selection. In this equipment selection I have not examined every choice available. What I have done is first told you what you need, and secondly, given you enough facts to enable you to ask intelligent questions about the most-used and favored types of this equipment currently on the market. From this you can form your own opinion of what's best for you. I feel that this is a better way to do it for what *I* like—you may not.

Part II gets you out on the river and into specifics. Getting the most out of your paddle for the effort you expend and maneuvering the canoe—sideways, forward, backwards, in circles, whatever is necessary—are gone over here. This is the part of the book that many of you may read first, it's the meat of river canoeing, and I've tried to be as specific as possible on exactly how to do the various techniques. Paddling a canoe is like many other things (playing a piano, for example). First you learn the way it's *supposed* to be done, then once you know the correct way, you can put your own little twists into it. But—it's important to know the correct and generally accepted way *first*, and that's what you'll find in the various chapters of this section.

River running is fun but it sometimes claims a toll for the pleasure. Part III delves into this. There are hazards on the river and there are hazards in the weather which require safety all the time and rescue some of the time. Repairs are necessary, too—no canoe goes down a rocky river for very long without requiring them to one degree or another.

And, while getting the canoe down the river is certainly the most critical part of any canoe ride, trips do begin and end somewhere on the shoreline, and you thus get into the sometimes mystifying and complicated intricacies of running a trip, whether it's one canoe or a flotilla of them.

In the various appendices you'll find other things that were a little dry to put in the main body of the book but were too important to even consider leaving out completely. There's more basic safety in them and more specifics about things mentioned in the bulk of the book.

When entering a strange land it's helpful to speak the language. Although all canoeing shares a basic terminology, each aspect of it has its own particular words and meanings. River canoeing is no exception. There are many specific terms related to it that you will find used quite often. You will also *hear* these terms used among canoeists. While it's not really vital to know the correct names or descriptions for everything, understanding them *will* make the explanations in this book easier to follow, will familiarize you with your basic equipment, and help you when communicating with other canoeists. It also makes you *sound* like you know what you're talking about even if you don't! In an appendix of this book, therefore, I have included a glossary of terms. It defines in brief form all of the words and expressions that you may find puzzling (or most of them—I probably missed a few). Use this glossary often—that's what it's there for. You'll find more complete explanations of many of the terms in various places in this book.

I have really made no effort to present an encyclopedia of canoeing or to cover every little contingency or nuance of the sport that could conceivably pop up out on the river. I *have* made a great effort to include all the necessaries. I have also made an equally great effort to include the practicalities of canoeing, the little often-neglected things that do so much to simplify the whole sport. All in all I've tried to give you what you need to know to have the most fun with the least work in the safest manner in the world of the river. I hope I've succeeded for most of you but, as I said, only *you* can vouch for that!

Oh yes, one final word. Lest I be accused of rank chauvinism, let me assure any female readers that the terms bow*man* and stern*man* used so consistently throughout this book may also be read bow*person,* stern*woman*, or any other way you care to read it. It's simply that I'm a lazy writer, and *man* has only three letters while even *lady* has four!

See You On The River!

DEDICATED TO MY WIFE MARTA WHO HAS
PATIENTLY SUFFERED THROUGH ANOTHER
BOOK; TO ALL THE PADDLERS WHO TAUGHT
ME MUCH OF WHAT I KNOW; AND TO ALL
THOSE THOUSANDS OF BEGINNING CANOEISTS
JUST ENTERING THE WORLD OF THE RIVER.

Contents

PART III: SAFETY, RESCUE, REPAIR, AND LOGISTICS

PART I
The Basics

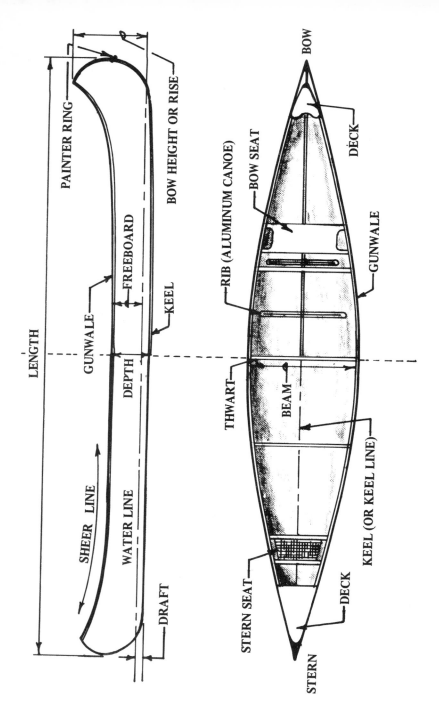

The parts of a canoe.

CHAPTER 1
THE SELECTION OF A CANOE

A basic fact of canoeing is that one cannot canoe without a canoe. Your canoe then will be the most important purchase that you'll have to make. As it will also be your single biggest investment, its selection deserves some thought and study. That's what this chapter is about.

THE ANATOMY OF A CANOE

Before we begin, it might be a good idea to look at the illustration of a typical canoe. All open canoes are basically the same insofar as the names of their parts are concerned. Some canoes may not have some of these parts (keels, for example) or they may be built-in so that they appear not to exist (ribs as another example). Because of manufacturing processes other facets may also be deleted, but despite the various idiosyncrasies of material and manufacturer, the basic canoe part names still apply.

The drawings shows a sort of composite 17-foot canoe plus a few common modifications. These parts will be referred to not only here in this discussion of canoe selection but also throughout the rest of the book as we go into the various phases of *using* this canoe we're about to select!

THE BIG QUESTION

"What kind of canoe do I buy?" is probably the most-asked question by the beginning canoeist. It also appears to be the hardest to answer partly because of all the possibilities of material and design available but primarily because the beginning canoeist has little working knowledge of what he really wants or needs.

Canoes are built in many lengths, widths, depths, weights, styles, stem heights, materials, load capacities, keel types—a veritable forest of choice in which the novice is liable to become lost. About the only thing they all have in common is that they are called canoes, are all more or less the same shape, and fall into a general range and relationship of size and weight that distinguishes them from most power boats.

Fortunately, the first big decision in the selection of a canoe is how is it to be used. I say "fortunately" because determination of the boat's major usage is usually pretty easy, and this will immediately eliminate many canoes from consideration.

In anyone else's canoe-selection guide this would probably be the moment to begin enumerating the mitigating conditions of usage as directly related to real life canoes and your own personal purchase of one. Not here—because I believe you can make your choice more intelligently if you know some of the very basic factors of the canoe itself that will affect that decision.

TYPES OF CANOES

"Canoes" may be *very* broadly classified into "cruising" and "special-purpose" canoes. The major groups within these rather crude boundaries are outlined as follows. Bear in mind that manufactufers tend to place labels like "downriver," "racing," "cruising," etc., on many of their boats but that *their* ideas of these classes may not exactly agree with yours. Too, small differences in hull design may make big differences in handling characteristics, but these differences are hard to detect on the display floor!

Cruising or Pleasure

This is the great, general class of canoe—the one that the public means when they say, "Look—there goes a canoe!" These boats are usually considered to be open-topped, with a keel, and designed for general-purpose use. They may have certain characteristics that make them somewhat more suitable for one use or another, but they are essentially multi-purpose boats.

There is probably more of this type canoe made than any other. As a result there is a great choice available of design, price, and material. It's this cruising type of canoe that most canoeists start with and keep throughout their career and one of the two classes that you are most likely to buy for your river running.

16

Whitewater or River

This is a rather general class in which some cruising and some racing canoes also fit. Whitewater boats are generally designed for more strength, more maneuverability, and less likelihood of swamping than most of the standard open cruising canoes.

Their maneuverability is enhanced by building them with no keel or a shallow, flat "shoe" or "whitewater" keel. Some are also slightly rockered (bowed fore and aft), which makes them pivot more easily. A higher bow and stern (usually) and more depth help them resist swamping. Aluminum versions are usually strengthened by having extra ribs.

Whitewater canoes *are* river running canoes. They are the other class of boat that you are most likely to buy.

Racing, Downriver, Slalom

Of these three types, the downriver may also be thought of as a whitewater boat or the other way around. In pure designs, however, these three are considered to be built either for speed (downriver or racing) or maneuverability (slalom) under competitive conditions, which may or may not include whitewater.

Downriver or racing canoes may be permanently decked (C1 type), open, or open with temporary spray decks. They are designed to get you there in a hurry in a relatively straight line. Consequently, they often sacrifice maneuverability and some stability to gain speed. Characteristically these boats are longer, narrower, and lighter weight than "cruising" canoes; low at bow and stern to cut down wind drag and wind effect; and with a keel or keel line to make them track better.

Slalom canoes are usually decked (again the C1 type), although there are a few open slalom canoes on the market. Slalom boats are built for maneuverability and sacrifice straight-line speed to obtain it. They are usually short, keel-less and rockered.

C1 Canoes

These decked boats are fast, maneuverable and tricky. They are built in slalom or downriver versions for the uses

17

described above.

Except for the cockpit the boat is pretty well filled with two inflatable airbags (one bow, one stern) that provide flotation, reduce water load if the boat swamps, and effectively prevent your carrying much more than lunch and canteen.

C1's are paddled from a kneeling position with a single-ended canoe paddle, and the paddler wears a spray skirt to seal between his waist and the cockpit ring. This type of canoe is also made in a C2 (two-man) and a C3 (three-man or two men and cargo) version. They *are* whitewater canoes but are better left to the more expert paddlers.

Square Sterns

Square-stern canoes look pretty much like any other cruising canoe that's had its stern chopped off and a flat back installed to keep the water out. They are built for use with a small motor but can also be paddled. With a paddle they handle like a double-ended canoe until the time comes to back up or do some maneuver involving backing such as a back ferry. The square stern then offers a lot of resistance to the water and makes for hard work and less control. Another real minus factor to the river canoeist is that most square sterns have flotation built in under the rear seat. This prevents your feet going under the seat and effectively blocks a well-braced paddling position.

Freight or Council Canoes

These are large, heavy, broad, high-capacity canoes used for carrying many people or large loads. They are definitely not one- or two-man river-running boats.

WHAT'S AVAILABLE?

Most modern-day canoes are built of one of four basic materials: wood and canvas, aluminum, fiberglass (or a version of it), or plastic (ABS or PVC). Each has its advantages and disadvantages.

Most of them are built in a good range of lengths, but there is a predominance of available models in a few lengths in each type of construction. It's these most commonly available models that I'll discuss in this chapter. The chart shows the general range presently available.

	Overall Range	Most Designs	Cruising
Aluminum	10'-20'	15'-16'-17'	15'-17'
Fiberglass	10'-20'	14'-18'	16'-17'
ABS	11'-17'	15'-16'-17'	15'-16'-17'

	Whitewater	Lightweight
Aluminum	15'-17'	13'-15'-17'
Fiberglass	16'-17'-18'	10'-11' (See Note 2)
ABS	15'-16'-17'-	----- (See Notes 3 & 4)

1.   Most of these canoes are available in approximate 12 inch length increments.

2.   Designs are limited between 10 feet and 12 feet and over 18 feet, 6 inches.

3.   Often labeled cruising and whitewater.

4.   Designs somewhat limited on foam core construction as of this writing.

Wood and Canvas

These are the old, original canoes, real beauties and, to many people, *the* canoe. They carry a definite charisma about them unobtainable from more modern materials and are un-excelled for romantic, moonlight cruises with your girl friend. They are strong and springy, of comparable weight with many canoes of the same length/beam ratio, are quiet, and slip over *rounded* rocks with ease. Flotation is inherent—wood floats, so does the boat.

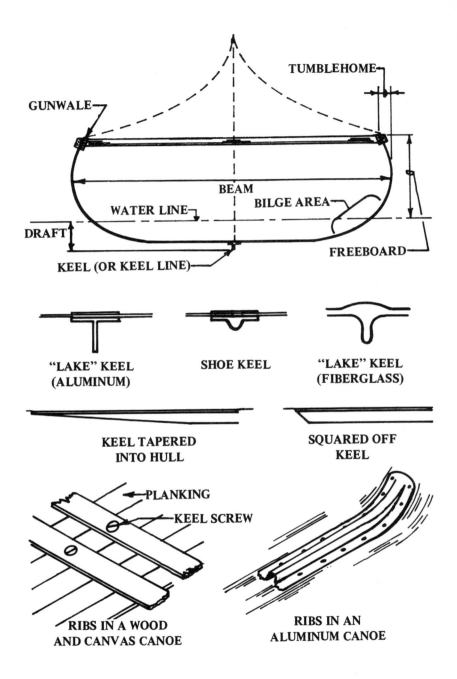

The parts of a canoe and some common modifications.

Despite their history of wilderness river usage these canoes have several drawbacks for river use in today's world. Sharp rocks gouge and tear the canvas, which is just not sufficiently abrasion-resistant for river running when compared to other materials. It takes time, but canvas *does* deteriorate and will do so more rapidly under river conditions and without proper maintenance. Periodic repainting of the canvas is necessary, not for beauty but for protection of the cloth, and each of these coats adds weight unless you strip off the old paint each time.

Replacement or repair of wooden parts is often more time consuming and painstaking than the repair of other materials. The wood, old or new, will require sanding and protective varnishing from time to time. In brief, the materials of a wood and canvas canoe will deteriorate naturally and require care and maintenance and good sheltered storage more than will any other canoe materials. I believe they are *suitable* for river running but that you could make a better selection for the shoals and rapids in the light of the *lasting* and *maintenance-free* service of other materials presently available. I will make some people mad at me, I know, but this is all the discussion I intend to have on wood and canvas canoes!

Aluminum

I would hazard a guess that at least 30 percent to 40 percent of all the canoes on the river are of aluminum. I'd probably be wrong, but there *are* a lot of them floating around.

Cuts, tears, and dents in aluminum are relatively easy to repair and the metal is tough enough and abrasion resistant enough for long, hard use. You don't have to worry about maintenance. Pull the canoe off your vehicle, hose it down if it's been in salt water, throw it out in the yard, and forget it. It won't rust or deteriorate.

On the other hand, aluminum *is* easy to dent, it's cold in the winter, hot in the summer, and noisy all the time. If it's painted, then the paint will wear off, and aluminum requires careful surface preparation to insure that the new paint will stay on. Aluminum also tends to "stick" when it slides over rocks.

21

The replacement of major parts of an aluminum canoe such as gunwales and keels is a tedious job but is sometimes necessary when a swamped canoe gets wrapped around a rock in a rapid. Aluminum canoes have been known to be ripped apart in such circumstances and a crease in the hull metal may become a crack when badly bent aluminum is straightened out. Nevertheless, aluminum is a good, sturdy choice for a river-running canoe.

The width, weight, and carrying capacity of various aluminum canoes are surprisingly standard. Almost all of them are 35 to 37 inches wide in the 15-to-18-foot range, with extremes of about 33 and 39 inches.

Carrying capacities and weights of standard cruising versions run about 650 to 750 pounds for a 14-to-15-foot canoe weighing about 69 to 75 pounds. The 16- to 17-footers will average supporting a hundred pounds more for a boat weight of 75 to 85 pounds.

Whitewater models have extra ribs, a shoe (whitewater) keel, or no keel and are made of standard weight aluminum. These models, therefore, usually weigh a few pounds more than the standard cruising canoe.

Lightweight models have additional ribs also, usually the same total number of ribs as the whitewater model of the same manufacturer. These boats run about 10 to 15 pounds less weight than the standard cruising canoe and are much less "bang resistant." I do not recommend them for river running. Both lightweight and whitewater models have carrying capacities comparable to the standard canoe.

Aluminum alloy (6061-T6), formed and heat treated, seems to be pretty standard on quality aluminum canoes. It is usually .050 inches thick, with lightweight models being of thinner material (commonly .032 to .040). Construction may be welded, riveted, or welded and riveted.

Nearly all aluminum canoes have aluminum gunwales and thwarts. Seats are usually formed aluminum or webbing stretched over an aluminum framework. Most of these craft are available with either shoe or lake keel.

Aluminum canoes obviously have no inherent flotation. Foam is usually fitted into bow and stern compartments (tanks) which are then riveted closed. Foam is also sometimes put under the seats.

A tandem 17-foot aluminum canoe.

Fiberglass

Another 30 to 40 percent of the canoes floating around on today's rivers are made of fiberglass. Again, I may be wrong, but there *are* a lot of *them* too.

Fiberglass canoes are quiet, slide over rocks easily, are maintenance-free, and very easy to repair even though repairs may be a little messy to do. Color is molded in or on, so repainting is not required except to brighten up a faded color or touch up a bad scratch.

Fiberglass boats generally run a little heavier for a given length/beam ratio than other materials. Some have little or no tumblehome and have limited depth for river-running use. Fiberglass canoes are relatively tough; however, fiberglass will only give or bend so much and then it's going to break. Pressure sufficient to bend an aluminum canoe around a rock will snap a

23

fiberglass canoe in two. A basic problem of fiberglass canoes is that they're cheap and easy to build and are thus a natural for the "fly-by-night" company. My suggestion is that you stick to well-known names and models that have been tried and proven by your canoeing acquaintances.

There are two basic ways of building a fiberglass canoe—the hand lay-up method and the blown or chopped glass method. Of these, the hand lay-up method is considered the best, giving greater and more equal strength for its weight and a more even thickness throughout the boat.

You may notice that some fiberglass canoes have a smooth inside finish; others have a rough, woven-looking interior; and still others have a sort of pebbly, matte finish similar to that often seen in fiberglass power boats. This makes little difference except that the matte finish could be a sign of a chopped glass lay-up.

Fiberglass canoes are made of epoxy or polyester resins and layers or "lay-ups" of substances called "glass," "roving," or "mat." Everybody has his own ideas of what constitutes the best resin and the best lay-up, and I couldn't tell you which *is* the best. The important thing is to get a *hand* lay-up.

Another construction is fiberglass reinforced with a material called Kevlar or a boat made of all Kevlar. This relatively new material is similar to glass cloth but has a much greater strength. Thus, a lighter boat for a given strength or greater strength for the same weight is easily achieved. At this writing, Kevlar is very expensive, and boats using it in their construction are priced correspondingly higher.

Although the widths of fiberglass canoes range from about 27 to 40 inches, most of the models designated as cruising or whitewater fall between 34 and 37 inches wide. The boats will weigh about 60 to 75 pounds in the 14-to-15-foot length and have a carrying capacity of 600 to 750 pounds. The 16 to 17 footers will weigh 60 to 90 pounds and carry 150 to 200 more pounds. Lightweight models weigh about 15 to 20 pounds less than the cruising version and have 150 to 200 less pounds carrying capacity. The width on these lightweight models runs from about 27 to 32 inches, which explains their reduced load capacity.

Fiberglass canoes may have metal (usually aluminum) or

wood thwarts and gunwales and usually molded fiberglass, cane, or webbing seats. A few have vinyl gunwales and ABS decks. They may be bought with or without keels. Some have tumblehome, and some have very low, almost flat, stems intended to *not* catch a cross wind. (This characteristic becomes a liability in heavy wave situations.)

Fiberglass has no inherent flotation, so foam is usually poured into the bow and stern compartments and sealed in with fiberglass. Some canoes also have foam under the gunwales and/or under the decks.

ABS

One of the newest materials out on the river is ABS. This cryptic symbol stands for acrylonitrile-butadiene-styrene, which doesn't matter at all but might interest you. ABS is a sort of wonder material. It dents when hit instead of breaking, it's hard to tear, it slithers over rocks like a snake, and it's very, very slippery, thus maneuverable. It's quiet, cool, almost maintenance free, and the color is molded in (or on).

Minor dents can be taken out with heat, although tears in the outer coating will tend to spread when the heat is applied. Other repairs are very easily made using much the same techniques as with fiberglass.

An 18-foot fiberglass canoe.

A foam core construction ABS canoe can be swamped and bent backwards around an obstruction until the bow and stern meet and, in most cases, the hull will not be ripped or seriously damaged! Obviously the gunwales will be bent or broken, and the thwarts, seats and other trim work may be damaged beyond repair, but the basic hull is quite likely to still be in one piece.

ABS is really the top of the line in materials as of this writing, *BUT*—do *not* run out and buy an ABS canoe on the strength of these magic letters alone. There are ABS canoes and there are ABS canoes, and what makes the difference is the construction and the way the ABS is used.

In what seems to be considered the best current construction, a one-piece, single-thickness, molded hull is made of a closed-cell foam core covered on both sides with the ABS material and that covered with an outer vinyl skin. The core supplies shape, strength, flexibility, and flotation, and the ABS and vinyl furnish a slippery, resilient, tough finish to protect the core.

A 16-foot ABS canoe paddled solo.

A 17-foot ABS canoe.

ABS canoes are remarkably uniform in width—35 to 38 inches in the 15-foot lengths, 35 to 36 inches for 16 footers, and 36 to 39 inches in the 17-foot lengths. Weights run 60 to 68 pounds for 15- to 16-foot boats and about 74 to 80 pounds in the 17-foot models. Carrying capacities are about the same as other canoes of equivalent length/beam ratio.

Gunwales and thwarts may be metal (usually aluminum), wood, or vinyl but are usually metal or wood. Seats are commonly of formed ABS or woven cane. Most ABS canoes of this construction have no visible ribs and no keel; they are one smooth finish inside and out.

Plastic (PVC)

Hulls of a single thickness of molded or formed plastic are what I consider in this group. These are generally cheaply priced boats and, although I have had little personal experience with them, what I have heard and seen leads me to believe that the quality of many of the boats is commensurate with their price. I could be wrong and there may be some good ones out; however, my main objection to them is that I have the feeling that they would tend to be somewhat brittle rather than flexible.

KIT BOATS AND PLANS

Many kits for canoes are available as are numerous canoe plans. Both kits and plans usually fall into one of the following four types of construction:

Fiberglass—preformed sections that you put together with fiberglass tape and resin. Usually flexible and thin-hulled.

Stringer and canvas—long wood strips (stringers) bent over and attached to a series of wooden ribs, covered with stretched canvas and painted. The canvas is sometimes also covered with a layer of fiberglass cloth. They are light and graceful but puncture very easily.

Plywood—a wood framework covered with 1/8-, 3/16- or 1/4-inch plywood. Sometimes also covered with canvas, which is sometimes layered with fiberglass. More puncture resistant than the stringer type. Usually unstable because of the impossibility of bending plywood into a real "canoe"-shaped bottom without elaborate and expensive equipment (such as a factory)!

Wood strip—built of edge-glued wood strips formed over temporary ribs. The strips are usually covered with fiberglass. These boats may be heavy or light, strong or weak, depending on the woods used and the care and skill involved. They are a lot of work but can be very strong, beautiful, and lightweight boats.

You might find it interesting and fun to build one of these canoes, but don't do it with the idea of using the finished product for your river running. The single exception would be the wood-strip construction, and even there I would reserve the construction and the use of this canoe for a time when you are a more accomplished and skilled river canoeist.

KEELS

The type of keel on your canoe will make a lot of difference in the way it handles. Basically canoes may have a lake keel (also called a standard or cruising keel); a shoe, river, or whitewater keel (all the same thing), or no keel at all.

Not all choices can be had with all canoes, however, as material and manufacturer dictate' what is available in a specific boat. In general, aluminum canoes will have either a lake or shoe keel, fiberglass canoes will have a lake keel or no keel, and ABS canoes (foam-core type) will have none. To divide further, most canoes designated as "cruising" or "pleasure" will have a lake keel on them, and those called "whitewater" or "river running" will have either no keel or a shoe keel.

Lake Keels

Lake keels usually protrude down below the boat from 1/2 to 3/4 inch and extend completely along the "flat" portion of the length of the canoe. They may cut off sharply at the ends or taper into the bow and stern. Keels make a canoe track better and make it easier to handle in a cross wind by resisting the "skidding" effect of the wind. By the same reasoning, a keel also makes the boat harder to *maneuver* sideways, which is a disadvantage in river canoeing. The keel protruding down from the bottom may also serve as a rock catcher in shallow water.

Fiberglass canoes that have keels may have either a molded-in fiberglass keel or a metal keel as on an aluminum boat. Lake keels on aluminum boats may be either a solid extrusion or a hollow forming. Of these the solid variety generally proves to be less subject to severe damage in river use.

A lake keel is a good choice if most of your canoeing will be done on unobstructed waters in a relatively straight line and where rapid maneuvering to the side is not often needed.

Shoe Keels

A shoe keel is a compromise keel. It protrudes less than a lake keel but obviously more than no keel. It usually tapers into the boat at both ends and laterally into the hull as well. Shoe keels protrude only about 1/4 inch and are usually in the shape of a flat bar. This keel offers reduced drag in executing maneuvers to the side, reduced likelihood of snagging on a rock, and yet offers a degree of tracking stability to the canoe as well as

Standard lake or "cruising" keel.

Shoe or "whitewater" keel.

some bottom protection and strength. It is a very good keel choice for all-around use on rivers and lakes.

No Keel

A smooth-bottomed canoe, one with no keel at all, is much easier to maneuver sideways or any other way because of its lack of sideways resistance. It is also less likely to hang on a rock in a shoal or rapid as it has nothing protruding below the bottom. But, it is very hard to control in a wind, and the beginning canoeist may find it a discouraging first boat anyway because of its rapid response to the paddle and poor tracking capabilities. No-keel boats take longer to adjust to, but the additional time is worth it. For pure river-running usage in shoals and rapids this is your best choice.

Molded-in keel on a fiberglass canoe. This one happens also to have auxiliary keels.

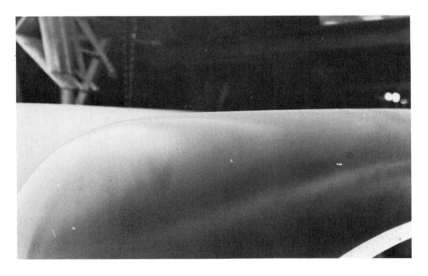

No keel at all. The ultimate in maneuverability.

31

WHAT DO *YOU* WANT?

If you've struggled through this chapter to this point it should be apparent that your range of choice for a river-running canoe has narrowed considerably. It should now be down to a factory-built, whitewater, standard-weight model with no keel or a shoe keel and made of aluminum, fiberglass, or foam-core construction ABS.

Other than keel type and material, the basic considerations in selecting a canoe are length, width, depth, bow and stern height, and load capacity. These in turn are pretty well dictated by usage, and all are completely inter-related.

Length

Your choice of canoe length should be most governed by whether your canoe is to be used solo or tandem the majority of the time. If in doubt, then buy the longer length.

Experience seems to indicate that a 15-foot boat is great for solo work or for two lightweight (up to above 150 pounds each) tandem paddlers without camping gear. A 16- or 17-foot boat is fine for tandem canoeing and for limited cruising. This length will be influenced by your size or your and your partners' size. The bigger the usual load, the longer the boat should be for a given width.

My opinion is that a canoe under 15 feet long is too small for practical river running. Despite its possible maneuverability and its probable light weight, it may not have the load capacity to give you adequate and safe freeboard. Another factor is beam—some short boats keep practically the same beam as their longer brothers, which means the short one gets a trifle "squatty," thus slower and harder to paddle. On the other hand, when the shorter boats are made narrower, they become tippier and have less load capacity. You can find canoes down to 10 feet long, 26 inches wide, weighing about 16 pounds, and with an advertised load capacity of almost 200 pounds. Do you want it? I don't know if *you* do or not—I don't.

A canoe 18 feet long or over may be great if you intend to do long-range cruising either solo or tandem and to carry a lot of gear. By long-range cruising, I don't mean a two-day trip down a local river—I refer more to a month-long trip out in the wilderness. For general weekend (or week) cruising, a 17 footer will easily carry all you need plus a buddy. *However*, an 18 footer *is* nice, if you're running pretty heavy water all the time. It will bridge some souse holes that a shorter boat won't and will have more of a tendency to ride higher because of its greater buoyancy. Its disadvantage is that its length may make it very hard to maneuver quickly.

Width and Depth

A canoe that is very narrow in relation to its length is unstable and tippy; a broad one is stable but is like paddling a barge. Usually a canoe 35 to 39 inches wide in the 15-to-17-foot range is a good choice. Depths available range from about 11 to 16 inches. River-running canoes need a little more depth because of the turbulent water they're usually in. About 12½ to 15 inches is a good choice here with the 15-inch depth giving you a little more insurance against taking on splash.

Load Capacity and Freeboard

The capacity of most canoes is given in pounds and is stamped on the boats' nameplates. Some manufacturers do not rate their boats. If you examine the capacity rating of various canoes you'll notice some peculiar differences in the advertised load capacities of boats with almost identical length and beam. Some of this can be accounted for by the shape of the bottom; specifically, how flat it is and how far the "wide" portion extends toward the bow and stern.

Any boat within the dimensions of the river-running craft that are suggested here will have adequate load capacity unless you're very big and heavy and are solo in a 15 to 16 footer or are paddling with an equally big and heavy partner in a 16 to 17 footer. The important thing is that when you're in the boat (with your partner if you normally paddle tandem) you have enough freeboard so that every little lean doesn't dip the gunwale and every little wave doesn't splash over the side.

Bow and Stern Height

This is a point disputed by some reputable canoe manufacturers, but most river canoeists of my acquaintance and most manufacturers of whitewater boats tend toward the idea that a bow and stern with some height to it does better in rapids by helping to prevent water pouring in over the bow when you dig into a standing wave. Somewhere between 22½ and 25 inches seems to be favored. I go along with this idea of a rising sheer. Too high a stem height, of course, serves as a wind catcher.

Weight of the Canoe

This is not really a tremendous problem. A lighter boat is more responsive, more fun to paddle, a lot less work to push along and easier to get into and out of the river at trip's start and end. However, lightweight canoes are likely to sacrifice some strength or rigidity for their lack of weight. A canoe that falls into the 60-to-80-pound range for a 15 to 17 footer is about right.

SOME OTHER THINGS TO LOOK FOR

There are several items to note before making your final decision. Some of these are very meaningful, some only comfort items. You can weigh their relative importance in your own mind.

First, be sure you can get your feet under the seats. Be equally sure you can get your feet *out* from under the seats. Much of your river paddling will be done on your knees with your behind nestled comfortably against the front *edge* of the seat. You don't want braces under that seat to possibly entangle your feet if you capsize. Similarly, some canoes have flotation built under one or both seats. With this arrangement there is no way to comfortably and securely brace yourself in the boat because there is no way to get your feet back behind you and achieve the desired "three-point" support.

You'll rarely find a canoe with its seats up even with the gunwale. If you do, don't buy it. Although you may not often sit on the seats, you'll have an awfully high center of gravity if you do. Look for seats well down below the gunwale and yet with room under them for your feet.

If you're thrown out of or around in a canoe you don't want any knife edges there to cut you, so run your hand along the under parts of the seats and gunwales and other turned-down edges of aluminum canoes. In some you'll find some sharp edges that are uncomfortable and dangerous. Look for rolled lips that are safe and a mark of quality, too. You may find these same sharp edges on fiberglass boats. Fiberglass can make a good cutting edge as well as inflicting you with a liberal selection of splinters.

While you're examining edges, notice the deck plate. You'll see a lot of canoes carried by the inboard edge of it or by hand holes in it or by door handles screwed to it by the canoeist. If it has hand holes or will be carried by the inboard edge, you'll find that life will be a lot more comfortable if the carrying edge or hand holes are padded or smoothly rounded in a fairly large radius. A heavy canoe digging into a paddle-weary hand at the end of a long day is just one of life's little irritations that can be avoided.

Some canoes have built-in sponsons, bulges on the outside of the hull running lengthwise of the canoe near the bilge. These air- or foam-fitted protrusions are primarily intended to increase the canoe's lateral stability. In so doing they decrease the canoe's lateral maneuverability. You don't want them. Do distinguish between sponsons (generally a bump on the *outside* of the hull, smooth inside the hull) and extra flotation (bump on the *inside* of the hull, smooth on the outside) located in this same area. The latter case is perfectly acceptable.

Some canoes also have bilge rails or what might be called extra keels along their bilge lines and sometimes on the bottom of the hull running parallel to the keel or keel line. These, too, decrease maneuverability and are unwanted on a river canoe.

BUYING A USED CANOE

Sometimes you can luck up on a good used canoe at a bargain, a bargain being defined as a canoe that meets your requirements, that's in pretty good shape, and that you can buy at a good discount from what the same canoe would cost you new. Apart from looking at it from the standpoint of all the things I've already mentioned in this chapter, here are some other things to check.

Aluminum: Dents, scrapes, gouges, holes, patches; loose, worn-down, or missing rivets; bent keel, asymmetrical gunwales (sight down it end to end for these last two items).

Fiberglass: Gouges, cracks (especially hair-line cracks) patches, holes, checked gel coat (the outer "cosmetic" layer that has the color).

ABS: Torn vinyl coating, dents, gouges, patches.

Examine any used canoe for overall appearance; for missing, broken, or bent fittings; hardware, seats, thwarts, gunwales, and decks.

Finally, check the canoe for leaks either by paddling it or by filling it with water to up above the bilges. You can check above this point by "sloshing" the water around in the canoe. One word of caution here—*never* put water in a canoe unless it's resting firmly on the ground for the length of its keel. If you fill it with water while it's bridged across sawhorses, oil drums, or anything you've come up with to put it up at a convenient height, you're likely to be buying it whether you want it or not.

Bear in mind that needed repairs need not stop you from buying the canoe. Consider the difficulty and expense of the repairs in the light of the price being asked and your own enjoyment of "tinkering." Also consider your own ideas of aesthetics; a rough-looking canoe may be perfectly serviceable.

Occasionally you'll find storm-damaged or otherwise damaged canoes that have been paid for by insurance settlements. They may be in the possession of the owner or the insurance company and may or may not be badly damaged. If you can find out about them, they usually go pretty cheaply. I

36

personally have one that I paid $35 for, and it took only $30 worth of parts (and two patches) to fix it.

FINALLY

Now it's your time to make a decision. One final factor that will affect it is what's available in your area. You'll find fiberglass the big favorite in one place and everybody out in aluminum boats in some other section of the country. ABS and Kevlar are the coming things, of course. They are your most expensive choices, but there is little doubt that they are the best materials currently available.

It may have occurred to you as you read through this chapter that there is no single canoe that will fulfill all requirements. This is quite true—there isn't. One thing to bear in mind, however, is that the river or whitewater canoe can more easily perform as a cruising canoe than the other way around. So, for an all-around, general-purpose recreational boat you'll probably be better satisfied with one designed for the river.

If you can afford to do otherwise, then never buy a new canoe on the basis of price alone. A high price does not always mean quality nor does a low price always indicate lack of it. If, in your opinion, everything else is equal, then most certainly buy the cheaper one, but base your "equal" decision on quality or on those things which *you* consider important in a canoe. After all—you're the guy (or gal) who has to paddle it!

CHAPTER 2
THE PARTS, PIECES, AND PURCHASE OF A PADDLE

GENERAL

Next to your canoe, paddles are your most important purchase. They are your motive power, sometimes your salvation, and the piece of equipment that you will use the most and expend the most effort on in your canoeing career.

PIECES AND PARTS

The drawing of the paddle should be totally self-explanatory. The only other thing you need to remember is that the upper hand is the one holding the grip of the paddle, and the lower hand is the one holding the throat.

GRIP TYPES

Paddles come with various types of grips. The one shown in the main drawing has a "tee" grip which seems to be the most favored in river running. The "tee" is comfortable and offers a large, firm handhold. With a firm hold the paddle is not so easily jerked out of your hand. You have better control of it, too, as you have more leverage for any twisting motion of the paddle you may want to do. Notice that the long dimension of the grip—the part where the palm of your hand goes—is lined up with the flat of the paddle blade. Apart from this being the logical location for the grip in standard paddling there is another, very important, reason also: you always know the position of the blade without looking at it. Later on in your river canoeing practice you'll find that this is very important. In a draw stroke, for example, you will fall right out of the boat if you try to lean on the *edge* of the blade.

Some of the other more common grips are also shown in the illustration. Generally speaking, you should avoid the very small grips—they're hard to hold and control and get uncomfortable after a long day's session with them.

Paddles are made in a variety of materials, combinations of

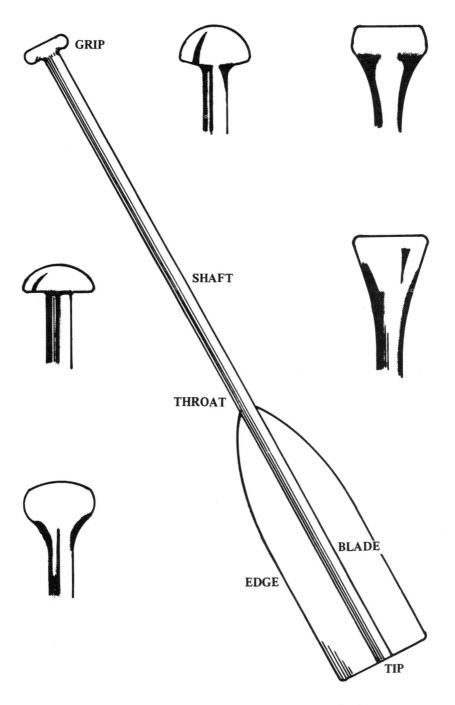

The parts of a paddle and various types of grips.

materials, methods of assembly, lengths, widths, weights, and prices. Wood or aluminum shafts; fiberglass, wood, or plastic grips; and wood, fiberglass, Kevlar, or plastic blades are the most common.

Blades come in various sizes and shapes. Some of the more common shapes are shown in the illustration. The sizes run from about 6 to 12 inches wide and 22 to 28 inches long. A 7-to-8½-inch by 20- or 22-inch blade is probably a good choice to begin with, but read on before you run out and get one.

Different paddle manufacturers have their own various combinations of sizes and shapes so, although a 7-to-8½-inch by 20- or 22-inch blade is probably a good selection to start with, your choice of size and shape will be influenced by the type of paddle construction and material you want, the price you want to pay, and where all this fits into who makes what and where you can buy it!

BLADES

Wooden Blades

Wooden blades may be one solid piece of wood, two "wings" laminated onto the shaft or numerous edge laminations. The laminations are usually glued up with waterproof glue, but at least one manufacturer puts his together with fiberglass cloth. Many of the laminated paddles are very pretty, being laid up with alternate strips of light and dark wood. The method of positioning the grain also adds strength to the blade. Most wooden blades are made of spruce, ash, cypress, cottonwood, mahogany, or, in the case of laminated blades, combinations of these. Spar varnish or polyurethane are the usual finishes.

Wood Blade and Tip Reinforcement

The tip of a paddle blade gets a lot of wear and tear and quickly gets rough and frayed. Some laminated paddles have the main blade pieces parallel to the shaft, and the tip portion laminations are laid perpendicularly to these. Other wooden blades have fiberglass-reinforced tips, either solid fiberglass laminate or

40

glass covered. Still others have the whole blade covered with fiberglass cloth. Cheap plastic blades are not usually tip reinforced, but some ABS ones are.

Fiberglass Blades

Fiberglass blades are extremely strong and wear resistant. There are two basic types of construction in both of which the shaft gradually flattens and widens as it enters the blade. In one, however, the shaft stops a few inches short of the tip and the grip. In the other the shaft continues on to the tip, then is attached to a flat metal piece inside the fiberglass. This metal piece extends all the way across the tip and up the edges of the blade. Some fiberglass blades also have an outside metal protector across the tip. This saves a lot of wear and tear on the blade. The fiberglass layups are essentially the same, but personally I favor the type with the interior metal-reinforced tip. Most fiberglass blades are solid but some have a urethane foam core (such as that used in foam-core construction ABS canoes) over which the fiberglass is laid. Kevlar, a super-strong cloth similar to fiberglass, is also now being used for blades and shafts either alone or in combination with fiberglass cloth. I have had no experience with these paddles, but they should be excellent.

ABS and Plastic Blades

ABS and plastic blades are the other choice. As for the one-piece molded plastic paddles—usually hollow—forget them. They are not the type you should even consider where any strain or reliability is to be placed on the paddle. ABS is better. Some ABS blades have foam flotation built into the blade. The only trouble I have ever found with the ABS blades are that some are too flexible even with ribs molded in. Some of these blades are sold separately and can be attached to a shaft with a screw. These do allow the advantage of being able to build your own paddle.

SHAFTS

Shafts are wood or aluminum. The aluminum shafts may

41

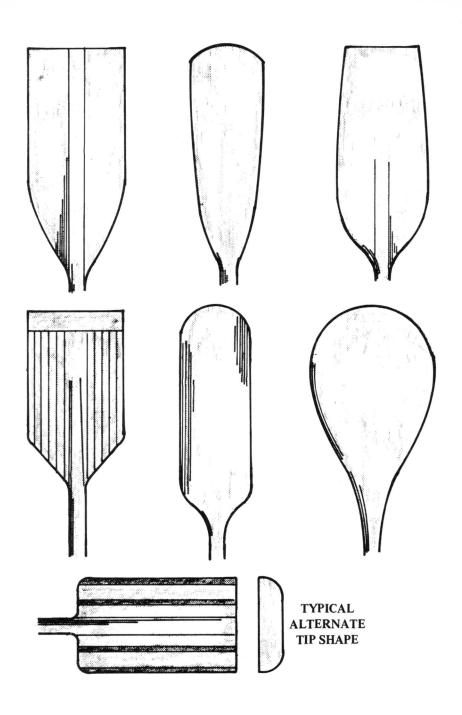

TYPICAL ALTERNATE TIP SHAPE

Various typical blade shapes.

42

be round or oval. The oval is more comfortable, I believe, and gives you still another guide to blade orientation. Some aluminum shafts are neoprene or plastic covered. This makes them more comfortable and also keeps the black aluminum oxide off your hands—for a while at least.

In the paddles with the fiberglass blades the shaft goes on down into the blade and is solidly laminated in. With ABS blades the shaft often fits in a collar and is secured with a screw, which is obviously a weaker method.

Wooden shafts are usually solid, some are laminated, and some are reinforced with fiberglass, hickory, or ash splines inset down the length of the shaft.

GRIPS

Grips are wood, plastic, ABS or aluminum. Once more, the ABS grips may be attached with a screw, the aluminum grips fiberglassed on, and the wood grip built into the shaft.

LENGTH

This is a purely personal matter. It depends on your usage of the paddle, your arm length, your paddling position, and the way the paddle "feels" to you when you use it. My suggestion is that you get a "starter" paddle about chin high. I also suggest that you start off with a relatively cheap paddle until you establish the length you really want.

Fiberglass, fiberglass and Kevlar, and the higher-priced wood paddles are available in almost any length you want. "Off the shelf," commercial paddles usually come in 6-inch increments. Any aluminum shaft paddle with a removable blade or grip can be shortened with the nearest handy hacksaw. You can also shorten wooden shafts, but it's more troublesome and you probably won't get the same strength as the original.

FEEL, WEIGHT, BALANCE—THE INTANGIBLES

There are intangible aspects to paddle buying—one being the "feel" of the paddle. If all else more or less suits you and the paddle feels right in your hand—then buy it. You'll probably not be sorry.

Paddles should not be heavy. By the time you've swung a paddle around all day you've done a lot of work and can lessen this work by getting a lighter paddle. *But*, don't sacrifice strength for lightness—try for a happy medium. Be particularly careful that aluminum shafts are thick enough to have plenty of strength.

A paddle should be well balanced when you hold it. This is another intangible factor and one that just has to be left up to your own judgment. The degree of springiness in the paddle is another thing that is purely personal. "Spring" is the flexibility of a paddle, the amount of "give" that you feel when paddling with it. This flexing, so some say, gives you a little extra kick at the end of a stroke as the paddle whips itself straight. By comparison with most wooden paddles, an aluminum shaft-fiberglass blade combination just simply isn't very springy. In the wooden shafts and blades, "spring" is desirable to some, not so to others.

PRICE

Good paddles do not come cheap. So, in addition to starting off with a "cheapie" because of paddle length, do it also because of breakage. You *will* break and lose paddles—more at first than later, and it hurts a lot less to see two halves of a cheap paddle floating down the river! Good paddles, of course, are stronger and won't break as easily.

FINALLY

Now—after all this discussion—what do you buy? I have no definite answer, because a paddle is really a personal thing. The wooden paddles are pretty, and, for what it's worth, they're warmer to the touch in winter. You can find those that are light, well balanced, and strong. A really good wooden paddle will cost you as much as a fiberglass one. They have the disadvantages of being less abrasion resistant, requiring more maintenance, and usually being weaker. They have the advantage of "spring" and the incalculable, purely personal aura of the old wooden paddle.

About chin high, a good beginning length for a paddle.

Fiberglass paddles are usually a little heavier and less springy but stronger, maintenance free, and very abrasion resistant. They are a very good choice for river running *after* you're more skilled and you know what blade width and paddle length you want.

Bear in mind that a narrow blade (5½ inches wide for example) doesn't push much water around but is not too much of a strain to use. On the other hand, a wide paddle, say 10 to 12 inches, will really move the canoe but takes a lot of energy to do it, and blades of these widths take a lot of getting used to. Somewhere in between—around 7 to 8½ inches—will probably prove to be a good choice. For now, buy a few cheap paddles and get out and paddle. Try your own, use other people's— experiment with length and blade widths and materials. Don't be in any hurry to order your own "custom-sized" paddle— you'll find your tastes will change as you learn more.

CHAPTER 3
YOUR LIFE JACKET

Your life jacket is the most important piece of personal safety equipment that you have. You should *always* have it with you; more importantly, you should always wear it if there is the slightest possibility that you may need it. This is presupposing that you can swim; if you can't then wear it *all* the time.

ACCESSIBILITY

Life jackets are intended to hold *you* up, so they don't do much good stuffed under the seat at the other end of the canoe. If you haven't got it on, keep it near you where you can quickly grab it. Don't tie it in the boat or tie it around itself in a compact wad that takes minutes to undo. Keep it loose and open, unzipped, unbuckled, or untied, as the case may be, and see that it's adjusted to your body *before* you get in the boat the first time. The best life jacket in the world will do you no good at all unless it's on your body or, as a *very* poor second, clutched in your desperate hand!

DON'T EXPECT MIRACLES

Your life jacket is not a magic carpet to safety or even to easy breathing when you're plummeting through rough water. I once heard a canoeist remark that there was something wrong with his life jacket. Inquiring, I discovered that he had an idea that it would keep his body completely *out* of the water from the waist up. It was a real shock to him when he sank chest deep!

And you will. Life jackets have different designs and different amounts of flotation, but none of them will sit on top of the water with you in it. You're going to go under and bob back up and be neck and chin deep most of the time. In waves you'll ride up, then probably cut through the crest which gives you a face full of water; as you plunge back into the trough you'll get another face full.

Your life jacket won't do you much good in frothy water

47

Three types of PFDs—the yoke or "horse collar," a short vest type with large pads, and a larger jacket with vertical tubes.

either. There's just simply too much air and not enough water to support you. You'll sink nearly as much as you would without the jacket.

But—a jacket will hold you up somewhat, and they do furnish additional flotation that may be vital. If you're unconscious, then they'll keep your face out of the water, and they'll even roll you over to a face-up position if you have the kind you should have and if you're wearing it.

KINDS OF JACKETS

There are five basic kinds of personal flotation devices (or PFD's) as recognized by the United States Coast Guard. Of these only three and preferably only two should be recognized by the canoeist. Here they are as defined by the Coast Guard: Type I and Type II—wearable devices designed to turn an *unconscious* person in the water from a face-down position to a vertical or slightly backward position. The only difference in

48

the two is that the Type I has more than 20 pounds of buoyancy, and the Type II has at least 15.5 pounds of buoyancy. Type III—a wearable device with at least 15.5 pounds of buoyancy that is designed to keep a *conscious* person in a vertical or slightly backward position. Type IV and Type V: a Type IV device is designed to be *thrown* to a person in the water. Cushions and ring buoys are examples. A Type V unit is a wearable device intended for some specific use. An example is a "work vest" for use on ships.

Of the preceding, only the first four are approved by the Coast Guard for use on recreational boats, and they require one of these devices aboard for each person in a canoe or kayak. The canoeist, however, should ignore this and consider only the first three and *buy* only one of the first two. He will probably find a Type II adequate, and it offers the advantage of less bulk.

INFLATABLE JACKETS

Do not use inflatable jackets. They are likely to be punctured or cut on rocks or sticks. If left stored and uninflated over a period of time, the material may deteriorate enough to leak or burst just when you need it.

Running rapids in a PFD!

PRACTICAL PFD'S

Life jackets come in two basic styles—the vest kind that covers your back and chest and attaches together in the front by zippers or ties, and the yoke or "horse-collar" kind that covers only your chest and usually has straps across your back that snap into "D" rings on the side of the jacket. Each style is (or should be) adjustable to fit snugly to your body. Vests ordinarily have laces or elastic sections or some kind of adjustment at each side and/or at the shoulders. The yoke's straps are adjustable.

Vests and yokes come in various sizes, each rated for a *very* general range of weight that they are intended to support. This weight range is important and will usually be found either on the label or stamped somewhere on the PFD. Obviously you should get one that is suitable for your weight.

Equally important is to get a PFD that fits you. One that is too small will be uncomfortable (and you're likely not to wear it), but even more important is the flotation aspect. While the basic amount of *buoyancy* in a PFD will not be less than that prescribed for its type, the actual *amount* of flotation material will vary. A size 46 PFD, for example, will contain more than a size 26. Thus, a PFD that is too small simply won't have enough flotation for your bulk even though its weight range is right.

A PFD that is too large for you will ride up under your chin and arms and float away from your body. This loss of body contact wastes a lot of the buoyancy of the PFD and is disconcerting as you feel like you're losing it. As it *is* possible for even a *snug*-fitting PFD to be ripped off your body in a strong current, this disconcerting feeling may well turn into reality if your PFD really is loose.

There are a couple of other extremes of PFD's of Type 1, 2, and 3 that might be worthy of mention. One is the very bulky, kapok-filled life-jacket type with about 30 pounds of buoyancy. They are often used on raft trips in really heavy water such as the Grand Canyon. They are too bulky, however, for active movement in a canoe. Another PFD on the market is a "sports"-coat style—Coast Guard-approved and just the thing for the impeccable canoeist, if not for the active one.

MATERIAL AND ADJUSTMENTS

PFDs are fairly standard in materials. The covers are some easily dried or waterproof material, often nylon, sometimes cotton drill. They come in various colors: red or orange are the most common for the yoke type, while many of the jacket types can be obtained in various patterns and more subdued colors.

Nylon laces and ties are common because of their strength and rot resistance, and zippers are usually nylon or metal. Zippers should have big, sturdy teeth and have pulls that are easy to grasp.

Elastic sections on the sides and the shoulders of some jackets provide a snug fit as well as flexibility of movement. On others adjustment of fit is done with cross-laced nylon strings. The yoke type has either cotton or nylon straps that are adjustable. All fittings should be rust resistant.

FILLER MATERIAL

Filler material in yoke-type jackets is usually kapok in sealed vinyl bags or a closed-cell foam normally all in one big bag or chunk in each side of the "yoke" plus the collar. Jacket types usually have closed-cell foam in vertical tubes, a series of square pads, or one big solid pad per section of jacket. Jackets with smaller pads are generally a little more flexible on bending movements, while the vertical tubes are handier for twisting movements.

One caution—any jacket with kapok in it is only good as long as the kapok is *dry*. Once a bag of kapok is broken—by sitting on the jacket, for example—the kapok absorbs water, gets heavy and stiff, and is useful only to drag you to the bottom!

STYLES

Yoke types end about your waist line or slightly above. Jackets may go to the waist or below. On those that extend below the waist, the zipper stops at the waist, and there is a flexible section at the waist so the lower section will flare out when

51

you're sitting down. Women should buy a jacket made specifically for women because they're cut fuller in the chest and are
longer in the front.

NICETIES

There are various little things available that make for nicer
living with a life jacket. Some have "fish net" inside that helps
you dry off faster under the jacket and also makes it a little
cooler in hot weather. You can also get jackets with leg straps;
these are useful for small children. The final thing is pockets on
the jackets, usually with Velcro fasteners—not waterproof but
awfully handy for carrying small items that *are* waterproof or
won't be damaged by water.

OTHER USES

Jacket type PFDs are hot in the summer, but they add
some welcome protection against wind and chill in the winter.
They also make fine back rests and seats (except the kapok
kind) and have served as pillows for noontime naps and night-
time camps.

FINALLY

Get a jacket that fits you comfortably and snugly, is suitable for your size and weight, and is good quality. Don't skimp
on the money for this—you may be selling your life cheaply.
Then, after you've bought it, wear it when the situation asks for
it: in fact, wear it when you think the situation *may* ask for it.

CHAPTER 4
OTHER EQUIPMENT

Hopefully you have now struggled through Chapters 1, 2, and 3 and have reached some conclusion on the three most important pieces of equipment you'll buy—your canoe, paddle, and life jacket. These are the basics, but the sport of river canoeing, like every other sport, has its own specialized accessory equipment that contributes various amounts of comfort, safety, and convenience to your canoeing. The selection of some of these items will be discussed in this chapter.

EQUIPMENT FOR YOU

Knee Pads

A lot of your river canoeing will be done in the kneeling position, and it doesn't take long for *any* canoe hull to get very wearing to bare knees or those covered only with pants. You can improvise some sort of pad out of a spare life jacket, a sweater or the like, or you can make kneeling pads in various ways. The easiest and most satisfactory method, though, is simply to trade a few dollars for knee pads made for the purpose.

Two types of knee pad are commonly used. One of these is the kind usually sold for athletic use. Ordinarily they are made of cloth-covered foam pads and have a wide elastic band to hold them in position. They slip up over your leg. To me, these have two disadvantages. First, the elastic band tends to "bunch" in miserable-feeling little ridges that get right in the bend of your leg when you're kneeling. Second, the pads get wet and stay wet long after the rest of you has dried.

To my mind the other kind of pad is the best kind you can get for canoeing. They're made of stiff rubber and are sold for gardening and mining use or for use by anyone who spends a lot of time on his knees. The rubber has "treads" on the outside to help keep you from slipping around, the pads buckle above and below the knee joints with two straps each, and they don't absorb water. Usually these straps are permanently attached to the "knee" portion but there is also a type sold that has replaceable straps. This is a handy feature as the rubber never wears out, but the straps do. When you buy these pads they usually have a thin foam lining in them. This lining frequently comes unglued and falls out. It's easily stuck back in, but I've never found that it makes any difference in comfort.

Another kind of knee pad is also sold specifically for canoeing. It's similar in construction to the rubber kind but slips on your legs with an elastic band like the athletic variety.

Canteens

I recommend the plastic variety for the simple reason that they're less noisy. Size will depend on heat, humidity, and how thirsty you get, but one- or two-quart capacity seems to be suitable for everyone.

If you buy a canteen with a cloth cover on it or a cloth carrying bag, it will stay cooler on a hot day if you keep the cover wet. Another summertime trick is to freeze the canteen the night before a trip. Leave the top off while you're freezing it, of course. During the trip keep the canteen under the canoe seat or shielded from the direct sun some way. The ice won't last all day, but your water will stay cooler longer. I hate to mention such an obvious thing, but carbonated drinks in a canteen rattling around in a boat, particularly under the hot sun, have a tendency to explode or at least bend the canteen!

A good way to carry a canteen that has a cover with a shoulder strap on it is to lay the strap over a thwart, then put the canteen through the loop of the strap. Otherwise, just tie the canteen in.

First-Aid Kit

River trip mishaps requiring medical aid are generally few in number, which is a good thing as you're usually miles or hours away from such help. However, it *is* a good idea to carry along a small first-aid kit to take care of the minor things that can happen. If you're preparing a kit for possible use by a group or for an extended trip, then of course expand its contents and range.

Miscellaneous but important—knee pads, canteen, first-aid kit, string, rainsuit, life jacket, and waterproof matches.

Cuts; scrapes; bruises; sun, wind, or fire burns; mosquito, wasp, hornet, or other insect bites; splinters (wood, metal or fiberglass); and possibly snake bites are the common canoe trip injuries. Most of these can be treated with essentially few items. Band aids, several 3 by 3 sterile gauze pads, an antiseptic and a burn ointment, tweezers, a small role of adhesive tape, a needle, a razor blade, and a snake-bite kit are the main items. Aspirin and antacid tablets are good extras to include, as are some waterproof matches that can be used to sterilize the needle or razor blade. Finally, a small first-aid reminder booklet might prove to be handy.

The snake-bite kit is one of those "Well, I don't know" items. Psychologically, the old "cut-and-suck" types are comforting to have along even though their use is no longer recommended. Antivenin kits are dangerous to use because of the likelihood of reaction of the antivenin, and most of the cold pack kits presently on the market are just too big to carry unless you're really in bad snake country. Small cold pack kits are available and might be useful but their cold-sustaining powers are limited by their small size. I suppose each will have to make up his own mind on this. Personally, I carry the old kind and just hope I never have to decide whether to use it.

Any special items that you personally and particularly need should also be included. If you're very allergic to any kind of insect sting, for example, you should take along whatever you require to offset its effects. If you're one of those unfortunates who merely has to look at poison ivy, oak, or sumac to break out, you may want to throw in a small bar of laundry soap to wash off its oils. Whatever *you* need, put it in. It's better to carry it around and never need it than to need it and not have it.

Pack or carry these items in something waterproof. Most "store" kits are in relatively *raintight* boxes but would quickly be ruined by total immersion. There is a waterproof kit available, but it is a little bulky for a personal kit. Put yours in your ammo box, or wrap it in tied or sealed plastic bags, or use one of the many watertight containers available—but do keep it dry. Your kit should also be compact enough so you're not tempted to leave it behind as being too weighty or space consuming.

Another factor to consider should you ever need first aid on the river is that you have a few useful items along with you on any canoeing trip. Your paddles would make good splints, for example, if padded with life jackets and tied on with belts, throw rope, or painters. They could also serve to immoblize an arm, leg, or back. The life jackets themselves would make a sort of splint if they were tied securely enough, and a canoe wouldn't make a bad stretcher (albeit a heavy one) if you had nothing else to use.

CLOTHING

Clothing on a canoe trip should contribute protection and comfort. What you are being protected from is a matter of season, but basically it will be sun and wind burn, rain, insect bites, the sharpness of rocks in rapids, and heat and cold. Clothing also helps prevent cuts, nicks, and abrasions, whether you're on the shore, on the portage, sliding around in the canoe—or in the rapids.

Rain Gear

Rainsuits, raincoats, and ponchos are about your limit of choices for rain protection. Raincoats are just not much good in a canoe. If they're long enough to keep the front of your legs dry, then they restrict your leg movements. They also leave the back of your legs exposed if you're kneeling. Ponchoes are not recommended for river canoeing because their flapping expanse could get caught on the boat if you spill or on an obstruction in the water if you're floating in your life jacket. Too, the open sides and sleeve arrangement on a poncho does little to keep you dry when you're paddling. A rain cape or cagoule version of a poncho has the same disadvantages as a raincoat—fine when you're standing up but sure to get at least your legs wet when you're paddling.

Rainsuits really give you better protection, are safer because they're more form-fitting, and don't restrict your movements. Two-piece rainsuits are standard, and they're usually made of Polyurethane or vinyl-coated, rip-stop nylon or cotton. One on the market is uncoated and consists of an outer layer of very tightly woven, water-repellent treated cotton and an inner lining of water-repellent poplin. It's supposed to be excellent from a condensation standpoint. Good rainsuits will have a seamless shoulder construction.

Don't buy a heavy, industrial-type rainsuit. They are sturdy, but they are stiff and movement-restricting, hard to pack, and just not needed. Don't buy the cheap plastic kind either. They don't last, and it won't take you many of them to pay for a *good* suit.

Condensation in a rainsuit is always a problem, because if the rain can't get in, your body moisture can't get out. The two-layer, non-coated type of rainsuit mentioned before can "breathe," so this problem is much relieved in it. To partially offset this problem, some coated rainsuit parkas have vents across the back of the shoulders and/or under the arms. The back-vent type is usually covered with a waterproof flap, but most of these flaps are too short to cover the vent when you stretch out to paddle. This means a leak. These vents do help the condensation problem some, but you'll still sweat in a rainsuit if you're exerting much energy.

A rainsuit (left). Though often used, ponchos are not recommended for river paddling (right).

Rainsuit parkas may be bought with or without hoods. For river canoeing you may find that the hood gets in the way, and you'll be better off with a hat. The hoods interfere somewhat with your vision and your hearing. In a rapid you obviously depend a great deal on your sight, but you also rely more on your hearing than you might think.

Parkas usually have a drawstring around the hood and elastic or a drawstring at the waist. Cuffs come with snaps, Velcro fasteners, or elastic. For canoeing the elastic is probably more suitable as it does a better job of stopping rain from running down your arms while you're paddling. Parkas may slip on over your head and have a short zipper or go on like a coat and have a full front zipper. Most of them will have a flap over the zipper. Don't buy rain parkas with buttons or snaps on the front opening; the zippers do a better job. Parkas may be had with or without pockets, and the pocket flaps may or may not be fastened. Personally, I find the pockets pretty useless in a rain.

When you open them to get something out, the contents get wet anyway.

Rainsuit pants commonly have a drawstring or elasticized waist and ankle closures. Some have snaps at the ankles. Make sure the cuffs open out big enough to comfortably get the pants on and off over your shoes.

Hats

A lot of folks don't wear any head covering, but I find a broad-brimmed hat very useful to keep rain off my glasses and from running down the neck of my rainsuit. It also helps shield my eyes from the sun. Occasionally a broad-brimmed hat does get in the way when you're paddling or cruising along under bushes or limbs, but to me its advantages far offset its disadvantages.

In heavier water you'll be more interested in skull protection. In that case it's becoming ever more common for canoeists

Wool "Long Johns," foundation for the non-wet suit winter outfit (left). Typical winter paddling outfit (right).

to wear kayak helmets. This makes very good sense and is highly recommended.

For winter wear a wool watchcap or bacalava will keep your head warm. As the head radiates a tremendous amount of body heat, it will also serve to keep *you* warmer all over.

Sun Glasses

These are nice things to have when the sun glints off the water and hides the rocks you're trying to dodge. They also cut down eye strain from general glare. Polaroid types are supposed to be much better for glare reduction. I don't know if they are or not, but if you think so, then use them. Whatever kind you wear, tie them on your head to avoid losing them if you spill.

Footwear

Do wear shoes. The rocks in shoals and rapids are frequently sharp and rough. They hurt when you have to step out of the boat. Even worse are the open cans and broken bottles that may be on the bottom. Shoes also offer protection to your feet if you're floating a rapid without your boat. They can absorb impact with a jagged rock a lot better than your bare soles. Still another reason is that a canoe hull gets awfully hot in the summer—sort of like stepping barefooted on hot pavement if the boat has been sitting in the sun awhile.

Wear shoes that drain easily (most of them do anyway after a few trips). Shoes that slip on also slip off in current, so use the lace-up kind.

Tennis shoes, sneakers, brogans, and low hiking shoes all make good summertime canoeing footwear. In the winter, wear wet-suit booties with a pair of oversized tennis shoes over them for protection of the easily torn bootie material. The booties are particularly advisable if you think you may have to get out and stand or wade in the cold water.

Boots are not recommended for river canoeing. While it's true that a tight boot won't get much water weight in it, the boots themselves are relatively heavy. I know canoeists who wear them summer and winter, but personally I'm afraid of them.

Shirts and Pants

These are purely a function of temperature and expected weather, although you should consider the protection aspect also. In the summer's warmth, shorts or bathing suits and a short-sleeved shirt might be cool but offer little protection against rocks in a rapid. Consider too that insects and sun and wind burn offer discomforts that could be offset by long shirt sleeves and long pants. On any summer trip you might want to carry along a pair of long pants and a long-sleeved shirt to put on if you need them.

In cool weather wool clothes are the thing unless it's so cold that a wet suit is called for. Wool retains some warmth even when wet and "wicks" the moisture off your body. Wool "long-handled" underwear and wool socks, pants, and shirt offer you maximum protection without a lot of bulk and without absorbing a lot of water if you spill. An outer layer of a windproof jump suit or parka will help cut chill factor loss.

Most wool outer clothes, of course, are not all wool; a blend of about 85-percent wool and 15-percent nylon is common. Wool underwear, too, is a blend, usually 80-to-85-percent wool and the rest cotton or a synthetic fabric. You should try to get as much wool as possible in them unless you can't stand the prickly feel of the material. If this is so, I suggest that you still use the wool outer wear and go to fish-net underwear. Don't buy cotton underwear. Cotton loses all its warmth when wet and "wicks" water into itself from any part of you that is wet.

Wool clothing is expensive, and it's also not readily available in many clothing stores. You'll probably have to buy or order it from an outdoor specialty shop. Dress in several lightweight layers rather than one big, heavy thickness. The layer system is warmer and also allows you to adjust your clothing needs as you or the day warms. You can roll up your sleeves, open your collar, pull out your shirt tail, take off a layer, and otherwise arrange to cool off without removing so much that you get chilled.

"Fish-net" underwear is good, too, although not as good as wool. It depends on its air spaces for insulation. Avoid quilted insulated underwear, or outerwear either for that matter. While

61

some of it, such as "Polarguard," can be wrung out and still be warm even while wet, it does trap water and gets very heavy until wrung out. This could be bad if you're in the water. Clothing of this nature is also bulky, so it restricts your movements. Down-insulated wear is useless for canoeing unless you're absolutely certain that you're not going to get it wet (which you never are). Down loses almost all of its insulating qualities when wet, so either rain, splash, or spill can turn it from a luxuriously warm garment to a bag of soggy feathers.

Wet Suits

Wet suits are *the* thing for winter canoeing if you're planning to enter rough waters where spills are likely or if the temperature is low. The old standby rule is that if the air and water temperature combined don't add up to 100 degrees—then put on your wet suit. If you're particularly cold-natured, wear it at other times, too. If the day warms up you may find yourself stewing in your own juices, but if you *do* hit the water, you'll be glad you had it on.

Wet suits are just what they sound like—suits that are wet, inside and out, when you're in the water. Their warmth comes from trapping a thin layer of water between the suit and your body. Your body heat then warms this layer of water, and your body and the thickness and insulation value of the suit hold this heat in. Obviously, when you first fall in you'll be cold as the river water circulates through the suit. In a few minutes, however, you'll warm up, and, if the suit fits you well, you'll stay relatively warm.

Wet suits are made of nitrogen-blown neoprene, which is neoprene with a lot of insulating bubbles and spaces in it. The suits may be smooth or rough finished on the outside, and the better ones will be nylon-lined on the inside. You'll appreciate a lined suit when you've tried to struggle into or out of an unlined one. Wet suits should fit snugly, and an unlined suit just doesn't want to slide over your skin. Getting out of a wet suit can be a real challenge at the end of a long day's paddling, and a lining makes it an easier task.

Zippers make entry and exit easier, too, as well as giving you a little temperature adjustment. Five zippers are best on full two-piece suits and a necessity on all one-piece suits—that's one at each ankle and wrist and one down the front.

A wet suit of 1/8-inch or 3/16-inch material is usually plenty for the average canoeist. They are available in 1/4-inch and 3/8-inch thicknesses, and you might want these if the weather is consistently very cold in your part of the country or if you're particularly susceptible to cold yourself. Generally, however, you'll find that suits of 1/4 inch and over material are too bulky and stiff for canoeing.

Wet suits come in various styles and in one- and two-piece outfits. For a full-length, overall suit I would only buy a two-piece suit. One-piece suits are just too hard to get on and off despite their zippers. Another advantage of two-piece suits is that you can wear only one part of it at a time if you want to. This is often done in cool but not cold water and weather.

Wet suits come in short, medium, and full styles and in vest and pants and the "Farmer-John" type. "Farmer-Johns" look something like the old bib overalls, and short suits of the "Farmer-John" type look like old-fashioned and very modest one-piece men's bathing suits. They have no sleeves, short legs, cover the chest, and usually have a snap and/or Velcro fastener at one shoulder. Medium suits have short legs and arms and a front zipper. Long, one-piece Farmer Johns have either no sleeves or short ones but do have full-length legs. You can wear a wet suit coat with any Farmer John. This gives your trunk double protection.

The two-piece suits have a "beaver tail" on the vest that

Short- and long-style "Farmer John" wet suits.

The full wet suit, perfect wear for winter canoeing.

loops between your legs from the back and fastens in the front of the vest. Two-piece suits commonly have normal "pants"-style lower parts that don't come up to cover your chest. The "tail" makes sure the vest and pants stay overlapped.

The suit *you* need depends on the average winter weather where you live and your own susceptibility to cold. A full suit gives you more protection than a shortie or partial one. A full-length Farmer John with a jacket gives you the most protection. For consistently milder weather you may well be content with a short or medium "Farmer John" or a vest only. It's all a matter of what *you* require.

Wet suits need to fit snugly enough all over your body to prevent the warm layer of water from being replaced so rapidly or in such quantities that you feel it. They do *not* need to be so tight that they restrict movement or circulation.

Your feet and hands are great conductors of heat (and, when cold, sources of misery on a trip), so if you buy a wet suit you should get wet-suit booties and mittens or gloves as well. These are of the same material as the suit and work in the same way. Hoods are also available. Both the booties and the gloves are absolutely great to wear on a winter's trip even if you don't have on your wet suit. There's nothing else that I know of that will actually keep you *warmer* when you get wet than you were when dry.

Wet-suit material is easily torn. Wearing a windproof jump suit or shell over it will protect the material and, by decreasing the effect of the wind, make the suit warmer. I've already mentioned wearing oversized shoes over the booties. If you do tear your suit, extra neoprene material and glue are usually available wherever you bought it, and it is easily fixed.

EQUIPMENT TO PROTECT YOUR GEAR

Waterproof Containers

One of the peculiarities of canoeing is that you and your equipment tend to get wet. Even if spills or splashes don't do the soaking, rain may. While wetness of the paddler is something every canoeist learns to expect, it's not too funny to find your "dry" extra clothes dripping wet, your sandwiches disintegrated from moisture, or your camera with water in its mechanism.

Depending on what you're carrying, your containers may need to provide protection only from water or from both water and impact. In other cases such as flatwater cruising trips where spills are not likely, a water-resistant (rainproof) container may be all you need. Several types and sizes of containers are useful to have so you can suit the protection and size needed to the particular trip involved. One general comment on all bags: they offer no shock resistance, so if you carry something fragile or breakable in them such as a camera, be sure it's well padded.

Ammunition Boxes

The best thing you can buy for both watertightness and impact protection is an army surplus ammunition box. Actually, "ammunition box" is not strictly accurate as many different things are originally packed in them, but you'll be understood if you ask for an "ammo" box. These metal containers are heavy and limited in practical size, but they do offer water-tight integrity, unsurpassed sturdiness, and will float even when loaded. They are also highly unlikely to come open even under repeated impacts such as floating through a rapid by themselves! These ammo boxes are available in various sizes, but from a weight and usefulness standpoint two sizes seem best suited for general canoeing. One is about 7 inches high, 10 inches long, and 3½ inches wide; the other also is about 7 by 10 but 5½ inches wide. Another useful box (also army surplus) is about 18 by 9 by 13 inches deep. It's handy if you carry a lot of fragile stuff that needs shock and moisture protection.

All of the boxes open from the top. Some larger boxes hinge on the long side, others have the hinge on the end. The end hinge types (such as those described above) are usually of heavier metal and, in my opinion, more likely to remain water-tight under stress and impact.

The big advantage of these boxes is their toughness and the protection they offer items such as cameras. They are also easier to open and close than most waterproof bags. They are, I think, unsurpassed for one-day trips, because you can get everything you need to take in one or two of them—even your extra clothes. One word of caution: these boxes are sturdy, but items such as cameras rattling around in them are not. You might find it helpful to put some one-inch foam padding in the box unless whatever you're carrying is already well cushioned with other items. Another value of the foam padding to a camera is its insulation value—it will help protect your film from being ruined by heat.

Not only film but any of the contents of an ammo box will get awfully hot sitting in the bottom of a canoe under the summer sun. Painting the box white or some other light, reflective color will keep these contents much cooler. A light-colored box is also easier to spot and less likely to be left sitting on the river bank.

Ammo boxes depend for their watertightness on the seal around the lid and on not having any pinholes in them from rust. Visually check the seals before you buy the boxes, then, before you use them on the river, float them overnight in a tub of water. Check for leaks the next morning.

Bags

Various-sized bags on the market are sold as waterproof or water resistant. Some are tightly woven nylon, others are rubber or vinyl coated nylon or all rubber, and then there are plastic and plastic-lined bags. Do bear in mind that none of these bags in themselves gives any shock protection at all.

Most of the bags sold as waterproof are of waterproof material, but some utilize a separate inner plastic liner that is tied or fastened in some manner and then an outer flap, also secured, to help ensure their watertightness. Usually the inner bag (or flap) is folded over on itself, bunched, and tied, and then the outer bag is done the same way. Some bags have Velcro fasteners and then are rolled and buckled with the fasteners well down in the rolled part. Bags with only a single shell (no liner or inner flap) normally use this bunch-tie or roll-tie method also.

Some bags such as army laundry bags or their commercial

Several types of waterproof boxes and bags.

equivalent are simply that—bags. They are coated on the inside with some waterproof lining such as vinyl, and in theory, you can fold, bunch, roll, or in some manner manipulate the top and then tie it so the assembly is waterproof. I have never found this to be so, but then maybe I'm just clumsy!

One type of bag also has a separate, inflatable air chamber that can be blown up after the bag is loaded. This could be a handy feature if the bag goes overboard.

One of the best waterproof bags that you can buy is a stiff, heavy, rubber-coated army surplus bag. These come in several back-pack styles and in larger sizes built something like trunks. Unfortunately these bags are rather hard to find as army surplus but, fortunately, they are on the market in a "civilian" model. This type of bag has an inner flap that is rolled into a series of flat folds, then has an outer flap buckled down over it.

It's obvious that all of these cloth or rubber waterproof bags depend for their water-tight integrity on the care with which their tops are closed. This means you have to do it right. For a one-day trip, I'd prefer the metal ammo box simply for its ease of use, but for bulky items these other bags are definitely the thing.

These bags come in two styles—flat bottomed (like a duffle bag) or just sewn together at the bottom like a pocket. They range in size from something about big enough for a couple of sandwiches up to about 2 by 3½ feet. They are all generally strong and resistant to punctures and tears, are relatively light, take little room when empty, and can be stuffed under a seat or in some out-of-the way place in the canoe where a rigid container wouldn't fit.

Plastic bags used for canoeing fall into two general classes—those made for the purpose and those you create yourself. Probably the best "made-for-the-purpose" one is a bag of 20-mil plastic with a sliding bar top closure. The plastic is heavy but *can* be cut or punctured by a sharp edge or point in the boat. To offset this a cloth outer bag can be bought with it that provides a lot of abrasion and cut protection. You can also use the protection method talked about under the "garbage-bag" packs.

These plastic bags are capable of carrying a surprising amount of weight. In fact, you can inflate them (added overboard protection) and then sit on them. They come in various sizes, all in the "pocket" bottom style; are good for bulky items; and really are very waterproof even though the locking bar *can* sometimes be pulled off by a strong current.

The plastic garbage bag falls in the do-it-yourself class. These bags are not very strong and are very prone to puncture and tear, so the best procedure is to load one bag, fold and tie the top, then put this bag into another one and fold and tie its top too. This gives you double strength and extra assurance of watertightness. Even with this double arrangement, however, beware of loading them with a lot of weight or items with points or corners.

Carry these "garbage-bag" packs in some protective outer bag such as an army laundry bag or something similar. This outer bag doesn't have to be watertight or even raintight; all it's there for is to provide abrasion, tear, and cut protection to your inner bags.

Plastic and Fiberglass Boxes and Packs

These are good for bulkier items. They are easy to open and close and lighter weight than an ammo box. They have the same disadvantage of the ammo boxes insofar as being able to stuff them some place out of the way, but they don't have the sturdiness and impact resistance of the ammo boxes.

The boxes on the market are, generally, rainproof and are more or less waterproof while floating in the water for a limited time. I don't know how they would react to floating through a rapid and hitting rocks, but I believe they would be likely to pop open, or at least leak and possibly crack. They come in limited sizes from a one-day variety to a backpack shaped box complete with carrying straps. They are excellent for cruising and canoe camping. Another plastic container that is absolutely waterproof is a five-gallon plastic bucket with a press-on lid. You may be able to pick one up free at a local hamburger place as they are originally packed full of such things as pickles. Generally they'll have a bail on them (the bail is the wire handle). That's handy for tying them in. The ones with which I have had experience took a lot of struggle to get the top off, so you don't have to worry about their leaking unless you get a crack or a hole in them. The only thing you do have to watch is the type of plastic from which the bucket is made. Some plastic will crack badly when it's cold and the bucket or lid is flexed—but then you don't have to use them in the winter!

EQUIPMENT FOR YOUR CANOE

Bailer and Sponge

A bailer is great for removing rain, splash, and the last quarts of water from a spill. What it doesn't scoop out can be mopped up with the sponge.

There's nothing on the market to buy for a bailer, but they're easily made out of a half-gallon or gallon plastic jug. Get the kind with a built in handle, leave the cap on it, and cut the bottom off straight across or in whatever "scoop" shape you care to. Your bailer can be made of a square or round jug. Either one will more or less mold itself to the shape of the hull as you bail. The round ones, however, seem to be a little sturdier when filled with water.

The sponge should be about 2 by 4 by 6 inches (or bigger) and tied to one end of a 2- to 3-foot cord or light rope. Tie the bailer handle to the other end of the cord. To carry it in the canoe, just loop the cord over a thwart.

Painters

A painter is a simple subject but worthy of mention considering what you see on canoes sometimes. You need neither hawser nor a thread. You do need a rope strong enough to hold your canoe down while it's being transported, one that is resistant to water and sun damage, supple enough to tie and untie with ease whether it's wet or dry and with enough friction to hold a knot such as a trucker's hitch or a taut-line hitch. I recommend 1/4-, 5/16-, or 3/8-inch polypropylene or nylon, both woven. The poly ropes are a little slippery and nylon slowly deteriorates under the sun but both basically answer all the requirements. Melt the ends of a synthetic fiber rope or whip the ends of a natural one to stop its raveling.

A painter only needs to be about 10 feet long. This will tie it down to almost any vehicle or to the shore. Anything longer is a foot grabber, could be dangerous, and will get in the way unless you keep it tied up some way.

Extra Flotation

Extra flotation in your boat comes in handy by taking up part of the space that water would otherwise occupy in a swamped boat. This makes the swamped boat lighter and higher riding due to the increased buoyancy as well as the reduced water weight, and both of these factors make the canoe easier to handle and rescue.

Large truck inner tubes and styrofoam blocks are the two most-used flotation devices for an open canoe. Of the two the styrofoam by far offers the most water displacement and buoyancy for its weight but is not as readily removed or installed as a tube. The styrofoam also chips easily but in large chunks is very unlikely to break out of the boat.

Inner Tubes

A single inner tube (about 8.25 by 20 or 10.00 by 20 or 22) is usually used. Its location in the boat may vary with boat length, whether you're solo or tandem, and your position in the boat. Commonly for either tandem or solo the tube is centered under the center thwart or in the center of the boat between adjacent thwarts. Here it's out of the way and yet leaves room for either paddler in a tandem boat or for a solo paddler to change position by one thwart if they or he needs to. The tube also helps to brace the paddlers in if they do move toward the middle of the boat. Be a little cautious here, though; don't locate your tubes so you're wedged in between tube and thwart.

For solo use the tube is sometimes put between the center and forward thwart so the paddler can more easily move up one thwart and paddle from nearer the center of the boat. In this position the weight of the tube also helps slightly to trim the boat.

When installing an inner tube, partially inflate it, push it into position, then finish inflating it. Leave the tube with a little "give" in it. A rock-hard tube is more likely to puncture if

71

Extra flotation using tubes---

---and foam.

struck by something sharp. Position the valve stem down toward the bottom of the hull so it won't be as likely to get torn off or to hurt you if you're slung around in the canoe.

There is no necessity for tying the tube in. If it's the right size, it will swell out around the thwart slightly and hold itself firmly in place.

Foam Flotation

This is much better for extra flotation. Usually only one large block is put in, although you can practically fill the boat if you want to.

The location of the block is the same as with the inner tube. The foam will need to be shaped to fit into the canoe, but this is easily done with a sharp knife or a saw. A common way of installing foam blocks is to remove the thwart or thwarts where the block will be and replace the rivets, screws, or whatever is holding the thwarts in with machine screws and wing nuts. This makes it easy to remove or install the block at any time. Fit the foam to the hull so that it fills the space from the keel to at least just under the gunwale. Notch out the top of the block so that the thwart can go back in place and replace the thwart. You may need to notch out the foam for access to the wing nuts, too. The replaced thwart holds the foam in place.

CHAPTER 5
GETTING FROM HERE TO THERE
WITH EVERYTHING YOU STARTED WITH

Watersoaked gear and lost equipment due to a spill can be expensive and irritating. You should get in the habit of securing everything you carry in the boat *to* the boat and of protecting anything that can be damaged by water.

CORD, STRING, ROPE, AND OTHER FASTENINGS

Select your tying in material for the job it has to do. I designate string as something moderately strong but that the average man can snap with his hands; cord as something heavier that most of us would cut with a knife; and rope (for tying in) as something about 1/8 inch in diameter.

Use string for tying in items you may want in a hurry or that won't matter too much if they get ripped loose (the exception is your spare paddle). Use cord for items you want to pretty well stay with the canoe and that you won't be taking out of the boat much. Use rope for things that you definitely want to stay with the boat even if it swamps.

"Other fastenings" includes such items as nylon straps with snaps and "D" rings or friction buckles. These are strong, easy to fasten and unfasten, and inexpensive. Use them anywhere you would use rope or cord. "Shock cords" (elastic rope) are also good, but get a type with a clip-on or other type of closed fastener on the end. Don't rely on an "S" hook and the tension of the cord alone.

A SPECIFIC WORD ABOUT ROPES

Rope is made of various natural and synthetic fibers, in various sizes and strengths. For canoeing, your critical rope needs will be confined pretty well to throwing ropes, painters, and cross tiedowns. You'll want a rope that's light, strong, flexible, and easy to work with, and for throw ropes, brightly colored and floatable.

Synthetic materials offer the best choice for canoeing,

specifically polypropylene and nylon. Nylon is usually woven construction, soft and pliable. Polypropylene rope may be woven (braided) or twisted and is a little stiffer than nylon. Both are water resistant, affected somewhat by the sun, strong for their size, and need the ends seared to prevent unraveling or fraying.

Get a rope that is strong enough for its usage but not too large. Remember that useful strength in a rope may only be about one-fourth of its breaking strength and that knots reduce a rope's strength tremendously. For most canoeing uses (except for the throw rope) you will find that in nylon or polypropylene a diameter of between 1/4 inch and 3/8 inch will serve most purposes.

WALLETS

This is an often overlooked item in the general waterproofing preparations. Put your wallet in something waterproof, or leave it in your vehicle for the whole trip. If you do leave it, however, you would be wise to hide it. Also consider the need to have your driver's license with you during the shuttle if you're driving and have left everything in your canoe ready for the trip start.

WATCHES

Another frequently overlooked item is your watch. A waterproof watch is a good investment if you do a lot of canoeing. If your watch isn't waterproof, then tuck it away with your wallet.

CAR KEYS

Car keys are still another often forgotten item. I remember one canoeist who lost his keys when he spilled in a rapid. His camping equipment, food, dry clothes, wallet, and all his possessions were tightly locked in his trunk. He had a wet and cold 300-mile drive home in a hot-wired car and was stopped at a routine Highway Patrol check! Fortunately, they believed his story!

Put your keys in your (tied-in) ammo box or similar container or tie them to your belt with a cord or strap long enough to let them stay in your pocket. Many canoeists attach a hidden spare key outside their vehicle somewhere in case they lose or forget theirs. One location is inside a parking light. You can break the lens with a rock if you have to.

GLASSES

Tie them on your head. Use two cords, one each knotted through holes drilled in the temples of your glasses or tied around the earpieces. Tie them together behind your head in a bow knot—makes them a lot easier to get off. You might also use the adjustable, elastic type of holders that clip or slip on your ear pieces and are sold for athletic use.

CAMERAS AND DELICATE EQUIPMENT

Use your ammo boxes for items likely to be damaged by shock as well as water. Get one you're sure doesn't leak, then line it with foam rubber to make a snug nest for your camera or whatever. Tie the ammo box in with rope such as you used for your painters and use hard knots or else use straps. Leave enough slack to open the box but not so much that the box can go over the side of the canoe if you spill or swamp.

BAILERS

Don't tie your bailers. If you have the sponge-scoop variety, then wrap the connecting string around a thwart once and let the bailer and sponge lie in the bottom of the boat.

CANTEENS

Use cord but leave enough slack to be able to drink out of it if you want to. Tie with a hard knot to the canteen and a bow knot around a thwart.

SPARE PADDLES

Position your extra paddle or paddles as shown in the

photo. The grip should be toward the paddler whose spare paddle it is. The blade lies on the bottom of the hull toward the center of the canoe, and the grip end of the shaft is *under* the thwart closest to the paddler and in easy reaching distance, but offering no interference to your normal paddling movements.

Correct location of the spare paddle—available yet out of the way.

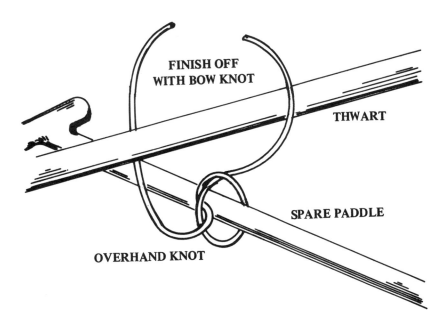

FINISH OFF
WITH BOW KNOT

THWART

SPARE PADDLE

OVERHAND KNOT

How to tie your spare paddle.

Tie an overhand knot around the shaft just below the grip (or just loop the string around the shaft), then pull the shaft up under the thwart, loop the thwart, and tie a single loop bow knot on top of the thwart. Use only one thickness of string.

Use string or light cord to tie the paddles in, something that can be broken with one sharp downward blow on the grip in case the knot jams. Tied in this way and in this position the paddle is readily available and yet not likely to be ripped loose by the current if you swamp. Even if it does break loose it's more likely to catch under the seats and thwarts than it is to take off alone.

IDENTIFYING YOUR GEAR

A lot of canoeists have identical gear so it's always a good idea to distinguish yours in some manner. The easiest way is to put your name and address on it. A felt-tip pen with a broad tip is excellent for paddles, ammo boxes, canteens, or any surface on which the writing will show. Felt tips are quicker, easier, and less messy to work with than paint, and the writing is waterproof (most of it is—check first). Put a strip of adhesive tape on objects such as knee pads, wet suits, and other dark-colored items where the writing won't show up; then write your name and address on the tape. Locate the tape where it's not likely to be torn or rubbed off when the piece of equipment is being used. Containers such as ammo boxes can also be marked on the inside.

USEFUL KNOTS

You have just read and will read throughout this book various instructions on tying things in and on using various knots. You may choose to simply ignore this, you may already know the knots, or you may have your own favorites that you use. This part of this chapter is for the rest of you.

There is never any need in canoeing for using masses of

This paddle isn't likely to go home with the wrong person.

knots; one knot applied correctly and tied correctly will usually suffice. The knots given here are simple and useful. They do an admirable and easy job for their specific application. All of them are easily tied and untied whether wet or dry, and all will hold either wet or dry when used correctly.

These knots, I am sure, are not the only ones that will serve. They are, however, proven in canoeing by long use, and are all good to know.

Trucker's hitch.

To Canoe

To Tie-Down

KNOTS

The Trucker's Hitch

This hitch is probably the most useful knot you'll ever learn. It gets its name from its use by truckers to tighten down tarps, and it's good for tightening down any rope. It holds best under strain and can be untied (deliberately) with one pull on

Trucker's hitch.

To Canoe

the free end of the rope. It is unlikely to come loose accidentally, but just for visual checking purposes it's best to tie it so the hitch is up above the hood or trunk and visible from the

Trucker's hitch.

driver's seat. It's unsurpassed for use on bow and stern tiedowns and rope cross tiedowns. It's also useful for hanging up a throw rope clothesline to dry river-wet clothes or to support a tarp for rainy-day lunches.

Trucker's hitch.

To Canoe

Overhand knot.

Bow knot.

Overhand Knot

If you can tie your shoes, then you can tie this knot. It's really not so much a knot as the first step in tying other knots.

Bow Knot

Again, if you can tie your shoes, this knot is a snap. In canoeing you'll probably find the one-loop version given here more useful than the two-loop type that you use on your shoes. This knot is often used to tie in extra paddles and gear and to tie your canoe to shore. Be careful of how you tie this one. If you get the load on the wrong end it will pull the knot loose. For deliberately untying it, however, it comes loose with one pull.

Half-Hitch, Two Half-Hitches

Half-hitches are handy knots for tying painters to canoes or ropes to anything. They hold best under a slight strain. They are very quick and simple to tie and untie and easy to pull tight. Actually, the half-hitch is nothing but an overhand knot pulled on its side.

Slip Knot

This is handy for just what it says—a knot that slips. You can tie it, then pull it up tight. It's also good for tying painters to your canoe.

Clove Hitch

This knot is useful to finish tying off the loose ends of a coil of rope such as when you finish coiling up your throw rope for storage or travel.

Bowline

The bowline is great for safety ropes and for tying around the hulls of swamped canoes for rescue purposes. It forms a loop that will not slip either way, yet is easy to untie.

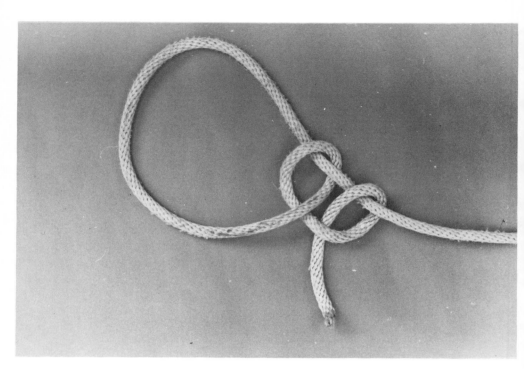

Two half-hitches.

Slip knot.

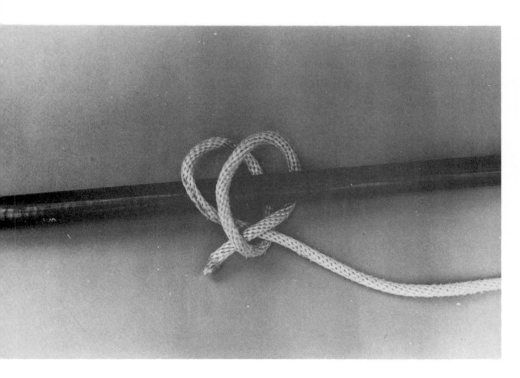

Clove hitch.

Bowline.

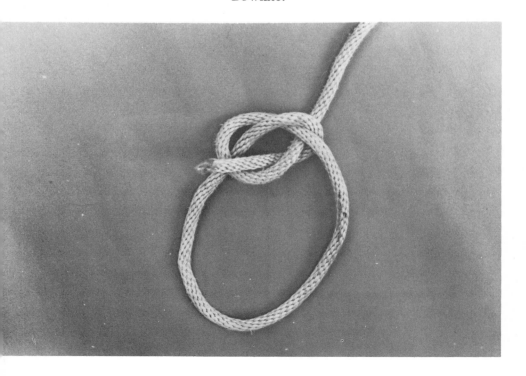

CHAPTER 6
TRANSPORTING YOUR CANOE

CAR TOPPING AND TRAILERS

There are two basic ways of getting your canoe to and from the river—by trailer, or by carrying it on top of your vehicle.

The trailer method is straightforward and simple and requires little comment. If you tie the upside-down canoes tightly to the trailer, make sure the trailer hitch is snug and a safety chain is on, don't sling the trailer around curves and, of course, don't forget that there *is* a trailer behind you, you'll have no trouble. This method is often used by church groups, Scout troops, canoe rental businesses, and the like and is a very practical way to transport a number of canoes that are stored at some common point.

A canoe trailer—probably the best method to use if all the canoes are stored at one place.

Despite a trailer's advantages to a group, "car topping" is the most common and most practical method for the average individual canoeist. "Car topping," of course, is only a general term that covers a multitude of types of vehicles and sometimes ingenious adaptations of the principles laid out in this part of this chapter.

Safely transporting a canoe by car topping involves creating a sort of pyramid of secure attachments. The racks must be firmly attached to the vehicle, the canoe to the racks (or held down on the supports in some cases) by cross tiedowns, and finally the canoe to the vehicle by the use of bow and stern lines. Here is a cardinal rule for car topping: *never* rely on the racks or the cross tiedowns alone to hold your canoe. They are there only to provide a stable platform for your canoe and to keep it from slipping sideways, forward or backward. Straps and ropes can break, clamps work loose, and vibration and wind pressure create loads that can rip canoe and rack right off the vehicle. Rely on your bow and stern lines, and *never* fail to tie them down securely. This is the *only safe* way to car-top your canoe.

Another good method for group canoe transport.

RACK POSITION

The strongest part of any vehicle top is around its edges near the windows, windshield, and sides. When using racks with "feet," locate the feet as near the edge of the top as possible. If you're using foam blocks, put them as near the front and rear of the car top as you can. On a car always put your rack crossbars as far apart as possible. For a van, camper, station wagon, and the like, locate the racks (or foam blocks) so that about 3 to 4 feet of the canoe extend beyond each crossbar.

RACKS—GENERAL

There is no doubt that racks made for the purpose are the

Racks for use on vehicles with rain gutters. This one has nylon strap cross tiedowns.

easiest, safest way to transport one or several canoes. Good racks and crossbars are sturdy, inexpensive, easy to use, and readily available. They come in various fixed or adjustable lengths to fit different-width cars and to accommodate one or two canoes directly on the racks. Those wide enough for two canoes side by side greatly simplify shuttles. They are only slightly longer than the one-canoe-width rack and will well repay their additional cost on the first trip you make that involves only two vehicles.

Two principal kinds of racks are available specifically for canoeing. Both of them are shown in the photos. One rack is typical of the type used on vehicles with rain gutters. Nothing touches the top of the car, and the racks are held to the gutters by clamps. Those shown have a knob to tighten the clamps down, others have a wing nut, and some have a lever or cam device. The method of clamping down is of little importance as long as it's sturdy, reliable, and relatively resistant to loosening from vibration.

The other style of rack is designed for vehicles without rain gutters. The padded feet sit near the edge of the top of the car, and the "gutter" hooks actually hook just above the car door. On the better racks these hooks are attached to the cross-

A rack for cars with no rain gutters. This canoe is secured with ropes.

bars by aircraft cable or some similar strong, flexible wire. An adjustment is provided for tightening up the cable. This type of rack is also available with longer "legs" on it to fit cars with high crowns on their tops.

These two types of racks provide a secure platform on which your canoe can ride safely. There are other types available, not made for canoeing, and often very cheap in price. These are usually stamped steel forms utilizing suction cups to hold the rack in place on the car top and cotton webbing straps to hold it down to the gutters. They are not reliable for canoe transport, and I would not recommend them for this purpose at all.

Another method of carrying a single canoe requires no racks at all and is also shown in the photos. It consists of four foam (rubber) blocks slightly curved to fit the car top. The blocks have slots that snap over the canoe's gunwales before you lift the canoe off the ground. The canoe is positioned on the car top, the blocks are moved to furnish support near the front and rear of the top of the crown, and the canoe is kept from sliding sideways by ropes or straps over the hull secured by gutter clips. This method is simple and cheap, but you can't shuttle another canoe with it.

Foam blocks are simple and inexpensive, but strictly a one-canoe-per-car method of transport.

Racks do not have to be bought complete. You can buy the clamps and attachments and put your own metal or wood crossbars on them. Doing this lets you pretty well tailor your racks to your own vehicle and needs.

CARRYING CAPACITY

All but the very shortest racks intended to carry one canoe will carry two canoes. Tie down the first canoe in the regular position, and lean the second one on it with one gunwale resting on the racks. Tie over the second canoe, rack end to rack end, pulling the cross tiedown tight. You may want to tie the bow and stern lines of the second canoe to the end of the bumper opposite the side it's on so that these lines are pulling more perpendicularly to its keel.

Two-canoe racks can easily carry a third canoe resting on top of the first two. The top one should be upside down just like the others, well secured to the racks with cross ties, and tightly tied down bow and stern.

OTHER SUPPORTS

Vans and most off-the-road vehicles will accept one of the types of standard racks. Pick-up trucks with covers or camper shells can have brackets attached to the covers and a slide-in or permanently attached crossbar in the brackets. Pickups without shells can use one rack on the cab and slip-in supports with crossbar in the sideboard holes at the rear of the pickup bed; or put both front and rear supports and crossbars in the side board holes.

CROSS TIEDOWNS

Cross tiedowns do *not* hold your canoe down against load. At least they should not be relied on to do this. Cross tiedowns are basically there only to prevent the canoe from slipping sideways on the racks and to hold the canoe down firmly enough to prevent its bouncing and vibrating on the racks. There are four common devices used for cross tiedowns. These are shock cords, rubber straps, nylon or webbing straps, and rope.

Shock cords, or "bunji" cords as they are often called, are made of a lot of individual elastic strands in an overall elastic sheath. They are available in various diameters and with or without end hooks and attachments. Shock cord is tough and strong but tends to get hard to stretch in the larger sizes. As it's not tremendously elastic anyway, you should size them more carefully than something with greater "give."

Rubber straps are weaker than shock cords (for any given size) and somewhat more susceptible to deterioration from exposure to sun. However, they are more elastic, easier to work with, usually cheaper and quite serviceable. For sheer convenience they're hard to beat even though you may need to replace them every year.

Flat nylon or cotton straps are often furnished with purchased racks and can also be bought separately. Of the two, nylon is more rot resistant and stronger for its size. If you buy cotton straps, get the heavier "webbing" kind. One inch wide in either material should be strong enough. These straps commonly adjust with a buckle-type arrangement or with "D" rings. Both are basically friction devices, and nothing actually pierces the straps.

Rope is the final tiedown. It is strong, cheap, and available. Use 1/4- or 3/8-inch nylon or polypropylene as either material

Homemade crossbars on factory clamps. This canoe is tied down with rubber straps with "S" hooks into eyebolts.

is sturdy and easy to work with, whether wet or dry. When using rope, keep your tiedowns simple. There is no necessity for masses of criss-crossed rope and knots. One loop over the hull at each rack is quite sufficient if you use the proper rope and knots. Use a clove hitch, bowline, or two half-hitches at the fixed end, pull the rope tight with the trucker's hitch or an overhand knot with "half" bow, and you'll have a good, simple arrangement.

There is another item on the market for use as a tiedown. It is called "rubber rope" and is a solid cord of rubber available in various diameters. Some rubber rope may be good (except for bow and stern tiedowns), but that which I have used has always turned out be very weak and unreliable.

HOOKS AND EYEBOLTS

Shock cords and rubber straps usually have metal "S" hooks at both ends. These hook around the under edge of the crossbar or into holes or eyebolts in the bar. On "factory" racks, the locations of these bolts are usually adjustable so that they can be placed within a few inches of the gunwales of the canoe and act as an additional safeguard against the canoe sliding sideways. Racks with holes only will usually have enough

Homemade crossbars on hand-fitted foam blocks.

A typical bracket and crossbar on a camper shell. Note the position of the eyebolts relative to the canoe's gunwale.

holes to provide a tiedown close to the gunwales, or you can install your own eyebolts.

The safest way is to put in the eyebolts; then even if a cross tiedown breaks, the bow and stern lines will still hold the boat down between the bolts. The bolts should be at this same location relative to the gunwale on homemade crossbars also. On a one-canoe-wide rack, you'll have only two eyebolts per bar. For a two-canoe rack, you can have one or two bolts in the middle and one on each end. Two in the middle will give a better gunwale fit for the bolts. Don't put these bolts so close to the gunwale that you have trouble getting the "S" hooks hooked in when the canoe is on the rack. Leave the bolts out about one inch from each gunwale. Position the bolts with the racks on your vehicle and the canoe(s) on the racks, because the distance between the racks will determine where the bolts go in relation to the canoe.

It's more convenient and easier to use your cross tiedowns if one end of them is permanently attached to the crossbar. Your fixed end on a two-canoe rack would, of course, be at the middle of the bar. For a one-canoe rack it makes no difference which end is fixed. If your cross tiedowns have "S" hooks, just bend the fixed-end "S" hook closed around the eyebolt, tight enough to stay on but loose enough to move around.

Straps and ropes can be rigged with "S" hooks, swivel snaps, or with small attachments made for the purpose of fitting on to eyebolts or into holes drilled in your crossbars. You can also tie the straps or rope. Tying is pretty safe if you tie to eyebolts or have some similar smooth, rounded edge to tie against. If you do tie around the bar itself, watch out for rough or sharp edges that might cut or wear your tiedown.

When the canoes are not on the racks, stretch the straps or cords, wrap them around the crossbar or clamps a few times to take up the extra length, and hook them in the outer-end eyebolt, hole, or what-have-you. Ropes and straps simply tie after being wrapped around the bars.

PULLING UP TIGHT

Shock cords and rubber straps stretch from crossbar and over the hull of the canoe to the other end of the same crossbar, so you're in good shape if you've bought them with a consideration for this total dimension less some "stretching" distance. Don't buy them so short, however, that it takes a mighty effort to pull them over and hook them. This kind of strain will shorten their life so much that you'll constantly be replacing them. Webbing straps are best bought complete with their buckles or "D" rings or you can use the trucker's hitch to pull them up tight. With buckles or rings the straps need to be at least 6 inches longer than the over-the-hull distance and for the trucker's hitch method about another 18 inches longer. This foot and a half extra will also about do for rope tiedowns. As with your painters, etc., sear the ends of your nylon or polypropylene cross tiedowns to keep them from raveling.

A SMALL TRICK

It's sometimes hard to get an elastic cross tiedown pulled across the hull of a canoe when you're standing on the ground. There's a simple way to do this. Just pull the loose end of the tiedown *under* the end of the canoe (between the rack and the end of the canoe), loop the painter through the "S" hook on the end of the tiedown, and hold this loop in your hand. Stretch the tiedown by pulling on the painter, and bring both out from under the end of the canoe and up over the hull until you can reach the elastic. This gives you a longer reach. Look at the photos and you'll see what I mean.

BOW AND STERN TIEDOWNS

I repeat here that your racks do *not* hold your canoe down—your bow and stern lines do. Again, use 1/4-, 5/16- or 3/8-inch nylon or polypropylene rope with the ends seared. Tie it firmly to your canoe's bow and stern rings, and check this knot from time to time to see that it hasn't worked loose. An even better attachment to a ring is to run the end of the tiedown through the ring, then splice it back into itself.

Bow and stern tiedowns need only be about 10 feet long. Commonly they are left attached to the canoe and used as its painters. Although some canoeists always run a line down from the canoe to each end of each bumper in a triangular arrangement, I've always found a single vertical line quite sufficient. However, as it's your canoe, do what *you* feel is safe; just be sure you have at least one good line bow and stern.

Bow and stern lines commonly attach to the bumpers themselves or to eyebolts in the bumpers. Bumpers may have ragged or sharp edges that will cut your lines; eyebolts in them eliminate this problem. Two bolts in each bumper, one at each end, near the frame support, will allow you to easily tie down all the canoes you're likely to carry or to use more than one line per boat. Use the trucker's hitch to pull these lines up tight.

THE TRUCKER'S HITCH

This is probably the most useful knot you'll ever know.

A small trick—hook the painter in the cross tiedown.

Pull the cross tie-down toward the end of the canoe---

---under and around the end---

---and over the hull.

Look it up in Chapter 5 and learn how to tie this knot if you don't bother with any of the rest. It is unexcelled for bow and stern tiedowns and for rope cross tiedowns.

HAND-CARRYING YOUR CANOE

If you paddle at all, you will have to hand-carry your canoe those last feet or yards to and from the water. Preferably this should be done without dropping the boat, falling down, running into anything, driving yourself to exhaustion, or developing a hernia.

Any carry at all will be easier at the start of a trip when you're fresh and sheer energy can offset lack of skill. At the end

Bow tiedown through bumper eyebolts and using the trucker's hitch. Notice that the hitch can be seen by the driver.

of the journey it's likely to be a different matter, and the easiest and most practical way to cover that distance will seem infinitely more appealing.

Various books show numerous skillful ways of hand-carrying a canoe. I have found that, on the short carries usually found in river canoeing, you'll normally see only four of them and, more commonly, only two.

One-Man Lift and Carry

This is a very easy method of carrying a canoe that has a center thwart. It's also a natural for loading or unloading the canoe at your vehicle as in either case the canoe is already upside down and ready to set off on the racks or your shoulders as the case may be. If you're strong enough for the "carry," you can easily handle the "lift" as this requires more rhythm than it does brute strength. The photos show the sequence of events in the lift. The key to the whole thing is in the snap of the knees and the swing itself. Usually the second and third steps are combined into one smooth, continuous motion by catching and continuing the momentum of the swing once you start it. Hit it just right (which only takes a little practice), and you'll barely feel the weight as you swing it up.

A one-man carry with initial help on the lift and a modified one-man lift are also shown in the photos. These are both good if you don't feel that you can handle the regular one-man lift. Even if you can, these two ways are useful.

"Portage" yokes are sold to fit on the center thwarts of canoes, and various methods such as tying paddles to adjacent thwarts are advanced to aid you in carrying the boat on your shoulders. In recreational river canoeing you will rarely have to portage far, so just wearing your life jacket will be enough padding.

Balance the canoe by holding to the gunwales ahead of you or to the ends of the next thwart. You won't be able to see very far ahead and not at all behind with this carry, so take it easy, particularly on the turns. Remember, too, that the stern may drag or catch as you go downhill, and the bow may do the same going uphill.

A one-man carry is just that—one man. You'll find that

The one-man lift, step 1.

The one-man lift, step 2.

The one-man lift, step 3.

The one-man lift, step 4.

A one-man lift the easy way. Lift one end and walk under the canoe until it's balanced.

Even easier. Someone else lifts and holds while the partner gets set at the balance point.

once you have the canoe on your shoulders, any well-meaning assist from bow or stern will unbalance you. Stepping on a dragging painter or catching one on something will also unbalance you (at the least), so either tie them to a thwart before you lift or have somebody hand them to you once the canoe is up.

One final note on the one-man lift-and-carry. For those who wear a broad-brimmed hat, prepare to have someone hand *it* to you, too. It almost invariably winds up on the ground!

Two-Man Carries

The photos of these should be self-explanatory. The over-the-head, upside-down version is another natural for loading and unloading at vehicles. The weight of the canoe is carried by positioning the stern seat on one person's shoulders. The person at the bow can also do this if the seat is near enough the gunwales to give him head room. Usually, however, he just supports his end by the gunwales, as moving back to the bow seat gives him a greater share of the weight. This carry also gives you the advantage of being able to lift the canoe up off your shoulders to see where you're going. It's a little tough on a tall and short guy carrying the same canoe, though. As in the one-man carry, your life jackets offer good shoulder padding.

The other two-man carry (with the canoe right side up) is best suited for the end of the trip because, once more, this is the position the boat is already in, and you don't have to lift it very far. Get on opposite sides and make some effort to progress as a team rather than in a series of uncoordinated jerks. This carry is *not* as easy and comfortable as the other two-man carry, but it's better when you have no path and have to struggle up a steep hill, possibly using one hand for balance or to grab bushes!

Door pulls screwed or bolted to the decks of a canoe make good carrying handles. Don't try this on fiberglass decks unless they are pretty sturdy. You might also want to put a flat plate under the deck where the handles are attached. The plate will distribute the strain. Some canoes come from the factory with deck-edge padding; if yours didn't, try splitting a length of garden hose and slipping it on the back edge of each deck. It

The one-man carry. On a long haul the life jacket would usually be worn for shoulder padding. This carry works only on canoes with a center thwart.

makes carries a lot easier on the hands.

Sliding the Canoe

This is the fourth method. When faced with a steep but relatively even hill into the water, just load your gear (within reason) into the boat, grab a painter, and let gravity slide boat and all right down the slope. Coming out of the water you may want to take your boat and gear up separately, depending upon how much gear and how much help you have. Naturally it's not as easy to pull a canoe *up* a hill as it is to slide it *down* the hill, but if you can't maintain footing to carry it, try dragging it. It's

Two-man, over-the-head carry.

Two-man, right-side-up carry.

Three-man carry.

Four-man carry.

Variations of the two-man carry—both recommended for short
distances only! They're a bit awkward!

Getting the canoe to the top of the vehicle from the ground. Notice the position of the hands ready for the swing up and over the head.

done all the time. Obviously, you should exercise some judgment as to what you slide your canoe up or down. Grass and mud are good; sharp-edged rocks are not. Whether sliding up or down hill, lay your paddles in the bottom of the boat, and either tie your gear in (or don't untie it), or stuff it in the downhill end of the boat. This way it doesn't all come falling out or go tumbling around in the bottom.

Carries When You Have More Help

A couple of other carries are also shown in the photos.

These are useful in carrying canoes longer distances or up or down steep places where you have room or anywhere you have enough willing hands.

GETTING YOUR CANOE ON YOUR VEHICLE

The easiest way is to get one person on each end facing each other, grasp both gunwales near the end of the canoe, and swing up and over until the canoe is upside down. Then set it on the racks. If you're using the little foam gunwale blocks instead of racks, you'll want to put them on before lifting.

If you're loading alone either do a one-man lift, or roll the canoe over, open side down, and put up one end at a time, sliding the canoe into position after it's on top of the vehicle.

PART II
Techniques, Paddle Strokes, And The River

CHAPTER 7
THE VERY BASIC, ABSOLUTE MINIMUM, FUNDAMENTAL DO'S
(AND SOME DON'T'S)

There are some fundamentals of paddling that the beginning river canoeist needs to know before he really starts canoeing. These fundamentals make the moving of the canoe easier, the maneuvering of it more effective, or the boat itself more stable at any time. Sometimes they even accomplish all three of these purposes simultaneously.

There are other fundamental things that you *don't* do in a canoe. Then there are some that are just simply practical and useful to know and make canoeing trips easier, safer, and more fun. You'll find a lot of these basics in this chapter. I think you'll find it very helpful in everything you do that's canoe-related, and I strongly urge you to go over it carefully *before* delving further into river canoeing.

BOARDING A CANOE

I suppose everyone has seen a comedy version of the fellow who, with one foot on shore, steps in a boat with the other foot and watches in dismay as the boat begins to drift away until finally he can stretch no farther and falls in. Out on the river you'll sometimes see novice canoeists doing this, and somehow *they* don't think it's funny at all!

There are good ways and bad ways to enter and exit a canoe. The sequence above is one of the bad ways. There are two basic rules to follow to avoid getting out when you don't intend to.

Steady the Canoe (Rule No. 1)

Keep the canoe steady and the center of gravity low. This is done by bending over, holding onto the gunwales with both hands, and stepping carefully along the middle (keel) of the boat, keeping your weight evenly distributed on both sides of the keel. This applies whether getting in or out of the canoe and whether the canoe is perpendicular to the shore, parallel to it,

Boarding a canoe from the shore without falling out. One partner braces while the other enters.

or anywhere in between.

Solo paddlers often put one foot in on the keel line, grasp the gunwales, and push off with the other foot. If the day is warm and the water shallow, you'll probably wade out and get in with the canoe already floating.

The approved (and driest) procedure for a tandem crew is for one member to enter while his partner steadies the canoe between his legs or by holding it. This steadying should continue until the first paddler aboard is settled down, paddle in hand. The first paddler then braces or secures the canoe by holding on to a limb or snag or by bracing against the river bottom with his paddle. He holds this brace until his partner is in and settled.

Stepping into a canoe off a bank is a little tricky. You'll need to carefully place one foot on the keel line, holding on to something on the bank, then shift your weight to the foot in the boat, grasp the gunwales, and gently settle down. With a high bank you may have to carefully stand up in the canoe to get out and slide both feet into the canoe to get in. Either way,

The other paddler enters as the first one braces.

use the bank as a support to hang on to or else pick out a spot with a nice limb, snag, or rock to grab hold of and be *certain* you put your weight vertically on the keel line of the boat. It should be obvious that in these situations all climbing in and out should be done at the tied-up end and the painter should be tied short.

Getting in or out at a sheer or slippery bank is a real test of skill and requires good balance and a certain amount of luck. I have no hints at all for this except hang on to anything available that's firm, get in or out at the tied-up end, and next time try to find a better place.

One Person at a Time (Rule No. 2)

The other rule is that only one person moves in a canoe at a time and that he gets firmly settled with paddle in hand before anyone else in the boat moves. Movements are made just as in entering or exiting—weight kept along the centerline, body bent low and both hands sliding along the gunwales.

Don't Bridge Your Boat

Don't step into your canoe when it's bridged between the bank and the water. Slide it off the bank so it's floating or nearly floating. Entering when one end is still resting on the shore is a good way to flip out of the boat and doesn't help the canoe much either.

Which End First?

The only time it makes any difference as to which end of a canoe is ashore (or the last to be boarded) and thus which way it's pointed when you're ready to go is if some maneuver is necessary immediately after you leave shore. In that case, it might be best to turn the boat around by hand before starting (if you can), or else to come in to shore when you stop so that you're facing whatever direction you want when you leave.

Changing positions in a canoe in the water—best done carefully!

CHANGING POSITION IN A CANOE

If you decide to shift bow and stern positions in a canoe, the sternman stays put and low braces (or gets ready to), and the bowman steps backward over his seat. Once he's cleared his seat he can continue moving backwards or turn (carefully) and face the stern. Either way he moves to near the middle of the canoe, holding the gunwales and keeping his weight low as usual, then crouches down as low as possible in the bottom of the canoe between thwarts. When he is settled the sternman gets up and, holding the gunwales, crosses over his bowman by straddling him (being very careful to keep his weight low and evenly distributed on both sides of the keel line), moves on forward to the bow seat, sits or kneels (preferably kneels), and takes paddle in hand ready to brace. Only then does the bowman get up and continue on to the stern position. The reason for the bowman moving first is that the sternman can watch all his movements and better balance the canoe at the beginning of the change. Other than this it makes no difference which one moves first.

PADDLING POSITIONS

Seats are put in a canoe to sit on, but only in smooth, easy water. *Before* you get to any rapid, shoal, standing waves, or other turbulence, *always* go to the kneeling position. Kneeling has the twin advantages of making the canoe more stable by lowering its center of gravity and enabling you to brace yourself more firmly in the boat. Both of these steadying influences contribute to safety and to better paddle control and thus to more effective canoeing techniques.

The basic kneeling position is shown in the photo. You are partially resting on and leaning against the front of the seat with the knees apread apart and braced into the bilges and the feet back under the seat. Your knee pads (essential for kneeling in comfort) grip the bottom of the boat so the combination gives you a three-point system of support. The bowman does not have as much room to spread out but is pretty well braced by the narrowing of the canoe at that end.

A variation of this position is to raise up off the seat and lean your thighs against the thwart in front of you. Use your

The basic "three-point" kneeling position, braced against the seat and in the bilges.

Alternate raised kneeling position used primarily for a better view of what's down the river.

spread feet to get a firmer grip in the bilges (sometimes even *under* the *seat*). This is *not* a good running position because your center of gravity is raised and you're not as secure in the canoe. It does have its momentary advantages in longer reach and a better view downstream. So, use it momentarily only; then go back to the regular kneeling position.

Paddle on Opposite Sides

In a tandem canoe the crew members *always* paddle on opposite sides. Do not swap sides unless your partner does also. Remember that the bowman can't see behind him, so the stern will have to tell the bow that he is changing over. Do *not* change sides to maneuver the boat; master the various techniques for moving the boat from the side on which you are paddling. A last-minute crossover by one of you so that both members of a tandem crew are paddling on the same side is an open invitation to a spill.

Do swap sides if you want to rest your arms. Just be sure your partner swaps too, and don't pick some time right in the middle of a maneuver to do it!

Holding the Paddle

The grip of a paddle is there to be held with the upper hand. The correct position is with the palm of the hand on or near the top of the grip and the knuckles parallel with the grip. Holding the paddle this way gives you maximum leverage for power or to twist the paddle (change the angle of the blade) and serves as a guide to blade position without your having to look. Holding the paddle below the grip is a very common fault of novice canoeists: don't do it. You lose control, leverage, grip, and also blade orientation. It is also distinctive as the mark of the rank amateur.

Another common beginning fault is holding the paddle with the upper and lower hands too close together. This results in a loss of leverage and control over the paddle that gets worse as the span between the hands gets smaller. A good, average span for the novice is to have your upper and lower hands a little more than shoulder width apart when one hand is on the

Correct paddle grip, the upper hand cupped over the grip and the lower hand firmly on the shaft.

grip. As your experience increases you'll shorten or lengthen this distance for various conditions. but this span will get you started.

It's essential that you hold the paddle *firmly*, not necessarily with a death grip, but secure enough for good control and security. A strong current or catching the blade on or in something can jerk the paddle right out of your hands.

Synchronize Your Strokes

Many canoeists will argue with me on this point. I think it's because they've never made the effort to establish a coordinated paddle rhythm and found out how smooth and powerful it is. This is basically a technique for stretches where there is no sudden maneuvering to be done. The bow sets the pace, as he always does in cruising, bearing in mind that the stern has varying amounts of correction to apply and can't keep the canoe on

A good beginning hand spread on a paddle—about a foot farther apart than your shoulder width.

course if the pace is too fast.

Ideally the power part of each person's stroke should be applied at exactly the same time, be the same length, and the same force. This is extremely hard to do and takes a lot of practice with the same person. If you ever hit it right, however, you'll immediately feel the difference in the way the canoe moves. Even if you never achieve this perfect synchronization, *do* paddle *together* and try to avoid progressing in "jerks." Move the canoe along smoothly and with as little side-to-side rocking as is possible. All of this combined means much less effort for a given speed.

Coordination of Strokes

In many maneuvers it's helpful, sometimes essential, that the two ends of the boat move in a coordinated and simultaneous motion. If the boat needs to move laterally to the left, for example, the bow and stern should coordinate their respective strokes so the boat does move *straight* to the side rather than ending up at an undesired angle. A more dramatic example of this is when a sharp, narrow turn with the current is to be made. Here the bow and stern might execute a simultaneous draw and pry respectively to twist the boat around an obstruction and into the chute. It does little good if one paddler gets his end around but the other doesn't.

Get Proficient on Both Sides and Both Ends

Most canoeists favor paddling on one side or the other, and it seems to have little to do with whether they're right- or left-handed. As a result, much of their skill is acquired only on their "good" side. Ideally you should practice all the strokes and maneuvers until both sides are your "good" side and you are as proficient to the right as to the left. This idea is rarely put into effective practice, with the result that "bad" side techniques are weak and awkward or even non-existent. Still, it's sometimes equally awkward or impossible to swap sides to do something on your favored side. In the long run it will pay you to work at this ambidextrous ability, even though it is initially tiring and wearing.

Similarly, you should be equally proficient in the bow and stern although, once more, canoeists seem to favor one position or the other. Both positions take their own particular skills, and the canoeist who can paddle bow or stern *only* is a long way from being really skillful in a canoe.

LOVE YOUR PADDLE

Novice canoeists often forsake their paddle and grab the gunwales when the going gets rough. Experienced canoeists also do this sometimes. I think it's instinctive—but it's the wrong thing to do.

Keep your hands on the paddle and the paddle in position to be used. Cling to it. It can slow you down, hold you up, steady your canoe, and get you out of trouble if you know how to use it and if it's *in the water and being used*. And even if it doesn't successfully accomplish all those wonderful things every time, it has at least done more good than your frantic clutching of the gunwales, which does no good at all!

SPARE PADDLES

First, always carry them, one for each paddler in the canoe, and *do* tie them in. An extra paddle floating in the river is no help to a canoeist without a paddle in his canoe. Neither is a broken paddle in your hand much help if you have no spare paddles. In the same line, spare paddles so heavily roped in that they can't readily be brought to hand are also useless. Paddles *do* break, always at unexpected moments and usually just when you need them the most. Your spare paddle should be instantly available, yet out of the way in normal paddling. Look back in Chapter 5 for the way to accomplish both these goals.

TRIM

With no wind and no current, a loaded canoe should sit dead level in the water. As most tandem teams fail to come in matched pairs, the boat often rests unevenly. To remedy this, some adjustment can be made by shifting equipment or paddlers. The sternman might move forward a little; simply going into the kneeling position will help. Both members might also turn around, get ahead of the nearest thwart, and paddle the boat stern first. This makes no difference in the handling since the canoe is symmetrical, but it *will* affect the trim.

It won't take you many trips on a river to discover that wind most often blows dead in your face or at some equally disadvantageous angle. Trim can sometimes be adjusted to turn this wind more to your advantage or at least to offset some of its effects. This is particularly useful in solo paddling, but the general principles apply to tandem boats also.

One method, useful in a direct head or tail wind, is to let the downwind end of the boat act like the rudder on a weather-vane and thus help keep you straight. As the current exerts more force on the end of a canoe deepest in the water, you would trim bow down when paddling into a head wind. With a tail wind trim stern down.

Cross winds are rough on a tandem canoe, rougher on a

solo boat. A solo paddler and the sternman of a tandem team should always paddle on the downwind side. In this way the canoe's tendency to turn away from the paddling side can be offset by the wind blowing on the other side. With luck, little or no "steering" strokes will be needed. Trim the canoe bow up. If you must paddle on the upwind side, then trim the canoe stern up. The effect will still be to neutralize the wind. Obviously, in a very strong cross wind you may have to use corrective strokes the *other* way, trying to overcome the wind's force. Another method useful in a cross wind that's blowing at 90 degrees to the canoe is to tack or zig-zag down the river. Again, paddle on the downwind side (solo or stern in a tandem crew) and trim according to whether you're tacking up- or downwind.

Exceptions to these hints are in waves, standing or otherwise. You don't want to trim either end down, but you may want to change the weight distribution. You'll find this discussed elsewhere in the book.

OVERLOADING YOUR CANOE

Don't! Keep your canoe as lightly loaded as possible; it will be faster, more responsive, and a pleasure to paddle. The added freeboard makes waves less likely to enter and the boat less likely to "submarine." An overloaded canoe is sluggish, hard to maneuver, more likely to swamp, and basically just a lot of work.

For river use on one-day outings, about 450 pounds total loading in a 16- or 17-foot cruising canoe and 200 to 250 in a 15-foot model should be set as maximums. Either length will easily support more weight, but you'll be happier without piling on extra pounds. You can load up a lot more on longer, flat-water canoe camping trips or anywhere that maneuverability is not as important.

TIE YOUR CANOE

Obvious? Not so, boats do drift away. Knots come untied, limbs break, the current works one loose that's partially pulled up on shore. Make sure your canoe is secure. If there is only room for one boat at the shoreline, tie it up, tie the next one to it, and so on. Just be sure that number one is secure. If you pull your canoe up on shore, pull it up until it's firmly settled. You don't have to tie a big knot—two half hitches or a clove hitch will do if tied to something sturdy. It's all relative to the current you're in and the wind that's blowing. Tie up or pull up commensurate with the conditions.

WHO'S THE CAPTAIN?

One paddler in a boat needs to be captain, but this position of importance may change many times going down a river. The sternman, with his forward view blocked by the bow of the canoe and the bowman, has only a more or less long-range view of the river. Normally then, he sets the course on non-obstructed waters, and the bowman contributes mostly muscle, but always with an eye out for a sudden ledge or rock.

In rapids, shoals, rock gardens, and the like, anywhere that quick maneuvering may be necessary, the stern will still set the general course but the bowman, with his close-up view of what's right in front of the canoe, becomes responsible for last-minute corrections.

When one of these corrective strokes is called for or done by the bowman, the sternman then executes whatever strokes are necessary to keep the boat aligned with the current and the stern with the bow. Thus, if the bowman spots a rock and pulls the bow to the left to avoid it, the sternman must do a quick complementary stroke to bring *his* end of the boat to the left also, thus avoiding the rock (maybe) and still keeping the boat parallel with the current.

Normally the captain will give the commands. The stern must speak (or shout) his commands, as the bowman can't see him. The bowman can either speak and/or do—preferably both because his spoken command may not be heard or understood above the noise of the water and also because he's facing forward, away from the sternman with whom he is trying to communicate. No matter who gives the command, however, it needs to be shouted out strong and clear. Muttering into your shirt front just doesn't get the message across!

Ideally the two members of a team will be equally skilled and have paddled together so much that they will instinctively know what the other is going to do. In this case commands may rarely be spoken. On the river, you'll rarely find this ideal situation, and the command and sometimes other choice words *will* usually be spoken. An old river adage is that you can tell how strong to make your stroke and whether to *really* work at it by the way the command is given—or yelled—or screamed!

COOPERATION

Every tandem canoe has two paddlers. If you're in the bow, it won't take you too long to realize that your sternman is not only *not* doing his share of the work but also does not know what he's doing anyway. While you are thinking this, the sternman is meanwhile coming to the same conclusions about you! These feelings tend to grow in direct proportion to the length and toughness of the trip. Knowing then, that this is the usual way of bow and stern, be patient, calm, and cooperative and try to remember that you won't always be stuck with the dumbest person on the river!

SOME DON'T'S

Standing Up in the Canoe

You will see this done. Canoeists do it who either don't know any better or who know *much* better. Those who know much better usually stand up to get a better view downstream, stand carefully and steadily, do it only occasionally and for a good purpose and, if they're in the stern position, make sure the bowman knows they're *going* to stand up before they actually do it. Those who don't know any better often fall out of the canoe!

Grabbing Bushes, Cables, and Limbs

Grabbing cables, wires, tree limbs, and the like as you canoe down a river is a good way to wind up in the water watching your canoe continue its trip alone. The faster you're moving, the more likely you are to be yanked right out of your boat. You will see canoeists holding on to limbs and such when they've stopped; you'll also see them grab limbs or logs *to* stop, but the wise ones only do this carefully and in *slow* current unless it's one of those "desperation lunges."

FINALLY

In this chapter I have used many weasel words such as "usually," "normally," and "often." As you progress on into the book and as your river-running experience increases, you'll begin to see why they were used. Except in instruction sessions, things are just not normally (there's another weasel) done in their pure form. They're combined and modified to suit the conditions of the moment and the paddler's own ideas. As no book could cover every variation and aspect and condition of river running, the only choice is to present the basic ideas and ways in a manner that is generally acceptable and that works. The weasel words are inserted so the novice river canoeist won't become rigid in his thinking and will be aware that there *are* different ways of doing things under different conditions.

It is essential, though, that the novice first know the *fundamental* ways and conditions. Remember that many of the rules *can* be violated but *only* if you know enough to violate them!

CHAPTER 8
WATER AND WATER READING

Moving water behaves in certain known ways, and a knowledge of these characteristics is essential if you want to be even a moderately adept canoeist. Forearmed with such know-how you can often avoid or offset a struggle with the current or even use these characteristics to aid you in your paddling and maneuvering. In addition, knowing what the current will do and the effects it will have on your canoe enables you to stay out of many unsafe situations.

WATER

A river doesn't run in one long, even chute from its headwaters down to level land. It usually starts off small and fast, flowing with a lot of slope to it up in the mountains or hills somewhere. As it descends toward more level land its drop will gradually decrease. It will flow along through pools, where it will slow down and get deeper. Then, at the end of each pool, it will descend more abruptly and swiftly to the next pool. These abrupt descents may be caused by hard layers of rock in the river bed that haven't been worn down as fast as the rest of the bed. They may also be boulders that have fallen or been pushed into the river and serve as a sort of dam, or they may be some obstruction that has been built up by deposits of silt and smaller stones brought down by the river. Sometimes they may be man-made, such as a dam. Whatever their source, we call the natural ones rapids or shoals or, in extreme cases, ledges or waterfalls. As the river continues its downhill run and the elevation of the surrounding land decreases, the river will gradually get deeper and slower or wider and slower and its pools will get longer and/or its abrupt descents less and less; finally it becomes a placid stream flowing through flat lands and basically unobstructed by natural causes.

WATERFLOW—WHAT'S A RAPID?

Water is heavy, noncompressible (at least as far as the

130

Where water reading is easy and a mistake makes little difference.

canoeist is concerned), occupies space, and runs from a higher to a lower level. These properties make a river that *flows,* but water has another important characteristic—it seeks its own level and in so doing fills all of the space into which it is confined up to the amount of water or space available.

As a river canoeist you will probably get into some rapids sooner or later. "Rapids" are just what the word says—a place in the river where the water flow is faster or more rapid than what is immediately before or after this place. What makes a rapid? Some answers could be that a rapid is formed by rocks in the river, a shallow place caused by these rocks, or a sharp change in elevation. All these answers are true.

A river has a certain amount of water flowing down it. On a free-flowing river this flow actually varies almost from day to day, depending upon such things as rainfall, water-table height, whether anything is being pumped out of or into it, and numerous other factors. Nevertheless, we can say that for any given moment at a given place, there is a constant amount of water

Rapids. An ability to read water is very necessary in a place like this.

between its banks.

    If a river channel is only so wide and so deep and enough water is flowing along it to fill the channel, this water has to go at some certain speed to maintain this flow. Otherwise, the river will run over its banks. To find out how much water is flowing at any given point, multiply the width of the channel by the depth and the speed of the water (in feet per minute). This will give the cubic feet of water going by at any one time.

    Using a theoretical river 100 feet wide, 5 feet deep, and flowing at 1 mile an hour down a channel with smooth sides and bottom and with a constant drop:

$$100 \text{ feet x } 5 \text{ feet x } \frac{5,280 \text{ feet per mile}}{60 \text{ minutes per hour}}$$

$$= \quad 4 \text{ x } 4,000 \text{ cubic feet per minute (about 27,280 gallons)}$$
$$\text{at 88-feet-per-minute speed}$$

Of course, real rivers don't look like this nor would these calculations be more than a guess. Real rivers get wide and narrow, shallow and deep; their drop varies all over the place; and their banks and bottoms are all sorts of shapes and cluttered with all kinds of obstacles that wreak havoc to this ideal flow.

The following chart, however, made on these ideal conditions, illustrates some fundamental facts about water behavior in a river bed.

WIDTH	DEPTH	MPH	FPM	VOLUME
100'	5'	1	88	44,000 (Ideal)
100'	2½'	2	176	44,000
50'	10'	1	88	44,000
50'	5'	2	176	44,000
200'	2½'	1	88	44,000
200'	1¼'	2	176	44,000
200'	5'	½	44	44,000

From the chart it appears that if the river narrows, the water has to get deeper or faster or both; if the river widens, the water must get shallower or slower or both. Conversely, if the speed of the water increases, the bed has narrowed or the water is more shallow; slower water means a wider river or a deeper bed. Out on a real river this means that deep water runs more slowly than shallow water, and shallow water will tend to have a wider bed than the same volume of deep water.

To return to the rapids again, it is easy to see what happens. Rapids are shallow so the water gets faster, or rapids stay deep but have rocks in them, and the rocks, in effect, make the bed narrower and the water faster.

VARYING WATER VELOCITY

The velocity of the water in a river varies, depending upon where it is in the river. It doesn't all flow along at the same speed. Generally the swiftest portion of any relatively straight-flowing current will be on and near the surface in the middle of the main flow. It is slowest near the bottom and near the shoreline because of the friction between the water and the bottom and banks. The closer the water is to the shoreline (or the bottom), the slower it flows.

To the river canoeist this is useful because it means that there is usually an eddy of sorts near shore which can be used to aid your going to or departing from the bank. This is true even on an outside bend, but in this case the eddy will probably be unnoticeable and unusable. This difference in the speed of the water near the surface and below the surface also explains why a canoeist floating in his life jacket with his feet down instead of up near the surface is likely to start tumbling—his upper body will be moving down river faster than his feet.

THE MAIN CURRENT

On a straight, unobstructed stretch of river, the main flow and thus the fastest current and deepest channel will be down the center of the river parallel to the banks. If one bank is higher than the other, the river is usually deepest and fastest near the higher bank. If an angled ledge occurs across the river, the main flow will probably be toward the downstream end of the ledge if all of the ledge is a constant depth under the water surface.

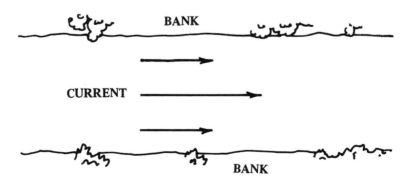

The fastest current.

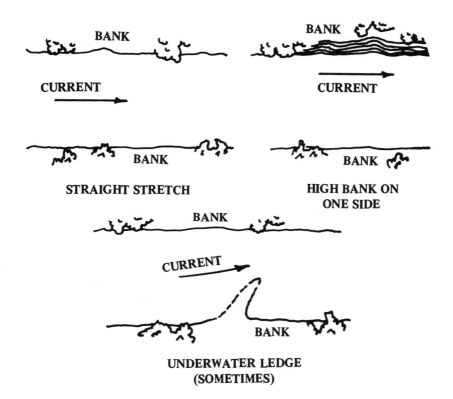

Location of main currents.

Obstructions in the river will also divert the main current, but where it's diverted *to* is a question of the placement of the obstructions. It could be flowing in almost any direction and path and could constantly change that direction and path.

In a bend the main current and deepest water will be to the outside of the bend. In multiple bends it will be from the outside of one bend, across the river, to the outside of the next bend.

The inside curves of these bends will have eddies in them— slack water moving much slower than the main current, possibly not moving at all, or even flowing slightly upstream. These inside bends are likely to be shallow because the slower current of the eddy has deposited silt and pebbles to build up a bar.

135

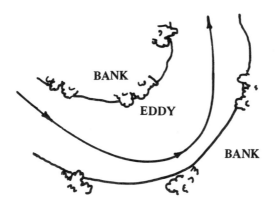

SINGLE BEND

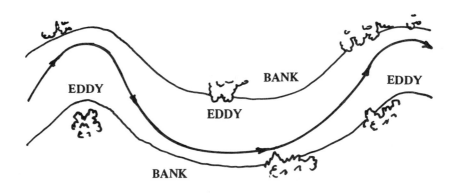

MULTIPLE BENDS

Location of main current in bends.

PARTICULARS ABOUT OUTSIDE BENDS

If standing waves occur in a bend, then they will be biggest on the outside of the bend because of the higher volume of water there. Similarly, because of this higher volume, the bank

136

of an outside bend is quite likely to be undercut or eaten away, which can present the very real danger of fallen trees in the water at these points. This danger is covered more thoroughly in Chapter 11.

WATER READING

General

If you want to progress down a river without using the pry-off-the-bottom, foot-against-a-rock, hit-it-and-bounce method of canoeing, you need to learn to read the water. Water reading is not a tough subject, but it does require practice and experience. You'll be fooled many times before you learn the fundamentals, and you'll still be fooled after you have some knowledge and experience—but not quite as often.

Basics

Water flows down a river in the easiest possible way for its speed and volume. This fact forms the basis for what is often called the "filament" theory of water flow. Basically, this idea of water travel says that an overall flow of water encountering obstructions breaks up into smaller individual flows or "filaments." These filaments then find the easiest path for their particular volume and speed and progress on down the river on their own until they all rejoin in the open water below the obstructions.

Translated into practical river *running,* this means that you should be able to select some filament that runs from the head of the rapid to its foot and follow it down. Theoretically, this is generally true. As these filaments meet in pools or separate into yet smaller flows, you will usually still be able to follow some basic flow on its course down through these obstructions. Some paths that this flow follows may not be floatable: they could be too narrow or too shallow, carry you into a place where you can't maneuver or make a turn or end in a hydraulic or some other danger, or for many other random reasons prove to be the wrong paths. But the idea of water reading is to find and follow one of these *navigable* filaments and, at some point before it

137

"Filaments" in water reading.

ceases to be navigable, find and follow the next one until you're to the end of the obstructions.

Navigability will depend to a great extent on your ability to maneuver the canoe, but in this case water reading is just as important. You may be able to handle the boat like no one else, but all the maneuvering ability in the world won't help you if you can't figure out *where* to maneuver to!

Water reading, therefore, really consists of two aspects— developing the ability to recognize and follow a series of float-able paths or filaments and recognizing and avoiding whatever obstacles may be in those paths.

Signs

To the beginner, running water usually presents an unfath-omable picture of confusion, and it *is* hard to define clear-cut categories for the purpose of instruction. The difficulty is that the categories are more often seen in combination than in their pure form. Nonetheless, there are some distinct signs to watch for and characteristics of water behavior to recognize that will give you abundant clues once you learn to see them. Once you do learn them the apparently random flowing of the water sud-denly won't be nearly as confusing.

Practice

Shallow water loaded with easy shoals and small rapids is an excellent place to practice beginning water reading. Make the run short, take your time, and conscientiously look for and fol-

138

low the various paths and "read the signs" to the best of your ability.

The best way to learn to recognize the various basic signs and conditions is to accompany an experienced river canoeist who can point them out to you on the river itself. You can expand these fundamentals by your own study, observation, and testing. If you live near a controlled flow river that is sometimes "turned off" or in an area where streams are seasonally very low or even dry, study the obstacles and paths at normal levels, then return at a time of low or no water and observe what is normally obscured underwater. Being able to relate the cause (boulder, ledge, etc.) with the effect (pillow, souse hole, etc.) will greatly sharpen your interpretive skills.

Get in the habit of stopping at the upper end of a practice shoal or rapid and "scouting" out your idea of a path. Try reading the rapid from the "bottom" up—finding a navigable outflow and tracing its filament back upstream to some point of entry at the top of the rapid.

All of this slow and steady practice will pay off. You'll soon find yourself beginning to distinguish the patterns of the water and automatically selecting a path. And while you're working on your water reading, give yourself an additional practice bonus by trying to *maneuver* all the way down through every shoal or rapid without touching or scraping.

FINALLY

In the following discussion of specific signs in the water, I quite often use the term "rock" or "rocks." The obstructions referred to are not always rocks—they could be logs, dirt, old bridge pilings, broken concrete structures, or numerous other things. I simply became tired of writing "obstructions," and as the principles are all the same anyway, just remember that in the following cases a "rock" may not *be* a rock—but it *is* something to dodge!

139

WHAT TO LOOK FOR

The Vee

The vee is your first and most obvious guide to a floatable path. There are two kinds of vees—upstream and downstream, referring to whether the "point" of the vee is pointing up or down the river. They mean two very different things, as you can see from the photos and illustrations.

Vees are created by moving water being deflected around a rock (upstream vee) or being forced in between two rocks (downstream vee). Obviously, you want to avoid the "point" of an upstream vee.

The downstream vee, on the other hand, offers a first choice of path. It probably has been scoured out to a floatable depth, and it's also a clear path (at least for the duration of the vee). Don't plunge blindly down vees, however; look where they're taking you. It may be a place you don't want to go.

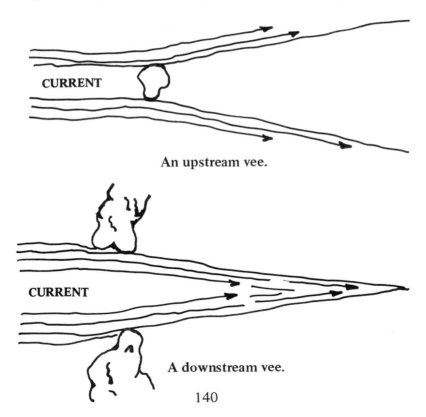

An upstream vee.

A downstream vee.

140

A very obvious upstream vee in the river.

A well-defined downstream vee flanked by two upstream vees.

Tongues and Chutes

A tongue or chute is sort of an overgrown downstream vee and the three terms are often used interchangeably. Usually a tongue or chute is thought to have a more distinct elevation change between its up and downstream ends than a vee and to have a higher volume and speed of water in it. Often they are formed by the water wearing down a softer section of rock in a ledge or ridge. They are also often found adjacent to large obstructions where the concentrated force of the water deflected around the obstruction has scoured out a deeper channel. The end result is that the water pours down through a sort of slot as if it were running down a chute—hence the name. Tongues or chutes may be straight or curved but will usually have a relatively deep path to accommodate their higher volume and velocity.

Dropping out of a chute into standing waves.

Pillows

Pillows are literally humps of water over underwater obstructions. They are caused where rocks are under the surface and the current or the rock's shape is such that the water just flows smoothly over it and is "bumped" up toward the surface. With very slow (or no) current there will be no pillow and therefore no warning of a rock unless you can see it. With relatively faster currents and bigger boulders, the hump will become more pronounced until finally the water begins to form standing waves downstream from it.

A pillow on paper—

Whether you have a pillow alone or a pillow and standing waves depends upon the current and the size and depth of the obstruction. Even in low-velocity water a small rock close to the surface may well have standing waves below its pillow. The waves may be only a few inches high, but they are standing waves nonetheless.

—and a small one in the river.

For a given volume, the farther downstream the waves are, the deeper is the rock. The point where you can float over it is a question of judgment. Just be aware that *something* upstream is causing those standing waves—big or little—and watch for the telltale pillow that tells where that something is.

Standing Waves

Standing waves are an easily recognized sign of clear water and will usually be found downstream from pillows and drops and at the end of vees and chutes. A standing wave is a wave that doesn't move or "break" as an ocean wave does. It "stands" in one place, and although the water in it constantly changes, the wave form and location remain the same. Standing waves are formed by fast-running water suddenly hitting deeper, slower-moving water. Thus standing waves, or "haystacks" as they are sometimes called, are a sign of deep, safe water.

Standing waves in theory—

Keep your eyes open, however; a solitary rock could be lurking along the edge somewhere or down in a long run of waves, and you might not detect the change in water pattern swiftly enough to dodge it.

Standing waves also offer a sign of danger. In a swift, flat current, the sudden appearance of standing waves means a rock upstream, so watch for the pillow over the rock that is forming them.

—and in fact.

SOUSE HOLES AND HYDRAULICS

A souse hole and a hydraulic "jump" are sometimes confused by the beginning river canoeist. The big difference is simple—a souse hole will spit you out downstream; a hydraulic either won't or will take its time doing it, possibly too much time!

Souse Holes

A souse hole is the deep trough just downstream of an obstruction and between the obstruction and the first standing wave. Souse holes are a product of high-speed and high-volume water running over a large obstruction, then suddenly slowing down. A good example is a large rock with a "pillow" over it. A trough is created as the water pours off the downstream face of the rock and suddenly slows down and begins making standing waves.

145

A souse hole.

Souse holes are a problem for two reasons. First, as a canoe rides over the obstruction it plunges into the souse hole in a bow-down position, the bow digs into the wave, and the boat takes in water and may swamp. The other problem is that even if you don't swamp (as with a decked canoe, for example), your forward speed may be checked so much (or halted completely) that you will broach with probable consequent swamping. In heavy water, souse holes can be deep, and you'll swamp in them despite your best efforts.

A combination of standing waves with a souse hole in the foreground.

Hydraulics

I have talked about pillows and souse holes, each of which is associated with standing waves to a degree that may sink you. Hydraulics are an aspect of water behavior in which you will *not* see standing waves but that can do more than just sink you. This distinction may be life saving.

If you are scouting a place and see standing waves running out below it (as in a souse hole), you know that even if you spill or swamp, you and your boat will be swept out downstream. If you do *not* see standing waves below it, however, look closely for an *upstream* current. An easy indication is flotsam drifting upstream on the surface, being pulled under, and reappearing downstream again to begin its upstream journey once more. This visible upstream current and/or lack of standing waves when there is a large volume of water pouring over something is a sign of a hydraulic—a whirlpool or giant eddy laid on its side, if you will, and one of the biggest dangers in canoeing.

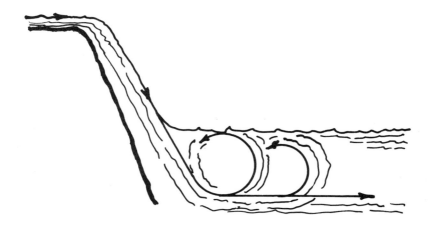

Currents in a hydraulic.

Hydraulics are usually found at the base of waterfalls, dams, ledges, and slopes where a large volume of water is pouring over the lip of the obstruction, hitting the relatively still water below and plunging toward the bottom. They are parti-

147

cularly easy to find and observe where solid sheets of water pour over a lip or down a smooth, inclined slope. On the slope the descending water just continues its natural path down the slope and begins to pull the slower surface water down with it. This results in a current on the surface that is first pulled upstream, then forced downward again by the descending water. This mass creates downward, reverse currents that can pull you under, roll and tumble you, push you up toward the surface, then pull you under again—all right at the base of the falling water. You can observe this action at the foot of any dam with a good flow of water over it. You'll often see fence posts, trees, or stumps vanishing in the froth beneath the falling water, then popping to the surface somewhere downstream and being pulled back upstream on the surface, only to be tumbled and sunk again. That post or stump could be you; the only difference is that the stump doesn't have to breathe!

Small hydraulics occur all over a river; almost any drop will have one. Unless the water volume is high, you can usually ride right through or over them and never know they're there. But when the river is high, the drop large, or the volume great, beware of them. Their danger under these conditions cannot be overemphasized. Hydraulics can be and are—killers!

STOPPER WAVES

Any medium-sized standing wave will slow you down if you dig your bow into it. If the wave is big enough or your momentum is not great enough, then it will stop you dead in the water. This is a "stopper" wave. Ignoring the fact that you may swamp anyway from digging your bow into the wave, the result of losing all or even most of your headway will probably be loss of control, broaching in the trough, and swamping.

Another aspect of stopper waves is the inability to paddle up their sides if you're down in a deep trough and have lost momentum. Both the "stopping" and this "hill-climbing" ability (or lack of it) are big dangers in souse holes.

DROPS, FALLS, LEDGES

These are all basically the same situation insofar as water

A 10-inch log caught in a hydraulic. Only half the length is above water. It was not stuck in the bottom but was being tossed into the air.

A ledge or small fall in the river.

reading is concerned. They all are vertical or nearly vertical descents over a short horizontal distance. At the foot of any of them you may find hydraulics whose size, depending on the water volume, height of the drop, and configuration of the obstruction, may be treated with caution or ignored.

Any flat, even-lipped drop is easy to spot from a canoe because the lip will form a sharp line across the river, and the downstream scenery will be noticeably lower. Sharp slopes and the beginnings of rapids with a marked elevation drop will also often present this sharp horizon. But usually you will begin to see the "whitewater" or water vapor in the air at or above the line as you get closer.

A series of ledges will be readily identified by the flat areas in between the drops and the froth and standing waves kicked up below them by the multiple (usually) chutes and vees. Hydraulics and souse holes also are fond of lurking at the bottoms of falls and ledges, so be careful. Be exceptionally cautious

150

when approaching the lip of a fall or what you think may be a fall. Remember that in high, swift water you may not be able to back off from it if you approach too closely.

EDDIES

Eddy water is distinguishable from the rest of the river because it moves at a slower speed than the surrounding current, apparently doesn't move at all, or moves slightly upstream. Eddies are found immediately downstream of obstructions that protrude above the surface of the water and thus break the speed of the current. The rock forming an upstream vee, for example, would have an eddy below it. Eddies are also found along the shore and on the insides of bends, as pointed out earlier.

Depending upon the current and the obstruction, the current differential between the main river and the water of the eddy will be greater or less. When the differential is large, a sharp and distinct line separates the main current and the eddy. This line of demarcation is called the eddy line. With less differential this eddy line becomes softer and less distinct.

As pointed out in a subsequent chapter, eddies are your haven of safety and rest in the turbulent world of moving water. You can run into one and sit securely while the water rushes by on either side of you. Eddies give you a place to rest, a place to plan your next move, or simply a place to sit and watch your fellow canoeists or the scenery. Eddies are very useful things; *however*, crossing the eddy line, either entering or coming out

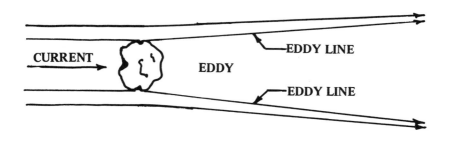

An eddy and its eddy lines.

of the eddy, can swiftly flip you right out of your boat, and the techniques of "eddy turns" and "peel offs" should be strictly observed. The sharper the eddy line, the more likely is the flip.

SLICKS, PEBBLED SURFACES, AND ROCK GARDENS

Slicks and pebbled surfaces are indications of shallow water. A rock garden may or may not be shallow, but in the usual sense of the term it frequently is.

A slick is just what it sounds like—a very smooth, slick-looking patch in the midst of the general rough surface of the water. Slicks are caused by a smooth and flat-topped ledge or boulder very close to the surface. It's best to avoid them as they're usually too shallow to float over.

Pebbled surfaces occur where the water is shallow and where the bottom is fairly even but has a lot of small obstructions of about the same height. Submerged gravel bars give a good example of this surface, as do sloping bars built up on the inside of bends in a river and at the outflow of streams and creeks entering a river.

A rock garden is a stretch of river with many rocks in it. While this could be called a rapid or a shoal, a rock garden is usually considered to be relatively shallow and low-volume water that is so obstructed with rocks protruding above the surface that it requires many maneuvers to negotiate its twists and turns. Rock gardens are good places to practice maneuvers and fun to work in if you're in no hurry. They are *not* fun when you encounter a really shallow one at the end of a long day on the river. It is at this stage of a trip that they're usually called powerfully descriptive things other than shoals, rapids, and rock gardens!

MISCELLANEOUS THINGS TO WATCH FOR

Cushions

When water hits the upstream face of a solid obstruction, it often banks up in front of it before being deflected and flowing on downriver. This mass of piled-up water is called a cushion and can *sometimes* be used to hold you off or whip you around

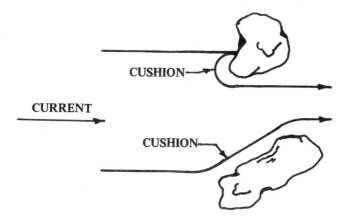

CURRENT

CUSHION→

CUSHION→

Cushions.

the obstruction. It may at least reduce the impact somewhat. Cushions are most frequently found and used where the water is banking off a rock whose face is sloping downstream and into or toward the main current. This buffer will often effectively send you on around the rock and through the chute. In connection with this let me repeat that water is *not* deflected by anything that it can pass through or easily pass over or under, such as most downed trees and logjams. *Safe* cushions are only formed by solid, comparatively massive obstructions, and their use is a matter of their size and your experience.

Color

The color of the water in a river sometimes offers a clue as to what's in it (or not in it). In calm water a darker color can almost be relied upon to mean deeper water and a lighter tone to mean shallower water. In rapids, although slicks and hard-to-detect pillows can also create dark spots, a darker tone will usually still indicate a *possible* path. You'll have to watch the general colors in the particular river you're in to become aware of just what changes mean what. Of course, color means little in a muddy river.

Terrain

The shoreline can offer you some clues as to approaching water conditions. If the banks start to get higher and earth banks begin to give way to rock formations and cliffs, you can almost rely on a shoal or a rapid coming up or at least a deep, swift, narrow channel.

Speed of Water

In conjunction with the last item you'll probably notice that as cliffs rise, river speed generally increases. In flat areas a drop in elevation ahead of you is usually signalled by accelerated current.

"Frothy" Water

"Frothy" water is water so full of air from being tossed up and churned around in a rapid that it can barely be treated as water. While it is not really a sign of anything except a lot of turbulence, you should be aware of its properties before you "read" the water, find a path, and paddle headlong into this "un-waterlike" froth.

Basically, frothy water is so "thin" and offers such little resistance, support, and body that your canoe will drop in farther than you expected it to, paddle strokes and braces may not be effective, and should you spill, your life jacket won't support you as you think it should. The degree to which this happens depends upon how much "white" is in this patch of whitewater. The more active the rapid and the higher the water is tossed, the more frothy it becomes and the more you can expect the above effects. Go ahead and paddle into it, but realize that it won't support you like a solid mass of water.

One More Sign

On any river your ears will usually tell you of an approaching shoal or rapid before your eyes do. This comes in very handy at any time but particularly so when rounding bends on strange rivers or when you're paddling in poor viewing conditions such as the late evening; dark, rainy days; or when facing into a late afternoon sun glinting off the water. Of course, just *hearing* something doesn't tell you much because *any* obstructed water or small drop makes a noise out of all proportion to its size and ferocity!

READING "IMPOSSIBLE" WATER

Early in your water-reading and canoeing career you will probably run across a lot of rapids that you will find "impossible" to read. Either there is no apparent path or none that you think you can follow, or there are drops that you're not willing to run, heavier volume and stronger current than you're used to, potential stoppers, or any number of things that make this particular rapid more than you're willing to try. As your experience and skill increase you will find that your rating of rapids decreases and that many of these impossible, no-path jumbles of water, froth, and rock *are* possible and *do* have paths. But, for your own safety, be cautious. Don't overmatch yourself! There are only two situations in which you should try to run a rapid that's "impossible for you." One is as part of a training program where qualified instructors are there to help you, and the other is when other experienced canoeists are along to help you. In both cases the run should be made with rescue canoes and personnel having throwing ropes stationed along the way (at least at the bottom of the rapid). If you're alone (and you shouldn't be) or if all in your group (no matter how experienced) find the rapid impossible, portage it. There is nothing cowardly or disgraceful about this; it just makes very good sense. It's your canoe, your equipment, and your life, and it's stupid to risk them because of what you think someone else may think.

CHAPTER 9
PADDLE TECHNIQUES

Your paddle strokes are wonderful aids in controlling your canoe. They can move it forward, backward, right, left, or diagonally; spin it in circles—or sink it! It all depends on what you do and when and how you do it!

In this chapter you'll learn the basic strokes of river canoeing—the strokes necessary to perform the maneuvers that you'll find in the next chapter and the paddle techniques necessary to move the canoe like you want it to move in all the directions mentioned above except, hopefully, the last one.

SOME RULES AND ONE DEFINITION

There are a few rules about paddling that should be strictly observed until they become automatic. They'll help you get more out of your paddle strokes and be a more efficient paddler, too.

Rule: *Put all of your blade in the water.* A paddle blade has just so much area. It does *no* good at all waving around in the air and only does half as much good as it should if only half the blade is in the water. The more of the paddle blade area that is *in* the water, the more work it's doing for you.

Rule: *Learn the various strokes—they all have their uses.* A river is rarely one long mass of rapids with no pools or flat places. Therefore, the river canoeist needs to learn how to negotiate the pools and other "cruising" areas as well as those full of obstructions. Then too, you won't always be running rapids. You may do more cruising than you think down rivers where holding a course or fighting wind effect is more important than making sudden maneuvers.

Rule: *Be aware of the difference in lake (or cruising) and river strokes—don't use the wrong one at the wrong time.* There are *many* different paddle strokes. Some are great for still waters or any unobstructed current, others work best in moving water, still others don't work at all in moving (or still) water. In this chapter you'll learn those that do work in moving water.

Rule: *Learn the pure strokes first and learn them well*

before you begin varying them. Paddle techniques are the foundation of successful maneuvering and *successful* maneuvering is the key to keeping your canoe (and maybe you) in one piece. Learning the *correct* way to do a pure stroke gives you a solid base upon which to build. "Slopping" through paddle strokes wastes energy, valuable time, and now and then a canoe!

Rule: *Pure strokes are rarely used.* The novice canoeist who learns his lessons well *will* use pure strokes until his paddling experience broadens, and these pure strokes will definitely yield the most result for his effort. But as his skill and knowledge increase, he will begin to incorporate (probably unconsciously) various little adjusting movements in his strokes to compensate for wind and wave and current and course corrections. For example, if the bowman is paddling along on his right as in "A" and desires to move the bow of the canoe slightly in that direction, he would probably *not* go to a full, textbook draw as in "B." Instead, he would simply put a little diagonal component in his forward stroke as in "C" or *would* do a draw but not with the motions or power of a full draw. He has thus modified the pure stroke and still accomplished his purpose with a minimum of effort.

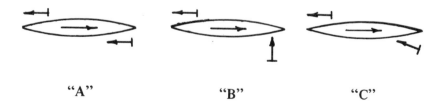

"A"   "B"   "C"

Another contributing factor to the absence of pure strokes on the river is that they often blend from or into some other stroke. In the "C" example, what starts off as a modified draw converts into a forward stroke, all in one smooth motion.

Definition: *Power Face.* Technically the power face of your blade is whichever flat side of the blade is being used to exert force on the water in any particular stroke or sequence of strokes. Either blade face may be used as the initial power face. For this chapter's instructional purposes, however, to insure that your wrist and arm motions and paddle orientation are right as you work on a particular stroke, the power face for any given stroke is *always* assumed to be the flat side of your blade that is facing and being moved toward the stern when you have the paddle in position for a basic forward stroke. The other side of your blade will be called the "non-power face."

DIRECTION OF FORCE

Always have the flat of the blade perpendicular to the direction in which you want the paddle stroke to have the most effect. Paddle strokes are most effective when all their power is aimed in the proper direction. This is done by positioning the *flat* of the blade so that the maximum area of the paddle is exerting that power 180 degrees in the opposite direction from what you want the canoe to do. This applies no matter in what direction you want the canoe to go.

Notice the difference in the two illustrations. In both you want the canoe to move straight forward. Disregard the tendency of the canoe to turn away from the paddle side (this will be discussed later). In the first illustration the blade is perpendicular to the desired movement and the force is being used effectively. In the second illustration the blade is angled, and part of the force of the paddle stroke is trying to move the canoe in some direction *other* than straight ahead or, as we're ignoring turning, there is *less* force devoted to moving the canoe *forward*.

FORCE

MOVEMENT

180° DIFFERENCE

FORCE(S)

MOVEMENT

**ANGLED BLADE
(LESS THAN 180°
DIFFERENCE)**

So, a paddle blade that is angled to the direction you want to go will force the canoe off to one side or force your partner in a tandem canoe to use part of *his* paddling force to correct the course. Either way means less movement in the direction you want to go with the same effort, or *more* effort for the same movement.

The same principle applies to the vertical part of your paddle strokes. In this illustration we're looking at a paddle stroke as viewed from the side. You'll see that in "A" some of the force is aimed downward, which serves to push up the side of the canoe on your paddle side. In "C" some force is directed upward—you're "lifting" water and pulling down on that side of the canoe. In "B" you're ideal—all your force is directed in a 180-degree direction from your desired movement.

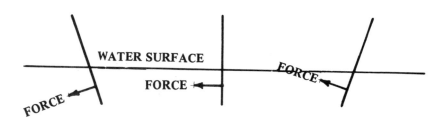

Most paddle strokes, then, can be broken into three segments: the entry where the blade is in "A" position, the power part as in "B," and the end of the stroke as in "C." Both the "A" and "C" positions in strokes such as the back and forward stroke should be relaxed, with the real power being applied for the short distance just before, through, and just after the blade is in the perpendicular position of "B."

Obviously, you can't keep a paddle in the "B" position all through a stroke without some awkward "rocking" body movements. You should try, however, to avoid a great percentage of your effort being wasted in up or down force components by not reaching too far forward (unless accompanied by a body lean forward also) and by cutting off the power of your stroke before it's doing more harm than good.

USE OF THE BODY IN PADDLING

Many muscles of your body are much stronger than your arm muscles, and to avoid undue arm fatigue as well as to generate more power, you should try to *use* these muscles to augment the power of your arms in paddling. Of course, regardless of the *way* you paddle, most of these muscles *will* come into play at one time or another and to one degree or another. Arm, shoulder, back, waist, and thigh muscles usually get the greatest workout no matter how unconsciously they are applied. Using these muscles take a little practice. Paddling (cruising) with both arms pretty straight out brings the back muscles into play. Some paddlers "rock" back and forth slightly with each stroke, leaning with it and thus using their waist muscles as well as their body weight. Using your body weight is also helpful, particularly in a backstroke, although in the backstroke torso weight and power seem to be instinctively used by all paddlers.

The majority of river paddlers I know rely primarily on arm, shoulder, and back muscle power in "cruising" situations and begin to lean more heavily on the use of their waist and leg muscles and upper-torso weight when the current gets swifter or the maneuvering more urgent.

You'll see many styles of paddling on the river. Your style will be governed by the way you learn to canoe and by what you find comfortable and effective. The main thing is to *use* the muscles and weight you have at the correct moment in the stroke. Don't try to do it all with your arms alone.

BRACING YOURSELF IN THE CANOE

A stable and well-braced position in the canoe is essential for effective paddling. The "three-point" kneeling position explained elsewhere in this book is about as good a position as you can assume for most of the strokes. As much as possible you want the canoe to respond not only to your paddle movements but also to your body movements and weight shifts as well. Thus, you have to be "locked in" pretty tightly. The smooth bottom of a canoe is not the easiest place to "lock in" on, even though rubber knee pads help a lot. This, incidentally, is an excellent reason for not using an old life jacket or anything

160

else not attached to either you or the boat for knee pads—they slide around too easily.

Some river canoeists glue or bolt their knee pads to the bottom of their canoes. This gives a pair of "pockets" into which to fit your knees. Another scheme is the use of "knee" or "thigh" straps, a single long strap laced into the canoe in the position shown in the sketch and into which your bent legs fit. Some canoeists don't like straps, fearing that their legs might get trapped in them in case of a spill. I personally have never used straps, but those who have think they're great. One caution here: to minimize the chance of entanglement, never wear knee pads when the thigh straps are in use.

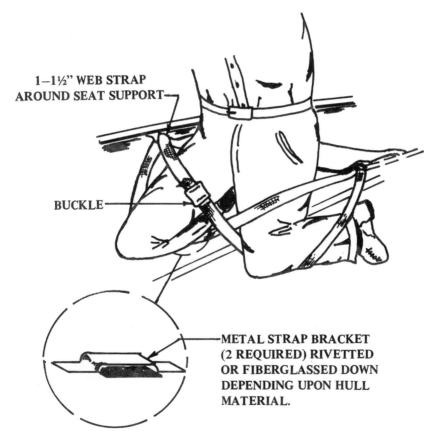

1–1½" WEB STRAP
AROUND SEAT SUPPORT

BUCKLE

METAL STRAP BRACKET
(2 REQUIRED) RIVETTED
OR FIBERGLASSED DOWN
DEPENDING UPON HULL
MATERIAL.

Knee (thigh) straps.

161

USE OF THE LEGS

Your legs are tremendously strong and are of great use in holding you braced into your canoe and in allowing you to use the muscles of your body while paddling. One of the surprises you'll probably have after your first rapids-running trip is how tired and possibly sore your thighs will be the next day. Sitting on the seat of a canoe almost neutralizes the power of your legs and waist. The "three-point" kneeling position locks you in so both can be effectively used.

FEATHERING

In the following descriptions of strokes you will often find the term "feathered" used in referring to your paddle. "Feathering" is the process of turning and keeping the flat of the paddle blade parallel to the water on the recovery part of a stroke. The paddle itself is then "feathered." Waves slapping at the flat of a blade with its face *perpendicular* to the water can jerk it right out of your hand, and wind blowing on it can greatly increase the work you do while paddling. By feathering the paddle during recovery, most of these effects are cut down as wind and wave have only the edge of the blade to strike.

The paddle in a "feathered" position.

FINALLY

The descriptions of some of the strokes in the rest of this chapter may seem to be unnecessarily long and detailed. They're not! I've tried to cover the motions thoroughly enough so that you don't make an error in some small but vital thing. It's amazing how many times novice canoeists can swap power faces or get their arms and hands contorted into some miserable-feeling and totally wrong position. Small things *do* make a big difference, so I suggest that you go through the descriptions carefully and pay particular attention to your hand positions as these (if right) will automatically put your paddle blade in the right position.

MOVING THE CANOE FORWARD AND BACKWARD

BASIC FORWARD STROKE

General

The forward stroke is used to propel the canoe forward. In its pure form there is no diagonal component to it at all. It is basically a bowman's stroke used for power but is also used by the stern as the beginning of the "steering" strokes or as a power stroke when no course-correcting is needed.

Paddle Position

For the forward stroke, the paddle shaft should be perpendicular to the surface of the water. You will find this an awkward and tiring position at first, but don't stop working toward its becoming automatic. It is the most efficient position, and your efforts in learning it correctly will pay off in the long run. This means that your upper hand will be out beyond the gunwale for most of the stroke and *may* mean (depending upon how supple you are) that your upper body will be twisted slightly toward the paddle side. For comfort you will probably be kneeling slightly to one side of the keel line of the canoe with your hip closer to the gunwale on the paddle side.

The power face is perpendicular to the keel, and the actual

Correct paddle orientation for basic forward strokes.

stroke itself is parallel to the keel or the keel line of your canoe. Your paddle does *not* follow the curve of the gunwale during the stroke. This is very important, for it is only in this way that the full power of your paddle stroke will be effectively used. Thus a forward stroke in the bow will begin with the paddle away from the gunwale and, as the stroke comes back parallel to the keel, the paddle will come ever closer to the gunwale. The opposite is true in the stern; the stroke begins near the gunwale and gradually gets farther away as the paddle follows through.

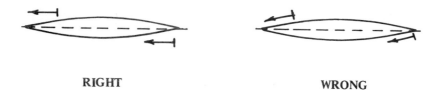

RIGHT   **WRONG**

Power

There are two basic methods of applying power in the forward stroke. One is for an easy, relaxed cruising situation, and the other is for use when you really have to pour the power to your stroke. This second version is very useful in forward ferries and peel offs.

In the cruising method the power of the stroke is furnished by *both* arms (and their associated muscles). Common mistakes are to "hold" the paddle with the upper hand and pull with the lower arm or to "hold" the paddle with the lower hand and push with the upper arm. Either way is more tiring and less effective than using the power of both arms.

The correct way is to simultaneously push with the upper arm and pull with the lower. This method gives you all of the advantages of the principles of the lever by multiplying the force of your pull, yet doesn't rely only on one arm.

In the "power" method both arms are kept extended, and the power is furnished primarily by the back and waist muscles. This method has a much shorter stroke but is much more efficient.

Stroke (Cruising Method)

Reach forward with the paddle a comfortable distance and put the blade in the water as vertically as possible. Your lower arm is extended straight or almost straight. Your upper arm is bent at the elbow, and the upper hand is about chin high, approximately in line with your upper hand side shoulder or your chin and about 6 inches or so in front of it. Obviously, this position does *not* give you a vertical paddle position, but this will be corrected as you begin the power part of the stroke.

Start of the forward stroke.

Begin the stroke by pushing with your upper arm by straightening it out. To get to the vertical paddle position, you will push away from your initial position, diagonally forward and out over the gunwale. At the same time pull with your lower arm, which will remain extended throughout the power part of the stroke. Thus, during the power part of the stroke, both hands are outboard of the gunwale, and the lower hand *always* remains in this outboard position.

Don't forget that for maximum efficiency, the power face

166

of the blade should stay as perpendicular to the path of the desired force as possible, so work to keep the blade as close to vertical as you can during the stroke without it becoming awkward. Relax somewhat on the beginning of a forward stroke, put the power into it when the blade is near vertical (actually a rather short "power" part), then relax at the end of the stroke.

Midpoint of the forward stroke.

Cut the power part of the stroke off even with or just ahead of your hip. Both arms should now be fully extended or almost so and both hands beyond the gunwale.

End of the forward stroke.

Recovery (Cruising Method)

Recovery is above the water. After stopping the power, relax your arms and let them continue on in the natural swing of the stroke so the upper hand ends about gunwale height above the water. The paddle blade will come to the surface naturally as you do this. DO NOT LIFT the paddle to recover it. Push down with the upper hand to raise the blade clear of the water a few inches, and swing the lower arm out and around in an arc toward the bow of the canoe so the paddle is more or less horizontal to the water and the power face of the blade is up. The knuckles of both hands will be turned down toward the water, and the lower arm will be bent slightly. Keep the blade feathered as you recover and the arms relaxed. Keep your upper arm more or less straight, and let it swing back in toward your body. As it comes in across the gunwale begin bending it and bringing the grip of the paddle diagonally upward toward your chin into position for starting another stroke. As you do this, rotate your upper hand thumb up and in toward your face; this will rotate the paddle blade so the power face will be in the correct position.

Stroke (Power Method)

For this method both arms are kept extended or nearly so throughout the entire stroke and recovery. This is a more powerful and efficient version of the forward stroke because the paddle stays almost vertical (position "B") throughout the entire stroke, and the full length of its travel in the water is all power component.

Hold the paddle with both arms extended, lean forward and slightly outboard, and place the paddle in the water perpendicular to the surface and with the blade face perpendicular to the keel. Put the blade in the water about 2 feet in front of your knee (this will vary with your height and arm length). The important thing is that the paddle be vertical with the water. Usually you will keep your "three-point" kneeling position but for a longer reach you may rise off the edge of the seat, provided you stay well braced in the canoe with your feet and knees.

168

The "power" method of doing the basic forward stroke.

Bring the paddle back parallel with the keel, keeping your arms extended and leaning back as you pull. This brings your back and waist muscles into play. Keep the paddle as vertical as possible throughout the stroke. As the stroke moves back, twist your body to the paddle side. This keeps the paddle travel parallel to the keel and the blade vertical.

The whole stroke is short and powerful. It's vital to keep the blade perpendicular to the direction of the force. Cut the power off near your knee or at whatever point near there that the twist of your body and holding the paddle vertically becomes awkward and the position weak.

Recovery (Power Method)

Keep the arms extended and bring the lower arm up and out in an arc away from the canoe, turning the knuckles forward and down to feather the blade, power face up. At the same time the upper arm comes down and inboard across in front of you, and you turn the upper hand thumb forward and outboard. As you swing the paddle back nearly parallel with the water, begin your forward lean again so that as the paddle is turned and brought back up in position for another stroke, you will have completed your forward lean.

The whole stroke and recovery must be synchronized with the lean of your body. It's all a very rhythmic, continuous motion.

BASIC BACKSTROKE

General

The backstroke is exactly what it sounds like, a stroke done opposite the forward stroke. The backstroke is used to slow down the canoe when you're going forward, to halt it, or to propel it backward. It is *the* basic stroke for the all-important back-ferry technique; it can offer you a little more thinking time if you find yourself being swept into some situation for which you are unprepared, and if "thinking" doesn't help, the backstroke is useful to reduce the impact!

The backstroke is done by both bow and stern. In its pure form it has no diagonal component and thus no steering effect.

Paddle Position

The backstroke techniques are done exactly as is the forward stroke except the power is directed *forward* instead of toward the stern of the canoe. All of the requirements for effective blade use apply: paddle perpendicular to the water, blade face perpendicular to the keel, stroke done parallel to the keel and not along the arc of the gunwale, face of the blade always as "square" with the direction of desired force as you can get it. As in the forward stroke, you will probably find it more effective and comfortable to have your weight closer to the gunwale on the paddle side.

170

Use of the Body

The backstroke usually requires more power than the forward stroke because you're contending with the current's efforts to push the canoe downstream. Therefore, the weight and strength of the torso is frequently needed and used when executing the backstroke. When doing this you are usually in your normal upright position at the beginning of the stroke, but as your paddle moves toward the bow, you lean back, throwing your weight into the pull of the upper arm.

Power

There are two basic methods of doing the backstroke, and each method has its own way of applying power to the paddle. In both, however, the principle of simultaneously using the strength of both arms still applies.

Stroke—Method One

In the photo notice that method one of the backstroke is done with the hands and paddle in exactly the same position as for the forward stroke. The only difference is that the force of the backstroke will be exerted by the *non-power* face of the blade, and the initial upper hand position is out over the paddle side gunwale. To change hand or paddle position may take time that you don't have, interrupt the rhythm of your paddling, and result in less-effective strokes due to reduced power.

Put the blade in the water behind your hip. Both your upper and lower arms will be extended full length or nearly so. Don't let the wrist of your lower arm bend so your hand is bent back to one side. Keep the hand, wrist, and forearm in a straight line so that you can get the most "push" and control out of your lower arm.

Simultaneously, push with the lower arm and pull with the upper arm, remembering to keep the stroke parallel with the keel. Continue the stroke on by you, and cut off the power part of it about even with your knee. Your lower arm will remain extended throughout the stroke, but you'll almost immediately start to flex your upper arm, bending it at the elbow and bring-

171

Hand position for backstroke method one.

ing it back toward your paddle-side shoulder. If you've kept the correct "paddle-vertical-to-the-water" position, this upper hand will be about even with the end of your shoulder or a few inches out beyond both it and the gunwale. If you need the extra power of your body, start the stroke as above, but as you begin the pushing and pulling with your arms, *also* begin to lean back with your body weight. Time your lean so it's over at the same time as the power part of your stroke. Straighten up at the end of the stroke during the recovery. For even greater power, you can lean forward at the beginning of the stroke and then lean backward during the power part of the "pull." This gives you a greater reach and a longer power stroke as well as better utilizing your body muscles and weight. You might also lean back at the beginning of the stroke to lengthen your stroke slightly.

Recovery—Method One

Recovery is above the water. Relax your arms at the end of the power stroke, and bring your upper hand in toward your body and down toward the hull, upper hand thumb facing up. This will lift the blade out of the water edgeways. Twist your upper hand thumb forward and away from you so your knuckles are down. Simultaneously, twist your lower hand forward with knuckles down toward the water. This will automatically feather the blade.

Swing your paddle out and back toward the starting position of a new backstroke. Your upper hand will be at about waist level during this recovery swing. At the end of the swing, as the blade enters the water, begin bringing the upper arm up in the "pull" of another backstroke.

Stroke—Method Two

The only differences between method one and method two of doing the backstroke are the position of the upper arm and hand and the use of the power face rather than the non-power face of your blade for the second method.

A glance at the photographs of methods one and two will show you the difference in the upper arm position. The method two arm position is *much* stronger as it allows you to use your biceps in the power part of the stroke. *Do not* change your paddle grip to arrive at this position. Simply twist your upper hand thumb inboard and back toward your face until the palm of your hand is facing you and the power face of your paddle is toward the bow of the canoe. As you twist the paddle with your upper hand, relax the grip of your lower hand, and allow the paddle throat to rotate in your palm.

You will notice that once the paddle is rotated to the correct position, your upper arm will be bent at the elbow instead of extended as in method one. Except for this the stroke is exactly the same, your lower arm extended and pushing with the hand, wrist, and forearm in line, and the upper arm pulling by "flexing your muscle." In both backstrokes you will find it easier and more natural to keep the paddle vertical in the water than it was in the forward stroke.

173

Backstroke method two hand position.

Recovery—Method Two

Take the blade out of the water edgeways by bringing your upper hand straight across in front of you and down toward the gunwale on the upper hand side. Stop about even with your upper hand shoulder. Lift with the lower hand. Feather the blade by twisting both hands forward so the knuckles are turning down toward the water. Swing the blade to the rear and into position for another backstroke.

Recovery on backstroke method two.

Stroke—Method Three

This is a combination form of methods one and two in which the grip is the same as in method one, but the power face of the blade is used as in method two. This version of the backstroke is most useful when some diagonal component is to be put into the backstroke as when steering while paddling backward or when holding an angle in a back ferry. It also has the distinct advantage of giving the paddler doing the steering a better view of where he's going. It is most used by the sternman.

Begin with the paddle and hands in the position of the forward stroke. Twist your body at the hips, and then keep twisting around until you are facing diagonally to the rear on the paddle side. Bring the paddle on around as you twist your body, but don't change your grip on it. You'll probably find it necessary to lean out and to the rear over the gunwale and to shift your legs toward the paddle side to achieve this position.

175

Backstroke method three.

Another view of backstroke method three.

Put the blade in the water as vertically as possible and as far behind you as you can. Both hands should be well out over the gunwale. The upper arm will be approximately horizontal with the water and at about the level of your chin and bent more than the lower arm, which is almost straight. Notice that the power face of the paddle is now facing the bow of the boat.

Start the power stroke by pulling with both arms. As the paddle moves toward your paddle side shoulder, the "pull" of your lower arm will gradually shift over to a "push" to the front, beginning about even with your hip. At about this same point, the pull of your upper hand will also stop and change to a "push" to the rear. As these arm movements occur you will also be rotating your body back toward the bow of the canoe and into a more "normal" paddle position. Continue this forward push with your lower arm until the blade is about halfway to your knee, then cut off the power.

Recovery—Method Three

As your hand position in the final stages of this stroke is the same as in the backstroke method two, the method of recovery is the same as for method two.

GUIDING THE CANOE BACKWARD

There are fundamentals of guiding or "steering" a canoe in the forward direction that will be fully explained in the next section. I feel that these fundamentals of *forward* control should be understood and practiced before trying to steer a canoe backward. I also hate repeating a lot of instructions that are essentially the same, so guiding the canoe while back-paddling is included in the next section.

STEERING THE CANOE

I dislike the word "steering" when used in canoeing because it implies (at least to me) that you are using some method other than the correct paddle stroke to control the direction of the canoe. The most common offense in this category is "ruddering," trailing the edgewise paddle along behind the canoe and literally using it as a rudder. Actually, in current and with no obstructions, on a leisurely trip there is nothing wrong with ruddering. You'll progress at the speed of the current, and you'll do fine as long as you have plenty of time and room to maneuver and no occasion to be very accurate in it. Obviously, you'll have no speed other than the river's speed, and following the current by drifting may take you some place you don't want to go. Like many other things in river canoeing, ruddering is all right—if you know better!

The second most common offense is swapping sides to guide the canoe. This is wasteful of energy and of time. It is also an absolute indication of the novice unless the canoeist is using that style of paddling as a race stroke. When used for down-river racing, it's a pretty good technique as it allows more of your power to be directed forward, but it also takes a lot of practice. For general river canoeing one of the methods given here will probably prove to be the best.

There are two basic strokes used to steer a canoe when it's moving forward. Both are strictly for open water, for the pools between rapids, or for cruising. Neither should be attempted in rapids—the results could be disastrous. There are paddle strokes specifically intended for quick and effective movements in obstructed waters, and you should use these other strokes in those situations. Both steering strokes are done only by the sternman.

GENERAL

The sternman exercises more control over the canoe in cruising than does the bowman. This is because the stern has a greater turning moment in the direction of travel. Normally, in open water the bowman will rarely do any course correcting. His basic job is to provide motive power with a forward stroke while the sternman sets the course and maintains it by the use of one of the steering strokes.

A canoe will always turn *away* from a forward stroke done in the stern unless wind or current prevents it doing so. The same stroke done in the bow has negligible effect. Thus, if there was no wind or current acting on the canoe and the sternman just kept using the forward stroke, he would keep turning away

178

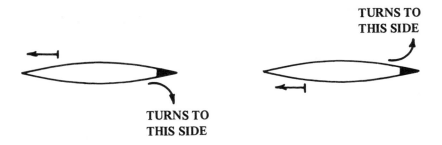

TURNS TO
THIS SIDE

TURNS TO
THIS SIDE

from his paddle side and, if he didn't run into the bank, gradually make a big circle.

To offset this tendency of the canoe to turn, some other force in a direction opposite to the turn is necessary. One direction is straight out from the canoe. This provides the force to turn the bow of the canoe *toward* the paddle side, and if this turning force and the force of the forward stroke are balanced, the canoe will maintain a straight course.

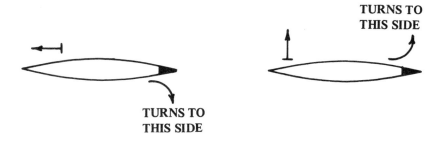

TURNS TO
THIS SIDE

TURNS TO
THIS SIDE

This is the principle of any steering stroke—to maintain your forward movement and yet to balance these two opposite turning forces so the end result is no turn at all or the amount of turn you want in the direction you want it. The method of application of the sideways force is the only real difference in the two basic steering methods.

"J" STROKES

The "J" stroke is the classic Scout, summer camp, and Red Cross steering stroke. It's hard to learn simply because it's hard to explain and to demonstrate so that anybody knows what you're talking about. It's a stroke that, for most, takes a lot of practice and one that you have to "feel" in order to really understand. It's also tiring at first. On the other hand, it's a quiet stroke and a very good-looking one when done correctly.

The "J" stroke is named from the shape in the water that the full stroke makes when it's viewed from above. There is a forward stroke component which moves the canoe forward but also tries to turn it away from the paddle side and an adjusting stroke component to the side which offsets this turning. Both components are blended into one smooth stroke. The difficult part of the "J" stroke is that the "adjusting" component is constantly changed throughout the stroke. It is infinitely variable, depending upon the wind, current, the strength of the forward part of the stroke, and the length of the stroke. Thus the blade angle in a "J" stroke is constantly being changed, and only experience can dictate the right amount of angle for any given moment. In addition, the force and the length of the two components may vary from stroke to stroke. You may put a lot of forward component force in and little adjusting force on one stroke but have to put more adjusting into the next one. This is what makes this stroke so hard to learn and to teach.

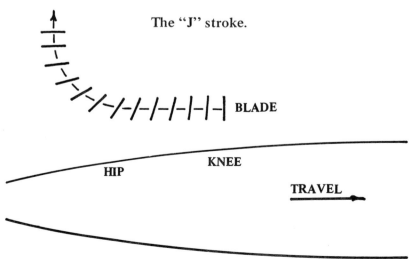

The "J" stroke.

Paddle Position

The paddle is held exactly as for the basic forward stroke, perpendicular to the water, the blade face perpendicular to the keel, and the forward component of the stroke parallel to the keel, not the gunwale. All of the basics of the stroke including the feathered recovery are also done exactly as in the forward stroke. The only difference is in the correcting "twist" that goes into the "J" stroke.

Stroke

Begin the forward component of the stroke as you do the forward stroke. As the blade reaches a point somewhere just behind your knee, begin twisting the paddle so that the power face gradually begins facing out away from the canoe. Do *not* stop the paddle's movement—continue your stroke all through this twisting movement. This twist is done by both hands, the upper hand thumb turning away from you outboard and forward and the lower hand knuckles rotating forward and inboard. The resulting angle on the blade causes some of your forward stroke power to be directed to the side as a correcting component, so even as your paddle is driving you forward it is also helping to offset the tendency of the canoe to turn away from the stroke. A common practice is to do all the twisting with only one hand, letting the other hand just follow around. This puts all the work on one wrist and is much more tiring than using both wrists.

The amount of "twist" you put on the paddle and *when* you begin twisting depends on the amount of correction you need to apply. A lot of correction would mean that the twist would start earlier in the stroke and possibly be more pronounced sooner in the stroke.

As the paddle reaches a point near your hip, the *flat* of the blade should be almost parallel to the keel with the power face facing out away from the canoe as in the sketch. For the remainder of the stroke the power will be directed *out*. This is the final correction, and the length of this part of the stroke will depend on how much correcting you still need to do.

181

The "J" stroke.

COMBINATION FORWARD STROKE AND PRY

General

This is an easier-to-learn, easier-to-do method. It is not as graceful or efficient as the "J" stroke, is noisy, and violates one of the basic paddle rules. Despite all this, it is restful and widely used. You can always tell when someone is using this combination to steer because each paddle stroke is accompanied by the "clunk" of the paddle shaft on the gunwale.

The stroke is nothing but a simple, basic forward stroke with a pry on the end. This pry serves the same purpose as the last part of the "J" stroke by furnishing a correcting force in the opposite direction to offset the tendency of the canoe to turn away from the forward stroke part.

Paddle Position

Observe all the basic position rules as you did for the basic forward and backstroke—paddle shaft perpendicular to the water and paddle face perpendicular to the keel. Variations in paddle position in the "pry" part of the stroke are described under "Stroke." You may need to slide your lower hand up the shaft a little to clear the gunwale during the "pry" part of the stroke, but this will depend upon where you normally hold the paddle with your lower hand.

Stroke

From the beginning of the stroke back to the hip, all movements are done exactly as in the forward stroke WITH THE EXCEPTION that rather than rigidly maintaining your stroke parallel to the keel, you let it gradually move in toward the gunwale. In other words, you violate one of the rules and somewhat follow the curve of the gunwale with the aim of ending up with the shaft of the paddle nearly touching the gunwale when the paddle is about even with your hip.

When the paddle reaches this hip position, twist the shaft forward, turning your upper hand thumb OUTBOARD AND DOWN toward the water. Make sure of this thumb *down* posi-

The "pry" position for the combination steering stroke. Notice the thumbs-down position of the upper hand.

tion or you will be reversing power faces, and in this stroke the same power face is used all the way through. As you rotate your upper hand, simultaneously turn the lower hand so the lower hand knuckles rotate outboard and down toward the water. These motions, if done sufficiently, will turn the paddle blade so its flat side (non-power face) is facing and parallel to the side of the canoe and its edges are straight up and down in the water. Your upper arm should now be nearly fully extended, with the upper hand above and about in line with the gunwale. The lower shaft of the paddle should be actually touching the gunwale, and your lower hand should be just above the gunwale but not touching the canoe. (This is the reason for shortening your grip.) The paddle will be angled forward, blade behind your hip and the grip toward the bow. All or nearly all of the blade will be below the surface of the water. You have now finished the power part of your stroke.

The correction part of the stroke is applied by swinging

the upper arm in toward the keel in a "prying" motion, using the paddle as a lever and letting it pivot over the edge of the gunwale, which acts as a fulcrum. The lower hand does no work but only steadies the paddle shaft and keeps it in contact with the gunwale. To avoid painful pinches, DO NOT LET YOUR LOWER HAND TOUCH THE GUNWALE. NEVER "CLAMP" THE PADDLE TO THE GUNWALE WITH YOUR FINGERS. KEEP THE LOWER HAND *ABOVE* THE GUNWALE.

Power

The power part of the forward part of this stroke is the same as for the basic forward stroke. The power for the "pry" part is something that seems to baffle a lot of people. The failure is to apply the force of the pry to the *side*, thus providing the correcting force. Instead, many novices apply most of their force upwards as in sketch "A," which does little correcting and pulls the side of the canoe down. The first problem is that they do *not* have their paddle turned enough. The upper hand thumb must be down; this automatically turns the blade 90 degrees to the surface of the water with its flat sides parallel to the side of the canoe as in sketch "C." As you apply the force of the pry, keep the blade in this position throughout the power of the pry. Don't let the blade twist into the position of "A" or "B" during the stroke. The power *must* be applied to the side. This gives you maximum effect for your force. The amount of pry will vary with the amount of correction you need to apply. Usually the length of travel of the blade in the water during the "pry" won't be more than a foot.

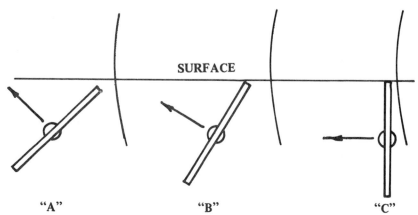

SURFACE

"A"   "B"   "C"

Recovery

Recovery is above water. Relax your arms, let the paddle float out of the water, and recover over the surface with the paddle feathered in the same manner as for the forward stroke.

Practice of Forward Steering Strokes

Initial practice of both the "J" and combination stroke is best done in slow-moving water in a straight stretch of the river. Pick out some stationary object down the river such as a tree or a rock, and try to get the canoe to it in a straight line, using *only* the stroke you're practicing and *not* resorting to "ruddering" between strokes. Use a minimum of force in your stroke, and concentrate on technique instead of on hurrying to get to wherever it is you're aiming. Don't let your bowman overpower you, and don't let him do any course correction at all while you're practicing. Vary the amount of forward and pry (or "J") on your stroke, and see what effect it has. You'll find that you can actually turn the canoe *to* the side on which you're paddling if you put a lot of sideways component into the stroke. After you've got the technique down, *then* increase your force and practice keeping a steady rhythm and length to your paddle strokes but varying the amount of force in the forward and sideways parts of it. Above all, watch your paddle blade during the pry part of the combination stroke and make sure that the blade is edge up in the water and parallel to the keel and that your "pry" force is directed *outward*—not outward and upward. Don't lift the water!

One thing to remember is that you do not necessarily have to do a "J" or a "combination" on *every* stroke to steer the canoe. The wind blowing against your off-paddle side, for example, may furnish the "correction" power, and you may need to use only a basic forward stroke, balancing its tendency to turn the canoe *into* the wind against the force of the wind.

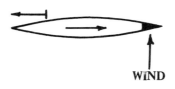

WIND

186

Sometimes, too, a tandem team will have a strong bowman whose forward stroke will offset or partially offset the turning of the canoe. In any event, use the "steering" strokes only when they are required. You may find that you need them on every stroke, every other stroke, or every now and then, and the situation may (and probably will) change all down the river.

STEERING WITH THE BACKSTROKE

Now that you (hopefully) understand and have practiced making the canoe move forward in the direction you want, let's return to making it go where you want to when you're using the backstroke. As paddling backwards requires some reverse thinking, I've tried to avoid confusion in the following discussions by always using the terms "bow" and "stern" and "bowman" and "sternman" in their normal forward-paddling usage. Do not forget, however, that the *canoe itself* is going *backwards*.

There are two basic ideas on steering with the backstroke. The first is that since a canoe is symmetrical, paddling backward can be done by simply doing the normal forward paddle strokes in reverse. This is quite true, and the only other factor is that the paddler's functions also reverse when backing. The bowman will find himself in the trailing end of a backing canoe and thus, in effect, in the "stern" position, while the sternman will occupy the front or leading end in the "bow" position. Because of this the bowman's stroke while backing will be a reverse "J" or combination stroke, and the sternman will do a straight backstroke for power. Obviously, the bowman and preferably both paddlers need to be twisted around somewhat and looking over their shoulders to see where they're going.

This method *will* work but has three drawbacks. First, the sternman has the better view of where he's going when backing and so should exercise more course control. (I realize that this is opposite to what I've said in going *forward*, but *backing* a canoe is usually a short-time, short-distance event involving somewhat limited vision anyway. Under these circumstances, the paddler with the best view should control the course, and that paddler will be the sternman.) Secondly, in most tandem canoes the sternman is usually the heavier of the two partners, which means that his end of the canoe will be deeper in the water and

187

the canoe will try to pivot around this point. When backing this makes it more difficult for the bowman to control the canoe. Finally, it's just awkward and hard to put any power into the correction component of a "J" or combination stroke when paddling backward.

Method One

If you want to learn this method, the sternman will simply follow all the requirements of paddle position and technique for the basic backstroke. The bowman will do the same for the "J" or combination steering stroke except that he will be doing this complete "steering" stroke in reverse, as shown in the illustration. For this, he will be using the non-power face of his paddle.

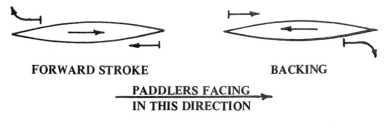

FORWARD STROKE   **BACKING**

PADDLERS FACING
IN THIS DIRECTION

Backing method one.

Recovery—Method One

Recovery for the bowman's reverse steering is above the water. Bring the paddle out of the water at the end of the "J" or pry part of the stroke by bringing your upper hand forward and down and your lower hand backward and up. This will slice the paddle blade, which is already parallel to the keel at the end of the stroke, out of the water to the rear. The blade will almost be in location for another stroke. A quarter turn of the wrist (do not *slip* the paddle in your hand), upper hand knuckles rotating outboard and down, puts the non-power face back in position for the next stroke.

An alternate method is to let the blade float out of the water at the end of the stroke (non-power face up) and bring it back in a feathered position. As you swing the paddle back for another stroke, rotate the paddle 180 degrees to bring the non-power face into position just before it enters the water. Rotation is done by the wrist (again, don't let the paddle slip in your hands) and by turning the upper hand thumb outboard and down toward the water.

Method Two

I find the second concept of steering while backing to be a much easier method. The sternman does the steering, and the bowman does a simple backstroke for power with occasional correction as called for by the sternman.

Although any one of the regular backstroke styles given before can be used by the sternman, I find the third method best as you're already twisted around and looking back. To me it's also easier to control the canoe and to apply more power to the stroke when you're in this position.

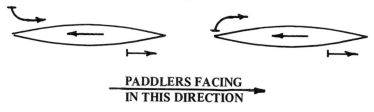

PADDLERS FACING IN THIS DIRECTION

Backing method two.

The sternman will be doing a reverse "J" or "combination" steering stroke. The "correction" part of the stroke is usually done by starting the stroke out from the hull of the canoe, pulling diagonally in toward the hull, then converting into a straight backstroke. This will move the stern of the canoe *toward* the paddle. Sometimes the correction will be needed to *push* the hull in the other direction, and the beginning of the stroke will start near the stern, be pushed diagonally outward, and blend into the backstroke. Occasionally, an additional little push or pull may also be needed at the *end* of the stroke. Correction at the beginning of the stroke is always best, however, as your paddle exerts more turning leverage the farther away it is from the center of the length of the canoe. As in the "J" or combination, the ratio of the length and power of the "back" to the "correction" parts of the stroke varies according to what you need at the moment. The bowman (now the sternman) can apply draws or prys to pull or push his end of the canoe to wherever the sternman wants it.

Recovery—Method Two

Recovery is done as for the normal backstroke method you are using.

Practicing Steering the Canoe Backward

Follow the same procedure as for steering it forward Paddling backward accurately is more difficult than paddling forward. You might want to find a lake to start off in, as current makes this procedure a little difficult to do until you have the hang of it. Don't use a lot of power, just concentrate on getting where you're going in a nice, straight line until you *can* get there in a nice, straight line!

SWEEPS

General

Sweeps are used to turn a canoe. Like the "J" and "combination," sweeps are lake-canoeing steering strokes and should never be used where any rapid or critical maneuvering is necessary. Use them *only* in the pools and on unobstructed rivers where there is plenty of room and plenty of time for course changing or correction.

Sweeps are useful additions to your paddling techniques. They are used by both bow and stern individually or simultaneously, depending upon what you want to accomplish. They are extremely useful to the solo canoeist as well. Although the draw and the pry are much stronger and more effective strokes, the sweeps can more easily be blended into the rhythm of your paddling when you're cruising. Sweeps are much more effective when done in conjunction with a complementary sweep or stroke by your partner. On a river, however, their use will probably be limited to quarter sweeps done by either bow or stern and used for minor course correction while cruising.

Principles of a Sweep

A "sweep" stroke is so named because the paddle blade "sweeps" *across* just under the surface of the water rather than burying down deep *into* the water as in the other strokes you've learned. Still another one of the rules is thus often broken as, in a pure sweep, the blade is usually *not* completely under the water. A sweep stroke has little inherent power. Its effectiveness comes from its turning leverage which, in turn, comes from the distance of the paddle blade from the canoe. Sweeps are always done as arcs of a circle, and for maximum effectiveness this arc should be as large as possible so as to reach far out away from the gunwale.

The basic sweep position.

Types of Sweeps

All kinds of names have been advanced for various sweeps, but basically they all come down to whether the sweep covers 90 degrees or 180 degrees and whether it's done forward or backward. A 90-degree forward sweep in the bow will turn the

191

canoe *away* from the paddle side. A 90-degree forward sweep in the stern will pull the canoe *toward* the paddle side. Sweeps of 180 degrees (solo only) also will turn the canoe *to* the paddle side. Here are some examples of what sweeps *can* do.

90° forward sweep—bow.
90° reverse sweep—stern.
Pivots canoe to left.

90° reverse sweep—bow.
90° forward sweep—stern.
Pivots canoe to right.

180° reverse sweep (solo).
Pivots canoe to right.

180° cross sweep (solo).
Pivots canoe to right.

Note that any reverse sweep will slow you down while turning you, so if your forward movement is important, don't use reverse sweeps. Also note that any sweep of more than 90 degrees done by a tandem crew very effectively cancels out the beginning part of your partner's stroke. In other words, tandem crews don't use anything more than 90-degree sweeps.

Here are some examples of how sweeps will most often be used on the river. Bear in mind that the sternman might object to arbitrary course changes by his bowman as the sternman may be headed exactly where he wants to go. This is one of those little things that have to be worked out by tandem partners.

Forward sweep—stern.
Turns bow away from paddle
side.

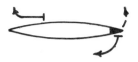

Forward sweep—bow.
Turns bow away from paddle
side.

Reverse sweep—stern.
Turns bow toward paddle
side.

Paddle Position

The paddle is held nearly parallel with the water throughout the stroke. All forward sweeps use the normal forward
stroke power face. Usually, the upper hand remains inside the
canoe or about even with the gunwale on the paddle side. The
blade face is perpendicular to the water and, because of the
angle of the paddle, is usually never completely submerged.

Stroke (Forward Sweep by Bow)

Turn the blade up on edge by turning the upper hand
thumb up. This will put the power face of the blade facing out
away from the canoe. The stroke starts near the bow of the
canoe, close to the stem. Now with your lower arm extended,
"sweep" the paddle blade out in an arc away from the hull. The
whole motion is a circular movement, so start the paddle
moving *away* from the canoe as soon as you start the stroke,

193

and reach out as far as you can so that the blade is as far away from the hull at the end of the stroke as you can get it. Keep the blade edge up all the time.

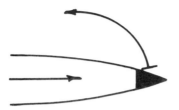

Cut off the stroke about even with your hip or when you have covered a 90-degree arc. If you continue beyond this point, you will begin to pull the canoe *toward* the paddle. At the beginning of the stroke your upper hand will be about in front of your body. As you sweep and your upper arm extends, this hand will move toward the gunwale on the paddle side. At the end of the stroke both arms will be fully or nearly fully extended.

Forward sweep by bowman.

Stroke (Forward Sweep by Stern)

The motions are exactly the same as for the bow forward sweep except that the paddle starts even with the sternman's hip and out about a paddle length away from the canoe. By pulling with the lower arm and pushing with the upper arm, the edge-up paddle is swung back in an arc toward the stern. The stroke ends very near the stern.

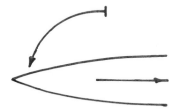

Forward sweep by stern.

195

Reverse Sweeps

Reverse sweeps should be self-explanatory if you understand forward sweeps. They are simply done backward, with the blade edge up and swinging in an arc. Ninety-degree sweeps by the bow begin away from the hull and end up near the bow; for the sternman they begin near the stern and end out away from the hull. All reverse sweeps will use the non-power face of the paddle.

Reverse sweep by bow.

Recovery

Recovery on sweeps is out of the water and with the blade feathered. On both forward and reverse sweeps, twist both hands outboard and knuckles down as the blade is removed from the water at the end of the stroke. This will turn the power face up.

Using Modified Sweeps To Steer a Canoe

As pointed out, sweeps are easily blended into your normal cruising strokes. Using a small amount of sweep in a forward stroke can be very useful for minor course corrections when you're cruising along in a straight stretch or want to make a big, gentle bend. These correction strokes can be used by bow or stern. For a small amount of correction, the paddle is not put out in the "sweep" position. Instead, the blade is swept out in a slight arc a little farther from the canoe than it would be in a normal forward stroke. The amount of arc and sweep depends on the correction necessary. The increased distance of the paddle from the canoe gives you more paddle leverage and turning moment. In cruising using these sweeps is much easier than using draws or prys.

ONE FINAL COMMENT ON STEERING

If you elect to synchronize your bow and stern strokes when you're cruising, don't forget that the bowman sets the pace, and the sternman follows this beat. *But* also do not forget that if the bowman sets too fast a pace, the sternman will not be able to keep up with him and still steer the canoe without resorting to ruddering.

MOVING THE CANOE SIDEWAYS

The two basic strokes for moving a canoe directly to the side are the draw and the pry. Both are strong, effective strokes and *are* river-running strokes, techniques to be used when avoiding obstacles, when sudden changes of direction are required, and when time and distance are *not* plentiful. Both of the strokes can be used to replace sweeps and even to steer a canoe down a river; however, they are a little awkward for cruising use on a continuous basis.

THE DRAW

General

The draw stroke is used to move the canoe *to* the paddle side. It is used by both bow and stern and in its pure state has no diagonal component. In addition to moving the canoe, the draw also relieves part of the *weight* on the canoe by letting the paddler temporarily put part of *his* weight on the blade. This not only enables the draw itself to be more effective as the canoe is lighter and reacts easier but also has another important use which you'll discover when you start doing eddy turns. There is one important psychological factor to doing an effective draw: always view your performance of a draw as planting your paddle firmly in the water and then *pulling the canoe over to the stationary paddle.* This is the object of a draw—to move the canoe to the side. Never look at it as pulling the *paddle to the canoe,* for that is *not* the object.

Arm Position

Arm position is important in a draw. The lower arm should be fully extended and the upper arm over your head with its bicep resting against the side of your head. To get this correct upper arm position, grip the paddle with both hands as you would normally hold it while paddling, then swing your outstretched arms straight up over your head so the paddle is parallel to the ground. Now try to swing the paddle over to what would be your paddle side. The upper arm will, of course, hit

198

The basic draw position.

your head, but keep it there *over* your head as that's the correct position.

Paddle and Body Position

A pure draw is done straight out to the side with the paddle in line with your hip and shoulder and the blade out as far as you can reach. The paddle is as perpendicular to the water as you can get it, and the face of the blade (power face) is turned toward you and parallel to the keel. The blade should be completely buried in the water. For maximum reach you should be leaning hard against the gunwale with your paddle-side thigh or hip and with your body out at an angle over the gunwale. Brace yourself in with your knees. For absolute maximum reach, get up off the seat or thwart, brace yourself in with your knees and feet, and extend your body from about the waist up out over the water and almost parallel to the water. However, don't try this posture until you've practiced and developed con-

199

Paddle position for draw.

fidence in the milder draws.

Stroke

A powerful draw will support part of your weight, so in drawing literally *lean* on the paddle. The harder you pull, the more weight it will support, and it won't take you long to discover just how much pull it takes to hold up how much weight! The amount that can be supported also depends on how much of your paddle blade is in the water and how perpendicular your paddle is. The more perpendicular the paddle, the more blade that must be in the water to provide the force to hold the weight up. Less blade in the water means that your paddle must be at more of an angle to provide support. It's best to submerge your paddle blade completely and get the paddle as perpendicular as possible.

Pull in with your lower arm, gradually bending it and straightening your body as the canoe comes in closer to the paddle. Keep the paddle nearly perpendicular to the water throughout the stroke and the force of the draw straight in toward your hip. Maintain the face of the blade perpendicular to the force of your pull, in this case, with the face parallel to the keel.

Cut the power of your stroke off about 6 inches *before* the paddle strikes the hull of the canoe. Your body should now be back in the canoe and your weight off the blade. If you let the paddle come on in and touch the hull, it's likely to hang there, especially in current. This unexpected "hanging" or a sudden current push on the flat of the blade could dump you or snatch the paddle out of your hands.

Recovery

Recovery on a draw is to the rear and above water. Slice the edge-up paddle out to the rear by bringing your upper hand down toward the gunwale and keeping your lower arm extended. Do not *lift* the paddle to remove it from the water. Rotate your upper hand thumb out and away from you so the power face of the paddle is up and parallel to the water, and swing the paddle back out in this feathered position. During the swing, turn the power face back over toward you by twisting your upper hand thumb back toward your face. Simultaneously, start lifting your upper arm back into its over-the-head position so that by the time the swing is completed, the paddle is back in position for another draw.

Important Points and Practice of the Draw

Remember that the more weight you lean on your paddle, the stronger must be your draw; also, you cannot maintain your initial posture of hanging far out over the gunwale to the end of the stroke or you'll find yourself leaning over a vertical paddle blade that offers no support.

Practice will soon teach you how far out you can reach with what paddle angle and when to get your body weight off the paddle and back in the canoe. After a few spills you'll begin to discover the various correct blends of weight, lean, power, and timing.

Using draws to spin the canoe.

THE PRY

General

The pry is used to move the boat *away* from your paddle side. It is the complementary stroke to the draw, which is used to move the boat *to* your paddle side. In tandem canoeing when one member draws and the other prys, the boat will move sideways—toward the side on which the draw is being done.

Don't Do a Push-Away

A stroke often taught in lake canoeing is called a push-away. It is intended to do the same thing as a pry. It is important that you distinguish the difference between a pry and a push-away. The push-away is just what it says—you *push* the face of the blade away from the side of the canoe. Try it, and you'll find that it's a weak stroke even though you can keep the paddle vertical and exert all your force to the side. A pry is also just what it says—you are *prying* the boat to the side, but in a pry you are using the principles of a lever which, while forcing you to sacrifice *length* of effective stroke, greatly multiplies the force within that length. The *pry* is a powerful, effective stroke, albeit a short one; the push-away is *not*.

The pure pry is done beside the knee—*not* the shoulder, and there is no diagonal component. It uses the bilge and gunwale as a fulcrum over which the paddle shaft rotates. In theory the shaft does not lose contact with the boat; in practice you will find that it sometimes does, because it's difficult to do a sequence of rapid prys and keep contact all the time.

Paddle Position

First shorten your lower hand grip—slide the lower hand up the shaft until it clears the gunwale slightly when the paddle is in position for the pry. Put the blade as flat as you can against the *bilge* of the boat; the blade is totally submerged and usually so is part of the throat of the paddle. The upper arm will be almost fully extended, and the upper hand will be well out over the water. The power face of the paddle will be in toward the

The basic pry position at the beginning of the pry.

The pry is done beside the knee.

hull, and your upper hand thumb will be turned toward your face with the palm facing outboard. The lower hand *knuckles* will be outboard.

Stroke

Apply a lot of power from the very beginning of the stroke and all the way through it; otherwise, the pry loses much of its effectiveness. *Roll* the throat and shaft of the paddle up the round side of the boat by pulling inboard on the upper hand. Keep the paddle shaft in contact with the hull at all times. Remember, never maintain boat and shaft contact by clamping the paddle to the gunwale with your lower hand fingers and thumb, fingers or thumb, or any other combination. This is a good way to severely pinch fingers and possibly yank a thumb loose. It also gives you a weak grip on the paddle. Maintain the contact with lower hand wrist action alone. Continue to pull on the paddle until the shaft touches the gunwale. Note that your

205

End of the pry. Notice the location of the upper hand in relation to the chin. The pry is a *short* stroke.

total stroke travel is only about 12 to 16 inches long. At this point your upper hand will be about in line with your chin if you're in the center of the boat. *This is the place to stop the stroke*—beyond this point the blade begins to "lift" water, thus exerting more upward than sideways force. If you don't cut the stroke off here, your effort is merely pulling the gunwale down instead of doing its job of prying the canoe sideways. The whole stroke is short but must be rapid and powerful.

Recovery

Recovery is done underwater. Rotate the paddle forward by turning the upper hand thumb out and away from you; this will put the blade face perpendicular to the keel and the power face facing you. Bring the blade back under the canoe to the bilge by pushing out with the upper hand. The lower hand is firmly holding the shaft in contact with the canoe hull, and the lower hand wrist is bending to allow these twists of the paddle.

Do not loosen your lower hand grip and let the paddle shaft slip through your hand as it twists. Keep a firm grip with both hands at all times. Just before the edge of the blade strikes the boat, turn your thumb back and inboard toward your face and, as the blade flattens out, bring its power face against the bilge once more.

If you need to, you are then ready to immediately go into another pry stroke. All this is done in one smooth, continuous motion. The strokes are short, rapid, and powerful, and the recovery must also be smooth and rapid. Doing a pry is a sort of four-part rhythm—pull, turn, recover, turn; pull, turn, recover, turn. Practicing slowly at first and gathering speed and power as you develop coordination will help you learn the pry.

The Stern Pry

Another use of the pry is to help execute a turning movement of the bow *to* the stern's paddle side. This is done by the sternman. Shift the pry back toward the stern by angling the paddle as you would in a reverse sweep. The blade should be very near the end of the canoe. Now do a short reverse sweep, except pry off the gunwale instead of pushing on the shaft. This blade position gives you a greater turning leverage, and the pry gives you more power. This also works in the bow by shifting the paddle blade *forward* and treating it as sort of a short forward sweep done with a pry off the gunwale.

HOLDING THE CANOE UP

Two basic paddle techniques are used to steady, support, or bring a canoe back upright when it is tilting or trying to roll. These techniques are called braces. One, the low brace, is used when the canoe is tilting (or tilted) *toward* the paddle side. The other, the high brace, is used when the canoe is tilting (or tilted) *away* from the paddle side. Braces are also a vital part of eddy turns and peel offs, as you'll learn in the chapter on maneuvers, and the low brace, in a modified form, is often used as a slowing and/or steadying technique in rough water. Both braces are done by either bow or stern and may be used simultaneously by

207

both partners in a tandem canoe as long as they are not using the same brace.

THE LOW BRACE

General

The low brace does two things. It provides a surface against which to exert force when you need to push the canoe back upright, and this same surface also gives you a platform on which to rest part of your weight while you're using the brace. This last use relieves part of the weight on the canoe and makes it more responsive to the brace. Remember that a low brace is used when the canoe is rolling *toward* the paddler's side.

Paddle Position

In a pure low brace the entire length of the paddle is completely outboard of the canoe, parallel or nearly parallel to the surface of the water, and below the sheer line of the canoe. The non-power face of the paddle is down and parallel to the water, and the paddle length is perpendicular to the canoe's keel. The brace is done out beside your hip or at a point roughly between your hip and knee on the paddle side.

Body and Hand Position

In the low-brace position your upper body will be twisted toward the paddle side with the torso leaning out over the gunwale toward the brace and your hip or thigh up against the gunwale. In a really strong brace your body down to the hips will be out beyond the canoe and almost parallel to the water. Use your knees and your upper thighs to brace yourself in the canoe. For a longer reach and more weight on the paddle, get up in the raised paddling position. You will probably do this all the time if you're short.

Do not change your normal paddling grip with either hand. Rotate the upper hand thumb outboard and forward. Maintain your lower hand grip, and do not let the paddle throat slide in your hand. Both hands will now be knuckles down toward the water, the upper hand thumb forward and the lower hand

208

The low brace in action.

thumb in toward the canoe. Do not bend your lower wrist; ideally, the back of your lower hand, your wrist, and forearm should all be in a straight line. This puts less strain on the wrist. Your lower arm may be almost extended or may be bent at the elbow; this depends on how far out you're reaching and the spread of your hands on the paddle. Usually, it will be slightly crooked.

Stroke

Lay the non-power face of the paddle on the water. The upper hand knuckles may be in the water or slightly above it. Press down on the paddle throat with your lower hand, and simultaneously pull up with your upper hand. You are using your lower hand more as a fulcrum, but by exerting force in both directions you increase the effect of the brace. Keep the blade face as flat as possible on the water. Shift part of your weight to the lower arm and thus to the blade. This gives you more push, lightens the boat, and helps it come back up. Don't continue to bear down on the blade or you will soon sink out of sight. All of this needs to be done as a quick, firm motion.

Recovery

Emphasis must be on the timing of the end of the "brace" and the withdrawal of your weight back into the canoe and off the blade. You should begin to pull your body weight back in near the end of the "lift and push" of your arms. After your weight is off the blade, twist your upper hand thumb back toward you to put a slight up angle on the front edge of the paddle blade. Slice the blade out to the front, and bring it just clear of the water and in position for another low brace if you need it.

Variations and Other Uses

In practice you should do a correct low brace as outlined above. In actual usage you will often not have the blade and paddle as horizontal as they should be and may possibly have the upper hand inboard of the gunwale. If the canoe is really tilting, you may not have to lean very far out (or be able to or have time to), yet your blade will still have a good, flat angle with the water because of the boat's inclination.

When low bracing in choppy water or waves, keep a slight up angle on the leading edge of the blade to prevent it from diving on you. When bracing in frothy water, your blade may (in fact, probably will) vanish below the froth until it finds "solid" water to rest on. In this case your whole paddle and both your hands may be completely submerged. In very frothy water the water may be too "thin" to support a brace at all.

Another use for the low brace is as a third point of support in rough water. Trail the paddle behind you at about a 45-degree angle to the keel, non-power face down and flat on the water. In this use your upper hand is usually inboard, and the paddle is at about 30 to 45 degrees to the water instead of horizontal. Exert more or less pressure on the blade to slow down or gain extra support. Be sure to keep a slight up angle on the leading edge.

Practice of the Low Brace

A good practice stunt is to dip your head in the water as you low brace, then recover without shipping water over the gunwale. You should be able at least to submerge the top of your head.

Try varying the amount of weight, force, lean, and timing until you arrive at what you can do under various conditions. You'll find that under some conditions you can lean on the brace a relatively long time. This becomes easier and more effective the greater speed differential there is between the boat and the current. Again—practice will show you what you can and can't do.

To be effective, braces must be done automatically. If the canoeist has to stop to think which brace to use, it usually is too late to use it by the time he remembers. Practice of the bracing stroke will get the technique down, but only experience can make bracing instinctive.

THE HIGH BRACE

The high brace is used when the canoe is rolling *away* from the paddler's side. It is a very simple brace to do if you have mastered the draw stroke. Get your body and paddle into position for a draw, but *don't* draw. That's all there is to it, but it's important that you *do* distinguish between a high brace and a draw.

A high brace in action. Note the similarity between a brace and a draw and the "over-the-gunwale" posture of the paddler.

USING THE BRACES TOGETHER

In the sketch the bowman is paddling on the left and the sternman on the right. Should the canoe roll to the right, the bowman could do a high brace and the sternman a low brace.

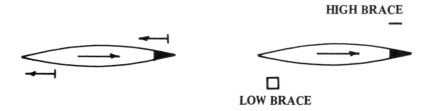

HIGH BRACE

LOW BRACE

The low brace *pushes* the canoe up, and the high brace catches the water to stop the canoe from rolling. If the canoe were to roll to the left, the two paddlers could reverse their braces, the bowman doing a low brace and the sternman a high brace. It's obvious that should *both* paddlers do the *same* brace, they would offset each other's efforts.

CROSS STROKES, DIAGONAL STROKES, AND SCULLING

CROSS STROKES

Cross strokes are paddle strokes done on the opposite side of the canoe from your normal paddle side *but without changing your grip on the paddle.* The strokes are accomplished by swinging the paddle across the canoe and twisting your body to that side until you can get the blade in the water to do the stroke. Cross backstrokes by the stern and cross draws by bow or stern in lieu of a pry are the most common in tandem canoeing. Cross strokes in solo canoeing are an integral part of the art, but they are discouraged for use by the novice tandem canoeist.

There are several reasons for not using cross strokes in a tandem canoe. One is that part of the weight of the paddler doing the cross stroke is suddenly relocated to the same side as his partner's. This not only makes the canoe unstable but could be disastrous if the partner, who probably didn't expect the cross stroke, was just about to shift his weight even farther out (to do a draw, for example). Another reason is that with both paddlers on the same side, a sudden tilt of the canoe in either direction leaves only one of them in a position to brace. The one doing the cross stroke has no bracing action at all if the canoe rolls *toward* his cross stroke and very little in the other direction.

Despite these drawbacks to cross strokes and the fact that a pry will do the same thing and is stronger, cross strokes are often seen on the river and do have their uses, particularly in back ferrying where one partner is weaker or less skilled than the other. Nonetheless, cross strokes are still another skill in canoeing that should be done only when you know enough *not* to do them.

DIAGONAL STROKES

Diagonal strokes are simple variations of the pure form of some strokes. They're useful when you want to maintain the rhythm of your stroke (diagonal components easily blend in forward, back, and draw strokes) or your forward or backward momentum and yet work in a change of direction or when you can use a diagonal change of direction rather than a sideslip. Bear in mind that if your canoe is in line with the current, diagonal strokes will result in an angle with the current, which is something you don't want to do except under certain conditions.

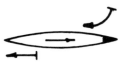

Diagonal on a bow forward stroke. Pulls canoe to the paddle.

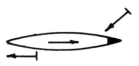

Diagonal draw, pulls canoe move sharply to the paddle.

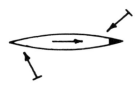

Diagonal bow and stern draw. Pivots canoe to the bow paddle side.

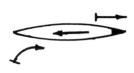

Diagonal on a stern backstroke, helps to steer and useful in a back ferry.

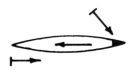

Diagonal reverse draw by bow. Slows canoe and turns it to bow paddle side.

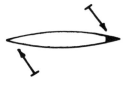

Diagonal reverse draws used to spin the canoe move swiftly.

SCULLING

This is a useful little paddle technique that's handy for short movements directly or diagonally to the paddle side. Sculling can be done by bow or stern. Don't scull when maneuvering is critical. Go to your draws and prys for that.

The stroke is a continuous "figure 8" pattern with the blade remaining under water the whole time. Put the paddle vertically in the water beside your hip or slightly in front of it. The power face of the blade will be parallel to the keel and facing the side of the canoe. Turn the paddle so that the leading edge is angled out from the canoe about 20 to 45 degrees. Do this by twisting your upper hand thumb inboard and toward your face so that the power face is facing slightly forward. Push the blade forward in the water about 1 to 1½ feet. At the end of this push, twist your upper hand thumb outboard so the leading edge of the blade is in toward the canoe and the power face is facing slightly backward. Get the blade at about the angle you had it going forward. Pull the blade back as shown in the sketch, pass your hip, and about 1 to 1½ feet behind your hip reverse the blade angle again and start forward. All of this is done in one smooth, continuous motion *without removing the blade from the water.*

The sculling stroke.

POWER FACE   POWER FACE

215

Although it's possible to do this sculling stroke in reverse and move the canoe *away* from the paddle side, you'll probably more often use a pry for that purpose. To move the canoe diagonally, either forward or backward using the scull, increase the length of the half stroke in the direction you want to go, and decrease the other half of the stroke.

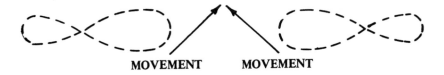

MOVEMENT   **MOVEMENT**

CHAPTER 10
MANEUVERS AND COMMANDS

Maneuvering a canoe is the art of making it go where you want it to go, when you want it to go there. The basic paddle strokes will pretty well do this for you when you're cruising in still or very slow-moving open water. On faster-moving rivers, however, particularly when there are obstacles to dodge and shoals and rapids to contend with, your maneuvering will require more and different techniques and skills. It's these that you'll learn in this chapter. You'll quickly find that some of these river-running maneuvers can *only* be done where a current exists and thus cannot be effectively practiced in still water. Others can only be executed where a current *differential* exists. Most of them are emphatically *moving*-water techniques.

As you practice these maneuvers you'll discover such things as how to nullify part of the current's effects on the canoe and how to sometimes use the current to help you maneuver; you'll put to good use the paddle strokes described in the paddling chapter and discover the importance of the body position, balance and bracing that you learned way over in "Fundamentals." You'll learn more about the current flow in the river, and the necessity for developing your water-reading skills will suddenly become important. You will, in short, begin to put many of the individual chapters into use and discover how one thing builds on another and fits into it. The best thing you'll discover, however, is that in doing this, your canoeing will begin to pull itself together, and when this happens you're on your way to really becoming a canoeist!

BASIC PRINCIPLES

Don't get crossed up in the current! Except during an actual maneuver (and there are a few exceptions to this, too), the length of the canoe is kept parallel to the river flow in all movements. This streamlined position reduces the effect of the current on the hull, making your movements more precise and reducing the amount of work you have to do by eliminating part of "fighting the current." It also decreases the "target" area of your canoe; 35 inches of width can slip through or around something a lot easier than 15, 16, or 17 feet can and is a lot less likely to get hung on some unseen underwater obstruction. The important thing is that the canoe be parallel to the *current,* not to the shoreline. Remember that the main current can run all over an obstructed river. Watching the shoreline to determine your angle with the current is another of those things in canoeing that you do only when you know enough *not* to do it. This subject will be covered more thoroughly under ferries, which is one of the places it really applies.

To keep your canoe parallel to the current, all ideal movements are done by moving the canoe to the side, thus assuming no angle with the current. In moving water, you do not *steer* a canoe through a series of obstacles or around a single obstacle. The two exceptions to this are where you have plenty of time and room to go around a single obstacle and can adjust your course far upstream and where there is such a definite path through two obstacles that the flow and power of the water carries you through by sheer force. In this last case, of course, you don't really steer, you just *ride*! Neither do you *power* your way around obstacles despite the theories advanced by some canoe books that the speed gives you better control and maneuverability. In this case, it doesn't!

In the drawing, the canoeist is going to try to avoid the rock by paddling forward and *steering* around it as he would in a lake. Look at what could easily happen. The current is already pushing him downstream. As he turns the canoe and paddles forward he is moving to the side of the obstacle, but he is also still being swept downstream by the current, so his course is a long diagonal.

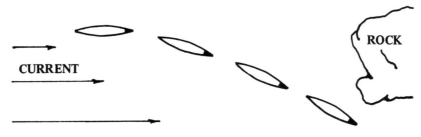

The lake method of avoiding (?) a rock.

As his canoe becomes more broadside to the current, the water force on the hull keeps increasing. This could increase his speed and will definitely increase the force with which he'll hit the rock if he doesn't clear it. The broadside position also increases the area that *can* hit the rock, making it even harder to dodge around it.

In the next drawing, the canoeist uses one of the river methods to clear the rock. It's called a sideslip. He's still being moved down the river by the current, but he's kept his hull parallel to it, thus holding his speed to whatever it was when he started and not increasing the hull force or the target area. Most importantly, he's accomplished his goal of dodging the obstacle a lot faster, and he *knows* when he's cleared it.

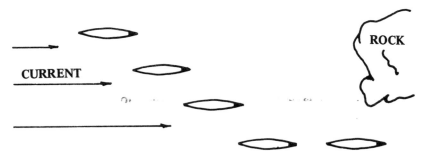

The sideslip method of avoiding a rock.

If he was close to the rock or if the current was very strong, he would use still another maneuver called a back ferry that allows him to move almost straight across the current, using the current to *help* him do it. If you look closely at the drawing, you'll notice that in this case he is *not* keeping his canoe parallel to the current. Ferries are one of the exceptions to the "parallel-with-the-current" rule.

The back-ferry method of avoiding a rock.

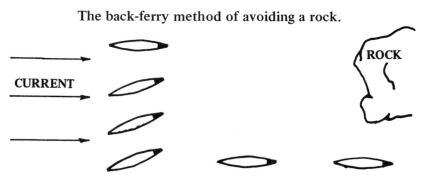

COMMANDS

Proper commands are essential in a tandem canoe. It takes a long time, many trips, and a lot of practice with the same person before two people can work together without commands or with a minimum of them. Even two experienced canoeists both proficient in bow and stern but strangers to each other would have problems for awhile until each became accustomed to the paddling style of the other and learned to anticipate the other's actions.

So commands are necessary. They should be simple and standardized and practiced until they are automatic. The most common basic commands are: "Back," "Forward," "OK," "Right," "Left," and one I like—"Ferry."

The commands "Back" and "Forward" are obvious: "Back" means to backstroke, "Forward" to go forward with a forward stroke. "Back" may mean to slow down, to stop, or to back upstream. To repeat myself, you can normally tell what's meant either by some modifying words or by the urgency with which the word "Back" is said (or screamed).

The command (or comment) "OK" is often used but may be confusing. It can, depending on the user and the circumstances, mean "What you're doing is fine, keep on doing it" or "We're OK now, stop doing it." If you're going to use "OK," clear it with your partner so he's sure what you mean by it.

"Right" and "Left" are self-explanatory. They mean take your end of the canoe to the right or to the left. It's understood that the resulting motion is to be to the *side* and not obliquely if you're doing any "avoidance" maneuvering. Substitutions for these two commands are sources of a very common and very bad practice. Instead of giving a command "Right" or "Left" and allowing the paddler to decide *how* to move the canoe in that direction, you'll often hear the actual technique such as "Draw" or "Pry" given as a command. Giving commands this way means that one of the two partners is thinking for both, which could lead to confusion. Use "Right" or "Left" and let him decide what to do. Once more, the urgency of the action will be pretty much inferred from the tone of voice.

The command "Ferry" is one I like to use more as an explanatory word than a command. It's more likely to be given by the stern than any of the rest of the commands. If you want to ferry and say "Back," which is the first thing to do, then the addition of the word "Ferry" (left or right) tells your partner that the backstroke he's doing is for more than just slowing down or stopping and is also serving a purpose as part of a maneuver. It also explains to him why the canoe is being put at an angle to the current so he won't try to straighten it up.

Now, who gives all these commands? "Who's Captain?" has already been covered in another part of this book, but let me jog your memory. The sternman is normally responsible for the general course through obstructions and is the only one in a tandem crew who can see the length of the canoe and judge its angle. Although he's facing the bowman's back, his voice is projecting forward so it carries better to the bow. The bowman is responsible for last-minute course changes as he can see directly in front of the canoe—an area partially blocked from the immediate view of the sternman. It's hard to hear what the bowman says unless he turns and speaks over his shoulder, and he may not have time to shout more than once or to look back at all.

So most of the commands will be from the stern, but there will still be some from the bow. Ideally, the stern will also react to whatever the bow does without spoken words. If the bow suddenly moves the canoe to the right, for example, the stern should assume there is some good reason for this and immediately get *his* end of the canoe over in the same direction, keeping the ends lined up parallel to the current. The sternman must not forget that when *he* initiates the evasive action, he *must* issue vocal commands to the bowman as the bow doesn't know what's going on behind him unless it's pretty drastic. Normally, whoever receives a command continues doing whatever was ordered until told to stop or commanded to do something else.

Whatever commands are given and by whomever, they should be given in a loud, clear voice so there is a minimum chance of confusion. As I've commented before, mumbling into the front of your life jacket just won't get the job done at all, as you'll find out the first time you try it!

FINALLY

One thought before turning to the actual "how-to" of the maneuvers. I defined "maneuvering" as making a canoe go where you wanted it to when you wanted it to. You won't always succeed in this, so don't expect to. Even after you're very good and even on familiar waters, the vagaries of current and wind, a momentary loss of balance, an unexpected catch of the paddle blade, or any number of other things can contribute to a sudden *not* making what you've made a dozen times before. This is nothing to worry about, and you've got plenty of company, because every canoeist who really gets out and canoes takes an unexpected bath now and then!

MANEUVERING THE CANOE

All of the maneuvers will use the same basic paddle techniques that you have already learned. These basic strokes and braces applied in various ways and combinations with body leans, canoe angles with the current, and the current itself will do most of what you want your canoe to do. You have already learned to maneuver your canoe forward and backward using the forward and back strokes, and you should be able to make it go approximately where you want it to go in unobstructed waters. As you go into the maneuvers you'll find that a sound foundation in the basic paddle strokes is vital. Without it your maneuvering will *not* be effective.

For practicing these maneuvers I suggest that at first you use a slow-running river with a few big, clearly defined obstacles. After you have the technique down, try a swifter river with a lot of small shoals. *Gradually* work your way up in skill level; don't get overconfident and careless.

SPINNING THE CANOE END FOR END

This maneuver is more useful than you might think. It can be used when you want to forward-ferry and there's no eddy to turn in or when you just want to paddle back upstream a little. When you spin your canoe, do it in a hurry and be sure you have room to do it in without getting hung on something either in or out of the water. Remember that in a current you're being pushed downstream as you spin around, so check downstream before you try it. Don't get caught broadside.

Spinning the canoe is simple. The bow and stern *both* do the same stroke, in this case either draws or prys depending on what direction they want to turn.

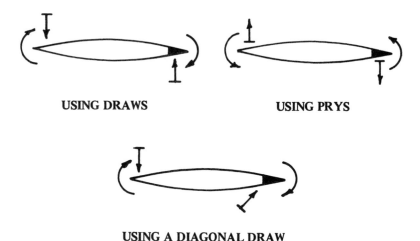

USING DRAWS   USING PRYS

USING A DIAGONAL DRAW

Spinning the canoe.

To help slow or halt your downstream drift, the bowman can twist around, reach out over the side and to the rear, and put a rear diagonal on his first few draws.

MOVING THE CANOE SIDEWAYS

There are two ways to maneuver your canoe directly to the side. In one, the sideslip, you still have some downstream component in your side maneuver even though the canoe stays parallel to the current. Because of this, the side slip is most often used for small obstacles close to you where only a minimum amount of movement to the side is necessary or where you have plenty of room and time and want to move over more leisurely.

Ferries are the other method of moving sideways. A good

223

ferry will not have *any* downstream component or will have less than a sideslip. This depends on the strength of the paddlers and the strength of the current. Ferries are best used for larger movements to the side or where time and distance will allow only a minimum downstream movement.

THE SIDESLIP

A sideslip is just as simple as spinning the canoe. The only criterion is that bow and stern do complementary strokes, one prying and the other drawing. The canoe will move *toward* the side on which the draw is being done. Either bow or stern may do either stroke, depending upon what direction the canoe is to be moved and who is paddling on what side. As the pry is a short stroke and the draw a long one, you will find that to keep the canoe parallel with the current, the partner doing the pry will have to do a lot of fast, hard prys to keep up with the draw of his partner. (This is assuming that both partners are equally strong and skilled.) In any event, in the sideslip don't let either pry or draw end get ahead of the other end and so put the canoe at an angle to the current. Keep parallel with the current by adjusting the draws and prys until the canoe moves evenly sideways.

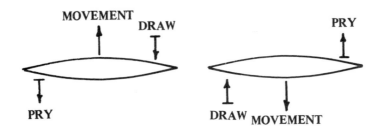

The sideslip.

THE FERRIES

Ferries are magic! Well, they're not really. But when you get out and do a *correct* ferry and suddenly experience the feeling of moving relatively effortlessly straight *across* a swift, rushing current of water and without being swept downstream (or very much downstream) in the process, you'll *think* its magic.

Ferries are probably the single most important river maneuver you'll ever learn. They are constantly used to dodge small obstructions and large ones. They are the *only* maneuver you can use to move along the lip of a rapid, shoal, or drop while looking for a place to run it. They allow you to maneuver to the side in places only slightly longer than your canoe, and they're great for just going from one side of the river to the other or for getting to shore in a current, pulling into an eddy, or crossing a current from one eddy to another. In two words, ferries are *useful* and *used*.

Canoe ferries get their name from the method of operation of the old-time ferries across rivers. Some of these ferries, often far out in the woods, had no power to propel them from shore to shore, so some ingenious person figured out how to make the river do it for him.

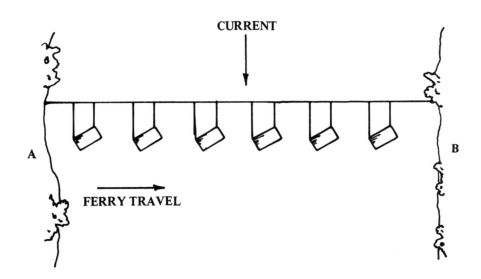

CURRENT

A

B

FERRY TRAVEL

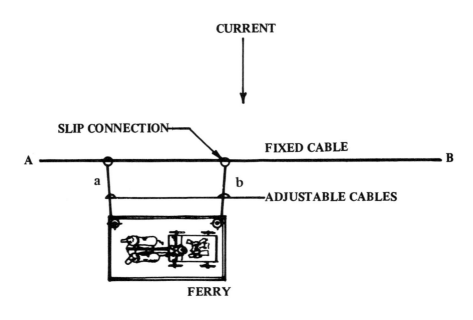

CURRENT

SLIP CONNECTION

FIXED CABLE

A ——————————————————— B

a   b

ADJUSTABLE CABLES

FERRY

An old-time ferry.

To get from side A to side B, the ferry operator would lengthen cable "a" and shorten up cable "b," and the river flowing against the side of the ferry, being unable to sweep it on down river, would push it to side B. To get back to side A, cable "b" would be lengthened and cable "a" shortened, and the river would push it back across. The physics or engineering student will recognize vectors at work here, but to the ferry operator, it just worked! Canoe ferries operate the same way except that a paddle stroke takes the place of the fixed cable.

Basics of the Ferry

There are two types of canoe ferries, the forward ferry and the back ferry. Each is named for the basic paddle stroke done during the ferry. The *back* ferry is done while the canoe is *bow downstream,* and the basic paddle stroke is the *back* stroke. The *forward* ferry is done while the canoe is *bow upstream,* and the basic paddle stroke is the *forward* stroke.

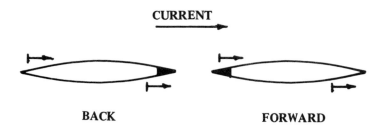

CURRENT

BACK   FORWARD

The ferries.

Two definitions are necessary to fully understand ferrying, whether forward or backward. One is for "parallel" with the current or "at an angle to the current." The other is for "increase" and "decrease" your angle. Here's what they mean. Parallel to the current means the length of the canoe is lined up with the current flow. It is at a zero-degree angle with the current.

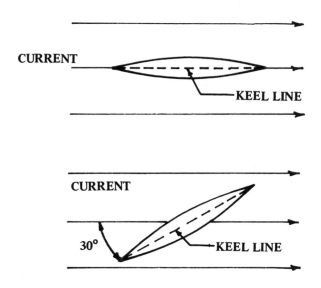

CURRENT

KEEL LINE

CURRENT

30°   KEEL LINE

An angle with the current means the angle may be to the side shown here or to the other side. This angle happens to be about 30 degrees but could be anything. In either of the above cases, the canoe may be facing upstream or downstream, depending on whether you are doing a forward ferry or a back ferry.

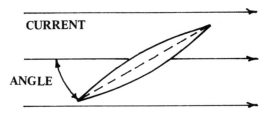

This canoe is at an angle with the current. If the canoe is moved so it is in this position:

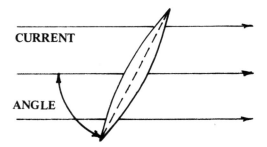

then you have increased the angle in respect to the current flow, approached more toward perpendicular or 90 degrees to the current. As you go back toward parallel with the current, you are decreasing the angle in respect to the current flow.

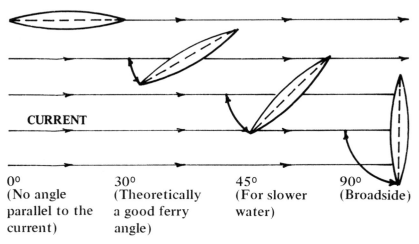

0°	30°	45°	90°
(No angle parallel to the current)	(Theoretically a good ferry angle)	(For slower water)	(Broadside)

Angles with the current.

228

Once again, the angles could be to the side shown here or to the other side, and the canoe could be facing upstream or down.

Why a Ferry Works

If you know what a resultant force is, you'll have no trouble seeing why a ferry works. If not, then here's a brief explanation. Suppose you had a tree you wanted to cut down but it had to fall in a certain place. You might tie ropes to it as in the drawing, cut the tree nearly in two, and pull on the ropes. You don't want the tree to fall on you so you and someone else get off to the side and both pull at an angle to the tree. Neither of you is pulling in the direction you want it to fall, yet if the pulls are equally hard and at the same time and angle, the tree will fall where you want it to—between the ropes.

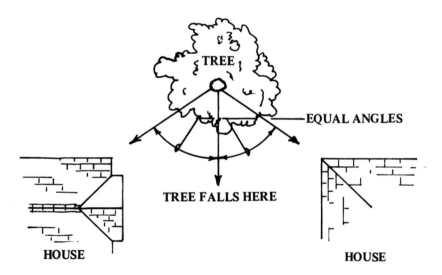

And that's the idea of the ferry. Two forces at an angle to each other are exerted on the canoe, the downstream force of the current and an upstream force of paddle strokes. These forces are balanced by varying the angle and the amount of paddle power so the canoe, unable to go in the direction of either force will, like the tree, move to the side.

Look at these drawings. They're all drawn to the same scale, and the length of each line represents how much force is being put into it. Equal-length lines are the same force.

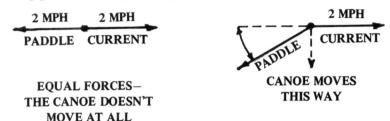

EQUAL FORCES—
THE CANOE DOESN'T
MOVE AT ALL

CANOE MOVES
THIS WAY

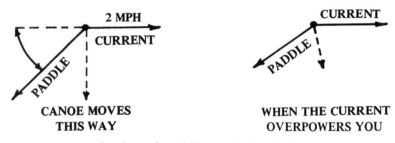

CANOE MOVES
THIS WAY

WHEN THE CURRENT
OVERPOWERS YOU

Angle and paddle stroke in the ferry.

Notice that the smaller the angle is, the less force you have to put into your ferry *but* the less movement you have to the side. Notice, too, that the canoe always moves in the direction of the angle or, in river terms, in the direction that the *upstream* end is pointing.

You will always have to paddle harder than the current if you want to move *directly* to the side, and you will often reach a point where the current overpowers you. When this happens you can settle for paddling equal to or less than the current speed and allow for some slippage down the river when the current overpowers you.

If you've followed the "why" of a ferry, the ferry itself should be very simple to you. Here's one of those cryptic diagrams with a canoe superimposed on it.

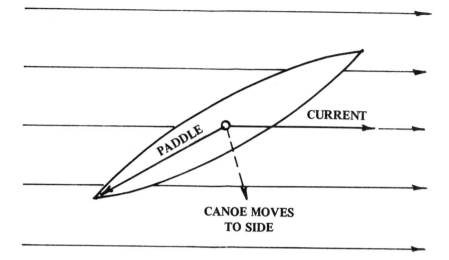

CURRENT

PADDLE

**CANOE MOVES
TO SIDE**

For a back ferry, the canoe remains in its normal bow downstream position. The basic stroke is the backstroke, thus the name "back ferry" as already pointed out. The sternman gives *all* orders on all ferries as only he can see the angle of the canoe.

The Back Ferry

On the river the procedure would be this. Upon deciding to back-ferry, the sternman would give the command "Back," and the bowman would immediately begin to do a pure backstroke. It's very important that *he continues to do this until told to do something else.* In a ferry the bowman's job is basically to do nothing but supply power.

As he gives the command "Back," the sternman moves his upstream end of the canoe in the direction he wants the canoe to move and sets the ferry angle by moving the stern as far to the right or left as necessary. He does this with a quick, powerful draw or pry, depending upon which side he's paddling on and in which direction he wants the stern to move. He may do several paddle strokes, but usually only one good one will do. He then immediately begins back-paddling. If the angle is right and the power of the backstrokes is correct, the canoe will move directly to the side except when you're overpowered by the current. It should not drift downstream. Neither should it be forced upstream by the paddle stroke. With both angle and backstrokes balanced it will take surprisingly little paddle power to keep the canoe moving sideways. You need only hit it right once and you'll understand the "magic" of a ferry. If you're having to struggle too much in a relatively weak current, then your angle is wrong. This is a matter of experience although an angle of about 30 degrees will be a good starting point. The slower the current, the wider your angle. Conversely, as the current increases, your angle should become smaller for the same amount of back-paddling effort. If you're in doubt about the initial angle, it's better to start off with a small one (you can increase it later in the ferry if you need to). On the other hand, it's much harder (sometimes impossible) to close up a large angle. You will often find variations in current in the river caused by obstructions. When ferrying across these, you'll need to adjust your angle for each different current speed.

The sternman is responsible for maintaining the ferry angle. He does this by quick prys or draws or putting diagonal components into his backstroke. Method three of the backstroke is especially good for this. In swift water, however, the sternman will need to contribute as much backing power as he can, so any strokes to correct the ferry angle should be done as fast and efficiently as possible.

It often happens that the sternman cannot hold the angle by himself or needs a faster or greater correction than he can supply alone without sacrificing too much of his back-paddling power. An example might be where the canoe is within a few feet of an obstruction and still moving toward it because of a bad ferry angle. The sternman would give the command "Right" or "Left," depending upon what correction is necessary, and the bowman would do *one and only one* swift, powerful stroke to accomplish this, then immediately go into his backstroke again. Although this "single-stroke" action violates the "Do what you're told until you're told to stop" principle, it is vital in a ferry that the backing power be maintained as much as possible. Simultaneously, the sternman would do the opposite stroke and, if this was enough correction, return to his backstroke. Obviously, the canoe will drift faster toward the obstruction during this momentary stopping of the backstroke, but this is a calculated risk, because if the correct ferry angle is achieved, you may still miss the obstruction. Without the ferry angle you'll be almost certain to hit it.

Once the canoe has cleared the obstruction, the sternman can do the correct stroke (draw or pry) to bring the canoe parallel to the current, directing his bowman to help if necessary. When the canoe is straight the sternman should tell his bowman "OK" or "Forward" (or whatever they have agreed on) so the bowman will stop back-paddling.

The entire sequence of a back ferry then is:

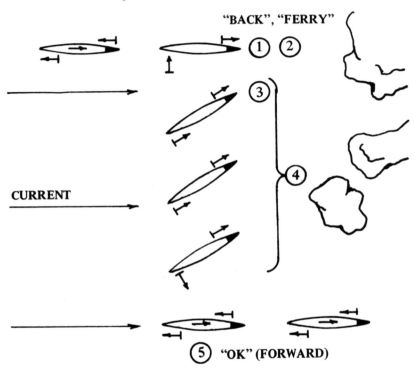

A back-ferry sequence.

1. Back paddle.
2. Point the upstream end of the canoe in the direction you want to go.
3. Get the correct ferry angle.
4. Ferry to the side of the obstruction.
5. Straighten the canoe and proceed.

The Forward Ferry

In the forward ferry the canoe is pointed bow upstream. This is an easier and more natural maneuver to most canoeists as the basic stroke is the forward stroke and the bow of the canoe is pointed in the direction you want to go. It's a very useful technique if you're coming out of an eddy or away from the shore or anywhere where you want to ferry across and are already facing upstream. It has two chief disadvantages: (1) you have to spin the canoe around to a bow upstream posture to do it, which requires a little time, room, and caution to avoid being broadsided on something, and (2) sooner or later you have to spin it back around, which lays you open to the same situation.

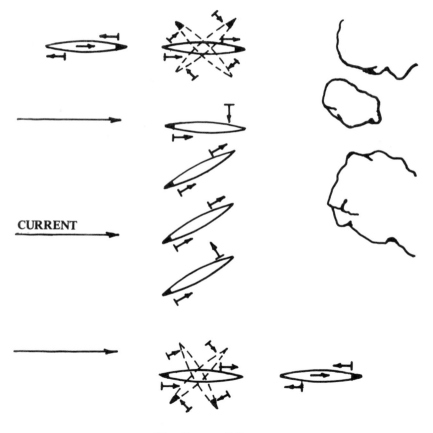

CURRENT

The forward ferry.

234

All of the techniques of the forward ferry are identical with those of the back ferry except that the forward stroke is substituted for the backstroke. Again, the bow is basically responsible for power only, doing swift, necessary correction as ordered by the sternman and immediately returning to the forward stroke. The sternman sets the angle and holds it and also furnishes forward stroke power. The balance of paddle power and angle is vital just as in the back ferry, and the movement of the canoe to the *side*, not up or downstream, should be maintained.

Once the obstacle has been cleared, the canoe may be spun around as rapidly as possible with due regard for the time, room, and obstructions mentioned before.

A very common use of the forward ferry is where a canoe has made an eddy turn and wants to cross a current to another eddy.

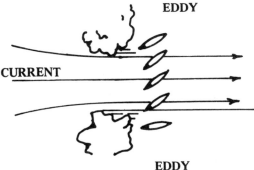

There is also another way to do this that you'll learn later in this chapter.

Which Side To Paddle On

I've heard various theories proposed as to which side is best to paddle on while doing a ferry, but all of these theories have been for *solo* paddling. For tandem-canoe ferrying, just paddle on the side you're already on when you start the ferry.

Practicing Ferries

Ferries are best practiced in relatively slow-moving water

until you begin to "feel" the correct angle. Experiment with holding the same paddle power and varying your angle until you achieve the most sideways movement for the current you're in. Remember, the slower the current, the greater the angle should be. When practicing in very slow current you may end up almost broadside to the current and be barely dipping your paddle in the water, but don't let that worry you. The important thing is that you *feel* the correct angle and that you don't drift downstream or paddle upstream.

To check that you are moving to the side only, pick out two stationary objects on the bank or in the river and ferry across between them, checking your alignment visually. Ferry to one side, then reverse your angle and ferry back across. If you're back-ferrying, then turn and do some forward ferries in both directions, too. It's all good practice. After you get the feel of ferrying and can maintain a straight-to-the side aspect, seek out swifter water and practice there.

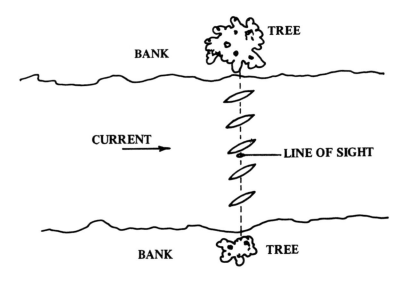

Practicing ferries.

Places Where Ferry Angles Will Fool You

I have mentioned that the ferry angle must be with respect to the *current* and that a common mistake of novice canoeists is to establish their angle with the shoreline or judge it by watching the shore. In an open, straight stretch of the river this may be fine, but in bends or where an obstruction protrudes from the shoreline or anywhere that the water cannot maintain a straight course, you should watch the *current* the canoe is in; otherwise, you may *think* you have an angle and have none at all. You may also have to continually adjust your angle throughout a ferry to compensate for changes in the current caused by varying river conditions.

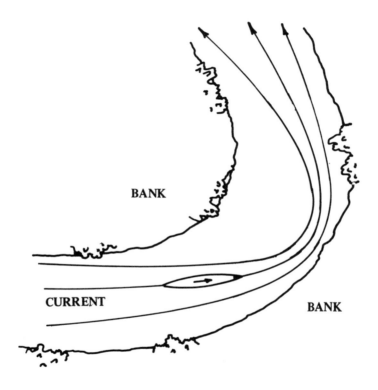

ANGLE WITH EITHER SHORE LINE

Typical spots with an angle with the shore but none with the current.

237

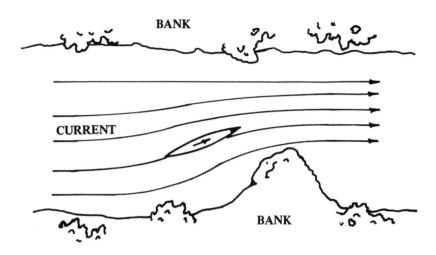

ANGLE WITH LEFT SHORE

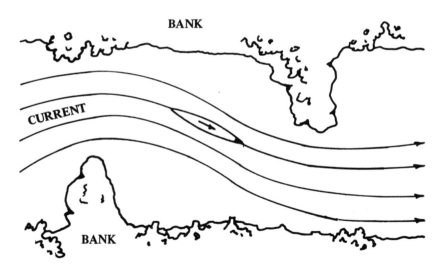

ANGLE WITH EITHER SHORE LINE

More typical spots with an angle with the shore but none with
the current.

238

GETTING INTO AND OUT OF EDDIES

As a river's volume and speed increase, so do its power and the velocity with which it pushes your canoe. As this power and speed build, the water's effects on the canoe hull become more violent, and precise maneuvering becomes ever more difficult. The water simply overpowers you. Where a sideslip or ferry could be used to enter or leave an eddy in a more moderate current, special techniques now become necessary.

The maneuver for getting out of the current and into an eddy is called an eddy turn and that of leaving the eddy to re-enter the current is called a peel off. Both maneuvers utilize the power of the current and the speed differential between the main current and the eddy to accomplish these goals. The river does much of the work. Note that both maneuvers *require* a current differential to work. Although both may also be used in moderate water flows with "soft" eddy lines, the greater the current differential, the snappier the maneuver.

Either maneuver may be done to the side on which the bowman is paddling (an on-side technique), or to the side opposite the bowman's paddle side (an off-side technique). In an eddy turn the canoe is heading downstream, spins around, and ends up bow upstream in the eddy behind an obstruction. For a peel off, the canoe starts from this bow upstream postion in the eddy, spins around, and ends up bow downstream once more in the current. Both are basically simple techniques but will definitely require practice.

EDDY LINES

Back in Chapter 8, I discussed eddy lines, those sometimes obvious, sometimes almost invisible divisions between the moving water of the current and the "dead" water of an eddy. Eddy lines play a vital role in eddy turns and peel offs, so if you can't identify them by now, I suggest you get out and learn to do so.

EDDY TURNS

If ferries are the magic carpets of canoeing, then eddy turns are the roller coasters. A properly executed eddy turn across a sharp eddy line is a real thrill and probably will do more to make you *feel* like an accomplished canoeist than any other maneuvering technique. It will also make you look good to anyone on shore, particularly if those ashore are non-canoeists!

Quite apart from thrills and exhibitionism, however, eddy turns are vital and extremely useful maneuvers. Although generally not used as often as ferries, they are, in their place, just as important and are replaceable by no other technique.

The object of an eddy turn may be as vital as avoiding going over a waterfall or as simple as wanting to stop and "park" to watch your companions come down through something. You may want to rest or to gain time to think or to use the eddy as a starting point for another approach to something. Whatever the reason, the eddy turn offers a way to enter the eddy safely and under control.

The "Why" of an Eddy Turn

Before a canoeist starts into an eddy, all of his canoe's hull is exposed to the current and thus subjected to more or less the same downstream water forces. As the end of the canoe crosses the eddy line, however, the part of the hull in the eddy is suddenly released from this downstream pressure and may even be subjected to a pronounced upstream pressure. The major part of the hull remains out in the current. This sudden unbalancing of forces has the effect of momentarily anchoring the end of the canoe in the eddy. This "anchor" also provides a point around which the rest of the hull can pivot as the current continues to sweep against it. The use of this current differential to spin the canoe around is the basic principle of the eddy turn. The paddles are used only to brace the canoe and to pull it securely into the eddy.

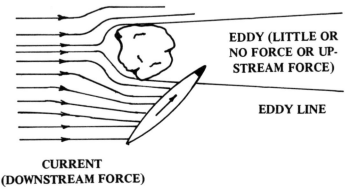

EDDY (LITTLE OR NO FORCE OR UPSTREAM FORCE)

EDDY LINE

CURRENT (DOWNSTREAM FORCE)

One other thing happens as the eddy end of the canoe crosses the eddy line: the canoe will tend to roll to the *outside* of the turn. That is the reason for using the paddles to *brace*. While the outside of the turn will be *downstream* for an eddy turn, it will be *upstream* for a peel off. To avoid any confusion whatsoever, forget down and upstream and just remember the roll is to the *outside*, which applies in *all* cases. This rolling to the outside of the turn may not sound too logical to you, and the idea of the canoe flipping you out downstream (on an eddy turn) may seem strange, but it is very true and is something that must be remembered and reckoned with. Without going into the complexities of relative velocities and water forces on the hull that cause this, just believe what I say; better yet, don't believe it and try making an eddy turn out of a fast current and across a sharp eddy line without the compensating braces and leans described later. You'll become a believer as soon as you fish yourself out of the water!

Lean and Brace to the Inside of the Turn

To offset this roll to the outside of the turn, the canoe must *always* be leaned and braced to the *inside* of the turn. This is a cardinal rule of all eddy turns and peeloffs whether on-side, off-side, to the right, or to the left and whether the bracing is done by the bow or by the stern. The sharper the eddy line and the faster you're moving, the greater this lean to the inside must be, the stronger the brace, and the more weight you should put on it.

The On-Side Eddy Turn

This is the easiest eddy turn to do. It's done to the side on which the bowman is paddling and the bowman does the lean and a high brace. The sternman aims the canoe into the eddy (with help from the bowman if needed) and provides paddle power. It's an easy, graceful, and effective eddy turn when done correctly. Step by step, here's how it's done.

241

EDDY

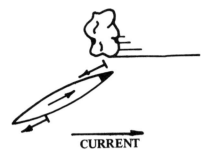

CURRENT

a

a. The sternman sets a course to approach the eddy at about a 30-degree angle and aims the canoe to barely clear the obstruction and enter the eddy just downstream of it. Both he and the bowman drive the canoe forward with forward strokes.

EDDY

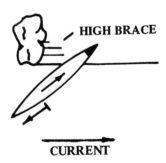

HIGH BRACE

CURRENT

b

b. The bow crosses the eddy line. As it does, the bowman instantly leans far out to the inside of the turn and high braces, planting his paddle firmly in the water of the eddy. He does *not* draw—he only *holds* his brace, which becomes an anchor for the bow and a pivot point around which the canoe begins to spin as the current pushes the stern downstream.

242

For a really effective brace and maximum reach into the eddy, the bowman should have his upper body, including his hips, completely out over the gunwales and parallel to the water, his thigh hard against his paddle-side gunwale and, as in any good brace, part of his weight on the blade. There will be a strong pull on the paddle until the eddy turn is almost completed, so he must grip the paddle firmly.

The sternman who is paddling on the opposite side from the bow and thus on the outside of the turn must be careful that he does not lean to the outside or position his weight in such a way that it makes it difficult for the bowman to lean the canoe to the inside. This is a bit awkward as the natural tendency of a tandem paddler is to sit closer to the side on which he is paddling. One suggestion is for the sternman to prepare for the lean by shifting his knee (the one on the inside of the eddy turn) to a position a few inches higher on the side of the canoe. Then as the bowman leans, some of the sternman's weight will be helping the lean or, to look at it the other way, less of his weight will be opposing the lean.

NORMAL KNEE   READY TO TURN   THE TURN
POSITION

Knee position to allow lean by your partner.

A very common fault of novices is to high brace too soon or not to reach out far enough. They miss the eddy, plant their paddle blade in the water of the cur-

243

rent, and watch the eddy vanish upstream as their canoe drifts past it. The high brace must be in the eddy or the eddy turn will not work.

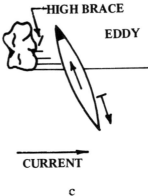

c

c. The canoe has spun around somewhat. The bowman continues to hold his high brace and lean, and the sternman continues to forward stroke.

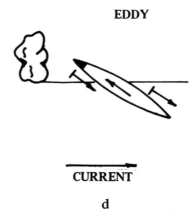

d

d. As the canoe pivots around the bowman's high brace, the relationship of the flat of the bowman's paddle to the canoe changes until, as the canoe approaches parallel to the eddy line and at about the point shown in the illustration, the blade will be just about in position for a forward stroke. By this time in the turn the rolling tendency of the canoe is weakening, and the lean and brace is no longer as important as it was. The bowman coverts his brace into a forward stroke and this, plus the still-continuing forward strokes of the sternman, drives the canoe on into the eddy as in the final illustration.

EDDY

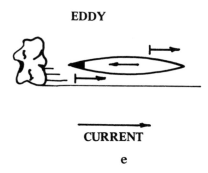

CURRENT

e

The on-side eddy turn.

On the river this entire eddy turn would have been completed long before you finished reading about it. It's all one smooth, continuous, and rapid sequence of events. Except for accurately aiming the canoe into the eddy, there is really little to it. Even a poor aiming job can be overcome somewhat if the bowman can only stretch far enough to get his paddle into the eddy. The bow of the canoe doesn't *have* to cross the eddy line first. A desperate stab with the paddle may succeed in pulling it in. The turn won't be as sharp nor will the canoe slip so neatly in close below the obstruction, but you'll have a chance of doing *an* eddy turn, if not a great one!

The Off-Side Eddy Turn

An off-side eddy turn is a turn made opposite to the side on which the bowman is paddling. The sternman braces while the bowman goes through a rapid sequence of paddle techniques that maneuver the canoe into the eddy. Off-side eddy turns are a bit awkward and difficult to do and require split-second reactions by the bowman and precise initial aiming by

245

the sternman. Consequently, off-side turns take a lot more practice than do on-side turns, and as we're all human, this often means that off-side turns never become as strong a maneuver as their on-side counterpart. But there may come a time when you *have* to do one, so it pays to practice.

Psychologically (at least to me), there is something that I dislike about being in the bow and trusting the lean of a canoe to some invisible being behind me. I always have the uneasy feeling that they're leaning the wrong way or have possibly abandoned me completely. I think this is the result of teaching too many novices, *but* if you too feel this way, then off-side turns demand that the bowman have a great faith in his sternman's brace and lean. The sternman, in turn, must rely rather heavily on his bowman as the quick movements necessary and the strain on the bow paddle in a sharp current differential demand both quick reactions and strong wrists.

Leans and Braces

Off-side eddy turns follow the same rule as on-side turns: *always* lean and brace to the *inside* of the turn. The only difference is that in off-side techniques the sternman does the bracing and uses a *low* brace.

Doing an Off-Side Eddy Turn

a. The initial drive toward the eddy, the approximately 30-degree angle, and the aiming to just clear the

EDDY

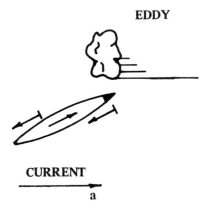

CURRENT

a

246

obstruction and have the bow cross the eddy line just downstream from it are all done exactly as in an on-side turn. *The sternman must be much more precise in his aiming, however. As pointed out, in an on-side turn, the bowman can often stretch out and get his high brace in the eddy even if the bow of the canoe has missed it. Not so in an off-side turn. The bowman has no such reaching ability and, in order to make the turn, the bow* must *actually be* in *the eddy. The sternman, then, must drive the canoe in without much error.*

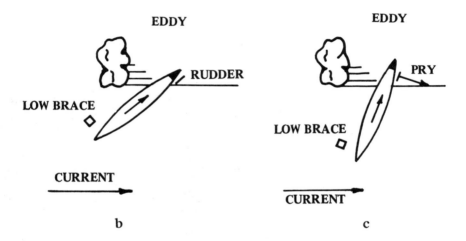

b., c. As the canoe crosses the eddy line, the sternman leans to the inside of the turn and low braces. *The low brace should be out as far as possible from the hull of the canoe, and the sternman should have his thigh up against the brace-side gunwale and his upper body out over the gunwale and must have part of his weight on the brace. The amount of lean and brace, remember, depends upon the conditions of the turn.* As the canoe's stern is swept downstream by the current, the paddle blade will "skid" along the surface of the water. The sternman continues to lean and brace until

247

the turn is nearly complete. The bowman has a more active job. At the *moment* that the bow slices across the eddy line and as the sternman leans and braces, the bowman puts his paddle forward at an angle of about 45 degrees with the water and with the flat of the blade parallel to the keel line. The blade *must* be in the eddy. If it's in the current, the turn won't work.

The bowman does not change his normal paddle grip to do this nor does he clamp his paddle to the gunwale with his hand. The paddle shaft is braced against the gunwale as in a pry, and the power face is turned in toward the hull. This is done by rotating the upper hand thumb back and in and the lower hand thumb forward and out. The photo shows the correct angle. The paddle acts as a rudder to help guide the canoe into the eddy.

The "bow rudder" paddle position for off-side turns and peel-offs.

As soon as the canoe is firmly in the eddy, the bow-man converts his "rudder" to a quick, powerful pry off the gunwale. *This pry helps force the bow of the canoe around into the eddy and also provides a pivot point and "anchor" for the canoe to swing around. This is not a standard "textbook" pry, and the bow-man shouldn't worry about the blade being down under the bilge; he just prys hard from the "rudder" position. The bowman should keep a tight grip on his paddle during his sequence and be prepared for a pretty hard yank as the blade enters the water.*

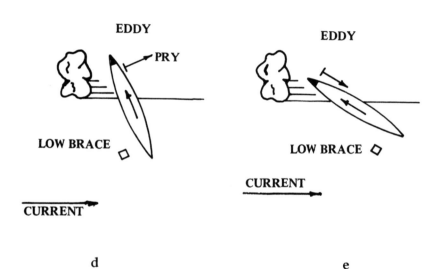

d   e

d., e. The canoe is now well into its turn. The bowman does a forward stroke to drive the canoe up into the eddy. *All of the bow motions of "b," "c," and "d" are done in three very quick, consecutive motions: rudder, pry, forward stroke; one, two, three, with each motion only lasting a few seconds and with as little superfluous paddle motion as possible.*

249

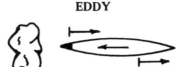

EDDY

CURRENT

f

The off-side eddy turn.

f.   The sternman holds his low brace until the canoe is nearly swung completely into the eddy. As the stern crosses the eddy line, he converts his brace to forward strokes, helping drive the canoe into the eddy.

You can now see why the off-side eddy turns require more practice. The bowman must react swiftly and instinctively to go through his three steps in the few seconds of crossing the eddy line. The sternman must put the canoe in place so precisely that the bowman can put his blade in the eddy with the very limited reach allowed him while using his blade as a rudder.

Practicing Eddy Turns

Eddy turns must be practiced in current and where there is an obstruction to form an eddy. In slow current (the best place for initial practice) you can "create" a snappier eddy turn by building up your speed as you paddle toward the eddy. The faster you paddle, the greater will be the speed differential between the canoe and the eddy and the more effective the eddy turn. Check your practice eddy before turning into it. It's disconcerting to start swinging in and suddenly broadside on some submerged rock. It's equally disconcerting to have your bow run aground on something behind the eddy-forming obstruction or to discover the whole "eddy" is full of rocks or logs or something.

Practice coming in close to the obstruction, making tight turns into the eddy, and holding the bow of the canoe close in behind the obstruction. Many eddies are small, but if you can swing in close enough and not be swept downstream, you can still use them.

Reverse Eddy Turns

Reverse eddy turns are also useful techniques to practice, as usual, *before* you really need to do one. Canoes often momentarily catch on some hidden rock, spin around, and wind up progressing down the river, stern first. Sometimes a reverse eddy turn is the quickest, easiest, and safest way to get turned around again or is the only way to avoid being swept into something backwards. Reverse turns are a little harder to do than forward eddy turns because you can't see as well, and they're more awkward because of the back-paddling and mental reversing of technique that must be done.

The technique of the reverse eddy turn is exactly like that of forward eddy turns. The man on the inside of the turn leans and braces, a high brace for an on-side turn, a low brace for an off-side turn. For an off-side reverse eddy turn the sternman will be doing the rudder-pry part of the movement behind him, and what would have been forward strokes will be replaced by backstrokes for both paddlers on all turns.

Aiming into reverse turns will be done with backstrokes, diagonal backstrokes, draws, prys, or whatever is required. Both paddlers will probably have to contribute to the steering and the corrections in order to hold the proper course, angle, and momentum on the initial run into the eddy. Once on the eddy line, however, they must immediately go into their leans and braces.

PEEL OFFS

The reasons for using peel offs to enter a current from an eddy are the same as for using eddy turns to exit from the current; that is, to cross the eddy line without the canoe rolling over and spilling you, to get the canoe turned in as short a distance as possible, and to use the force of the current to do most of the work. The reasons that peel offs *work* are also the same as for an eddy turn except that in a peel off the *stern* remains anchored in the eddy while the bow is swept around and downstream by the current.

Because the reasons for eddy turns and peel offs are the same, so too are the rules. Peel offs require leaning and bracing to offset the tendency of the canoe to roll to the *outside* of the turn, and these leans and braces must be to the *inside* of the turn. Peel offs use the normal high or low braces, and these and the leans are done in the same manner as for eddy turns. Peel offs can be on-side or off-side techniques, depending on which side the bowman is paddling and, to repeat, the paddler on the inside of the turn is the one who leans and braces, regardless of whether he's paddling bow or stern.

Because of the identical techniques used in peel offs and eddy turns, I won't go into detailed descriptions of the braces, leans, whys, and wherefores of either on- or off-side peel offs. Instead, I'll just launch straight into descriptions of their mechanics. If you do have any questions on the basic technique, refer back to Eddy Turns. Now here's how to do peel offs.

Doing an On-Side Peel Off

a.　With the canoe in a bow upstream position both bow and stern drive hard toward the eddy line with for-

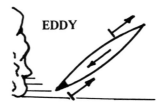

252

ward strokes. *The canoe is positioned to cut across the eddy line and enter the current at about a 30-degree angle. This angle can be adjusted for the current differential by using a bigger angle (up to about 45 degrees) for slower current and a smaller angle for faster current.*

Try to build up enough momentum so the canoe will not be immediately halted by the current and then swept downstream before enough of the hull gets out into the current to present enough surface to the moving water to create an effective turn. The canoe will usually keep some upstream speed and direction even as it begins to turn. The idea is to get a lot of the hull out in the current as the peel off progresses and yet make the turn in a snappy manner. With a small current differential the pattern will be somewhat of a circular shape. Remember, however, that you do want the bow to be swept downstream—you do not want to forward-ferry.

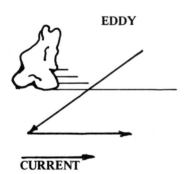

**WITH LARGE
CURRENT DIFFERENTIAL**

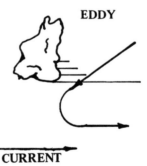

**WITH SMALL
CURRENT DIFFERENTIAL**

Basic pattern of a peel off.

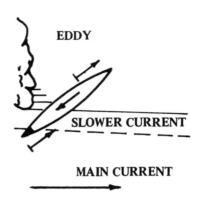

EDDY

SLOWER CURRENT

MAIN CURRENT

b

b. As the bow crosses the eddy line, both paddlers continue driving forward until the bowman can reach out
and high brace in the current. With a sharp eddy line
it will probably be necessary for *the bowman to lean
and brace as soon as the bow crosses the eddy line.
Often, however, there will be an area of slower current, and the main force will be a little farther out.
This enables both paddlers to drive a little more.*

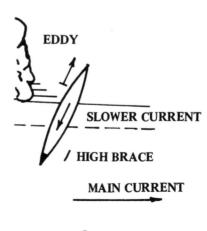

EDDY

SLOWER CURRENT

/ HIGH BRACE

MAIN CURRENT

c

c. The bowman leans and high braces. The flat of his
blade is perpendicular to the current. He does *not*

254

draw, but only holds his brace firmly, allowing the paddle to help pull the bow downstream as well as support his lean. The sternman continues paddling forward.

The body posture and high brace are exactly as for an on-side eddy turn. The bowman's brace should be in the main force of the current with his blade perpendicular to the current. A high brace in moving water but not the fastest-moving water will make for a sloppy, hard-to-control peel off. If this fastest-moving water is so far out that the canoe's stern will no longer be in the eddy, then either peel off as you cross the eddy line or forward-ferry out and convert to a peel off when you can brace in the main flow. This last ferry-peel off combination won't be very effective, however, unless there is a pretty good current differential between the main flow and the slower flow flanking it.

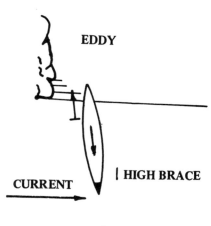

d

d. The bowman holds his lean and brace until the canoe is nearly swept around and the peel off nearly completed. The stern continues to forward paddle.

As the canoe comes around, the bowman will rotate his paddle face to keep the blade perpendicular to the current.

255

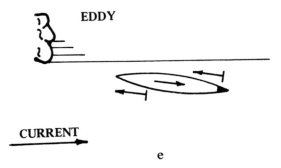

EDDY

CURRENT

e

The on-side peel off.

e.   The bowman converts his high brace to a forward stroke as the peel off is completed and the lean and brace are no longer required.

Doing an Off-Side Peel Off

As I said before, there are two ways of doing an off-side peel off. The correct way is for the bowman to use the rudder, pry, forward-stroke combination as in an eddy turn. All instructions for the angle and initial drive out of the eddy are the same as for the on-side peel off. The sternman leans and low braces as the bow hits the main current, and he holds this lean and brace until the peel off is almost through and the overturning moment on the canoe is weakened. The bowman uses his rudder to aim the canoe into the main current, does a powerful pry to help the bow turn, and converts to a forward stroke as the canoe is swept around.

The other (and easier way) is for the bowman to omit the rudder part, just pry when he can reach the main current with his blade, and then go into his forward stroke. The sternman leans and low braces as usual. Normally the forward momentum into the current will be enough so that a rudder isn't necessary anyway. Besides this, it's very difficult to control the paddle used as a rudder when the current is hitting hard against the flat of the blade.

In an off-side peel off the bowman must keep a very firm grip on his paddle. Coming from an area (the eddy) of little or

256

no blade pressure into the full force of the current and having the flat of the blade perpendicular to that current results in a sudden and powerful jerk on the paddle blade. This jerk will try to yank the grip out of the bowman's upper hand and force the blade under the canoe. A lot of upper-hand control is required to prevent this. (You might also make sure your spare paddle is readily available!)

Practicing Peel Offs

For practice purposes, peel offs should have a little more current differential than eddy turns; however, a good way to start is to do a practice peel off out of the eddy into which you did a practice eddy turn. A small current differential or indistinct eddy line will give you a slow, gradual turn instead of a sharp one, but at least you'll get the idea. Select a current that's wide enough so you don't drive right across it into the far-side eddy or end up going downstream broadside with both your bow and stern in an eddy.

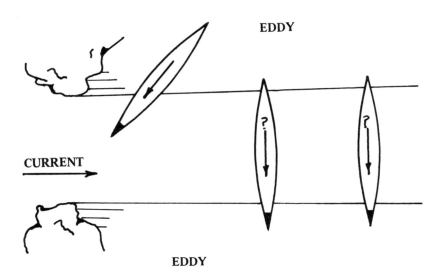

A mis-whack!

Gradually work your way up to stronger currents as you get more accustomed to the techniques. Be sure to try varying your angle of attack as you cross the eddy line to get an idea of what happens in different current speeds. Just once try *no* power across a sharp eddy line. Coast up to it from the eddy, and you'll be surprised at the actual "bump" the eddy line will give your canoe. It feels almost solid and won't let you cross it if there's a big current differential.

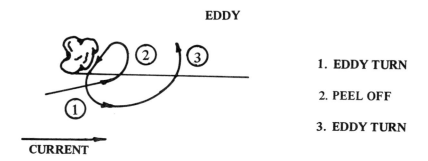

1. EDDY TURN

2. PEEL OFF

3. EDDY TURN

A practice place.

An excellent way to combine practice peel offs and eddy turns is to find a big eddy, do an on-side turn into it, and peel off out of it, then drive back into it farther downstream and eddy turn into it again. Now swap sides and do the above as off-side techniques.

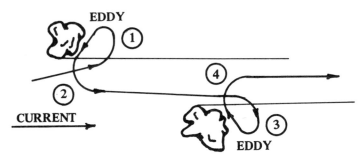

1. ON-SIDE EDDY TURN   3. OFF-SIDE EDDY TURN

2. ON-SIDE PEEL OFF   4. OFF-SIDE PEEL OFF

Another practice place.

258

Even better is to find two convenient eddies as in the sketch. Sometimes, though, they just don't build rivers as conveniently as this!

A COUPLE OF OTHER MANEUVERS

"S TURNS"

Here's a good way to work in some practice on partial peel offs, forward ferries, and eddy turns. It's also a useful maneuver to know and remember when crossing a strong current.

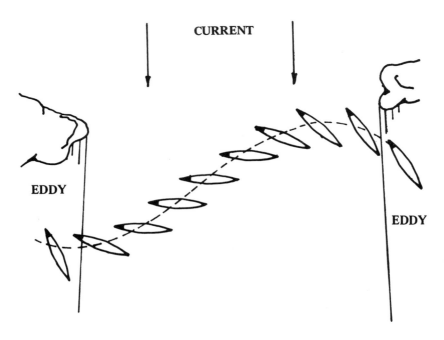

"S" turns.

It utilizes the upstream momentum and circular turning motion of a peel off for the first part of the maneuver, but instead of turning you use this diagonal motion to help you across the river.

In the sketch you could cross from eddy to eddy by driving upstream out of the first eddy with a small angle and a lot of momentum and then forward-ferrying across the current. In a very strong current, however, you might easily lose your angle partway across and find the canoe turning broadside. Should this happen, don't try to recover your angle, just drive on across with forward strokes and do an eddy turn into the other eddy.

Remember that entering the far eddy, you will have to lean and brace to the inside of the turn to avoid a possible roll-over.

SURFING

Surfing is a fun maneuver and a good test of balance, bracing, and judgment. Apart from its playground aspects, surfing can also be used to move a canoe rapidly and effortlessly from one end of a wave to the other.

Surfing on a river is not the same thing as surfing on an ocean. The big difference is in what you're surfing on. Surfing on an ocean wave means that you are riding a wall of water that is moving toward the shore. Usually, the wave gets bigger and bigger as it nears land until finally it curls and breaks on the beach. Surfing in a river means riding a *standing* wave, one that doesn't move anywhere and has a fairly constant height and size.

There are three basic ways of surfing. In one you are bow down in a trough with the hull of the canoe on the upstream face of the wave; in the second you are balanced on the crest of the wave; and in the third (for small waves) you are bow up on the crest.

The first two methods are far better done by solo paddlers but the last, bow up, position is quite adaptable to tandem canoeing. It can be used in place of a forward ferry to cross a current provided, of course, that you have a standing wave where you propose to cross.

All surfing is based on the forward ferry, so you have to be able to do that before you attempt to surf. If you *can* forward-ferry, then here's how to surf across a current. As in a forward ferry, the bow points in the direction you want to go.

Drive up onto the wave at a slight angle. As in ferrying the angle depends on the water velocity which, in this case, will be measured by the height of the wave and the water flowing through it. To start, keep a sharp angle with the wave.

Drive on until you feel the canoe is balanced or nearly balanced on the crest (at least well up on it). When you reach this point you should feel the canoe begin to move sideways along the crest of the wave. If you're perfectly right with your angle and balance, you won't have to paddle at all, but *do* be prepared to lean and brace downstream, because if you get carried over the crest a slight bit too far you'll be rolled upstream by the wave.

If you're not perfectly balanced on the crest, your angle is wrong, the wave is too small, or the water volume too low, you may have to forward-paddle some as you would in a forward ferry. This paddling will keep you on the wave as the wave moves you to the side.

FINALLY

You now have been exposed to all of the basic river maneuvers. If you've practiced them, you should be able to face some shoals and rapids with utter confidence and others with less trepidation than you felt at the beginning of the chapter. As I've pointed out many times in this book, there *are* other ways of doing things and combinations of strokes and maneuvers that I haven't covered, but what you know *now are* the essentials and should be making a great deal of difference in your canoeing and your confidence. To quote myself from the beginning of this chapter: "The best thing you'll discover (in fitting together your skills) is that your canoeing will begin to pull itself together and when this happens, you're on your way to really becoming a canoeist!"

You should now be well on your way.

CHAPTER 11
RUNNING THE RIVER

By now you should be well equipped in basic technique and should have been out running some rivers for fun instead of practice. If so, you may have discovered that just knowing *how* to do a maneuver or paddle stroke isn't enough—you have to know *when* to do it and how to put it to *use* on the river. You may also have discovered some things and places you didn't know how to handle. In this chapter, I'll talk about some of these common situations and water conditions, point out some of the places your basic strokes and maneuvers become highly practical, and go over some general river-running practices. A few of these things are mentioned elsewhere in the book. Where I repeat it's because these things are either important enough to bear hearing again *or* I'm enlarging on what were only comments before and applying them to really practical river running.

LOOKING AT THE "PROS"

One thing you've probably already noticed on your trips is that experienced canoeists sometimes (change that to "often") do things that apparently violate the basic safety tenets that I've tried to instill in you throughout this book. While this may occasionally be because their training in the field of safety has somehow been neglected, most often it's because they have learned through experience just what they *can* do under certain conditions. Usually their apparent foolhardiness is actually solidly based on the knowledge and skills they have accumulated through a lot of practice and paddling and trying one thing and another.

This does *not* mean that you should emulate them, at least not at this stage of your development! I once heard a canoeist remark, "There's no reason to be afraid of the water; all it can do is drown you!" Personally, I think that's reason enough to have a great respect for the river and not hurl headlong into something beyond your skill level. Continue to obey the basic safety rules, don't get overconfident, and don't begin to take

Standing up to scout a small shoal—often done when you know enough *not* to do it!

unnecessary chances. Basic safety is really very simple and its practice will quickly become automatic. It will in no way interfere with the fun of your canoeing. Test and expand your skills on training trips under the guidance of experienced and skillful canoeists or in some other safe situation. Let your own experience and practice tell you what you can do: go slowly, with small steps; giant leaps forward may only land you in trouble!

A CHECKLIST

It's very easy to forget something important or necessary on a canoe trip. Here's a brief checklist for one-day trips in the summer and winter that will help you remember the basic items. Some are necessary and some you can do without, but even the not-so-vital items may be nice to have along now and again.

You might be surprised how often some of the most basic

263

things are totally forgotten until it's too late. As an example, I once started down a high winter river in a kayak. I had on my wet suit and helmet and my glasses were tied on. I was nothing but ready. Three miles down the river and firmly caught in the current just above a drop, I suddenly realized that I was missing one vital thing—my life jacket! The rest of that trip was, for me, a very cautious one!

In case you think my lists somewhat long, I have a simple personal theory on equipment. From experience I have concluded that it's far better to have something and not need it than it is to need it and not have it.

Summer

Life jacket	Compass
Knee pads	First-aid kit
Bailer and sponge	Rainsuit
Paddle and extra paddle	Waterproof matches
Canteen	Duct tape
Lunch and snacks	Hat
Maps, river guidebook	Sunglasses

Winter (Add to the Summer List)

One complete change of clothes	Fire-starting fluid
Small towel	Small plastic tarp to
More waterproof matches	use as rain shield or
	wind break.

Group Items

A throwing rope—no matter how small the group. More than one for larger groups.

An expanded first-aid kit, again depending on the size of the group.

Miscellaneous Items

Camera, film	Fishing gear
Cigarettes, tobacco	Identification books (tree, bird,
Binoculars	whatever your hobby may be)

Don't forget to pack everything susceptible to water damage in something waterproof and to tie everything in.

And—speaking of tying in, *don't* forget to take plenty of cord—nobody ever seems to have enough of it with them when they assemble on the river bank. Finally, tie your glasses on if you wear glasses, stick your wallet away safely, and be sure you have your car keys with you or tucked away somewhere they won't be lost.

SNACKING

Canoeing takes energy, more for some than others. If you're one of those folks who, like me, are starving two hours after every meal, you might want to throw in something to nibble on all during a trip. Candy or anything with a lot of sugar in it is about the handiest thing you can take, although some prefer nuts or mixtures of nuts and candy. The candy gives you quick energy, the nuts a more lasting energy, but eaten along through the day they both serve to keep your energy level up and your stomach from growling.

Try not to get to the exhausted and famished stage before you start eating because this means you are really out of energy. Snack along a little at a time but fairly constantly to maintain your energy at as steady a level as possible. Even if you don't maintain it you'll at least slow down the using up of your reserves.

Snacking makes good sense in warm weather just for giving you energy to paddle. In winter it can be vital. Part of your energy is given off as heat to keep you warm, and you need the warmth to ward off the various dangers of cold weather to which canoeists are heir. This subject is covered elsewhere in this book but it's a good thing not to forget.

Two rather obvious points here but as *I* have been known to forget both, I'll bring them up for the benefit of other absent-minded people. Some candy *will* melt in the summer's heat whether in your pocket or in your waterproof container sitting in the sun. Similarly, some of it will dissolve into a gooey, sticky glob when exposed to water as from a spill, splash, or rain. It makes a real mess in your pockets! Get a kind that melts in your mouth only or else keep it out of the heat and the wet!

CRUISING DOWN THE RIVER

Be Prepared

Don't take off unprepared. If the river or section of the river is new for you, do your homework before the big day comes. Run through your sources of information, and possibly scout out the roads. Settle preliminary matters such as how to get to the put-in and take-out and how you're going to run the shuttle. In general, prepare yourself as well as possible so you know not only where you're going but have some idea of what to expect.

Tell Somebody

Tell somebody about your plans, when and where you're starting and ending and when you expect to be back. Don't plan too long a trip for the weather, water, and time. Many a canoeist has ended up stumbling through miles (or at least what *seemed* like miles) of pitch-black woods or along old dirt roads because he underestimated a trip's time. Remember that a summertime trip may prove to have very low water (maybe even non-existent in places), and a winter trip may prove to be so rough that it requires a lot of time-consuming scouting or portages. Too, there's always the chance of a spill and a lost or badly damaged canoe in high water or at best a lot of fire building and "drying-out" time. If *you* don't care about you, at least think of those left behind who, however mistakenly, may be worried if you don't show up on time. Finally, should a real emergency arise and a search for you prove necessary, there's a greater possibility of your being found swiftly if someone knows your planned route. This, incidentally, is a good reason not to make a last-minute change of plans on the river bank and go somewhere else.

Painters

The loose ends of your painters belong *in* the canoe when ou're paddling, not trailing out in the water where they're :ely to catch on something. *In* the canoe doesn't mean a random pile of rope shoved under your feet in the bow or stern. Loose coils can be foot grabbers, are uncomfortable to kneel on, and, if you *are* kneeling on them, make your position insecure. Coil the loose ends of the painters neatly, finish off with a clove hitch or some other simple knot, and keep the coils out of the way of your feet.

General Choice of Path and the Subject of Work

You'll usually judge your entire general path down a river on the basis of water level. In low water this will usually be around the outside edge of bends and always in the deepest channel and the main current, wherever it may be. At higher water levels you may elect to follow the outside of the bend if you're on a familiar river, if the current is not too swift, the standing waves not too large, *and* if you keep an eye out for the inherent dangers of the outside of bends (logjams, undercuts, downed trees, and the like). In really high, swift water you'll stick like glue to the inside of the bend as this is the safer path.

In unobstructed waters (and with due regard to water level and your ability to move around over the face of the river), use your knowledge of the current path to adjust the river's push on your canoe. Depending on the speed of the current and the pace at which you want to travel, you can let it do most of the work and reduce your forward paddling effort greatly (or to nothing) by staying in the main current (down the middle in straight stretches, on the outside of bends). On the other hand you can cut down the river's push by staying *out* of the main current (moving closer to the shore or hugging the inside of bends).

Use the slack water of eddies. They make it easier to pull into shore, to wait, to rest, or to pause and observe what's coming up. It's amazing what a tiny eddy it takes to firmly hold a canoe or reduce the river's push so much that only an occasional paddle stroke will hold the hull in behind whatever is making it. Remember, the eddy doesn't have to be as wide as your canoe to be usable.

Stay out of a strong wind if you can unless (and this *rarely* happens) it's blowing from behind you and helping you along. Unless barred from doing so by water conditions or obstructions, try to paddle on the side of the river that's sheltered from

267

the wind by vegetation or the shoreline. This alone can make a big difference in the amount of paddling work you do in a day.

In short, don't work yourself to death unnecessarily by fighting a strong current or wind or paddling more than you really have to unless you just love to paddle. Move around in the river, avoid the wind, use the current and the eddies. Be lazy when you can and save your energy; you'll probably use it up later in the day anyway!

The Ins and Outs of Eddies and the Shoreline

I combine these two apparently different subjects into one because actually their mechanics are the same. Going to and from shore is most often done in an eddy so what applies to one applies to the other. Thus, they usually present the same problems—lack of an appreciable eddy, or the presence of a very sharp eddy line, or the necessity for being very precise in your maneuvering because of limited room or the presence of an obstruction in or below your position.

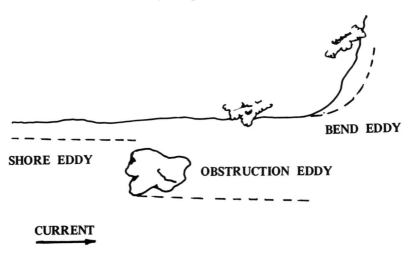

Types of eddies.

There are three types of eddies: shoreline, obstruction, and bend. Of these, shoreline eddies are generally the smallest and least defined and thus, from an effort standpoint, the hardest to use and the easiest to leave. Even though they may be an "eddy" only from the standpoint of having slower-running water in them, they are normally quite usable even though you may have to keep paddling a little to stay in them.

Obstruction eddies are easy eddies to use. Be wary, however, of pulling in between two obstructions if the lower one extends farther out into the river than the upstream one. When you leave your eddy in this situation be sure to drive out into the current enough to clear the lower obstruction before you turn, or otherwise you may end up broadsided on it.

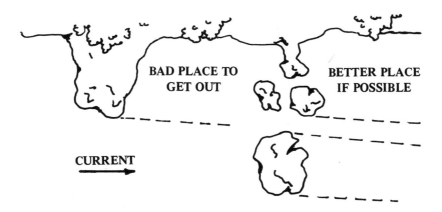

Bend eddies are usually convenient for two reasons. The shoreline on the inside bend is usually lower and thus a good place to go ashore, and bend eddies are the easiest of all to enter and leave.

Your maneuvering method of going to or from shore or entering or leaving an eddy depends on current speed, your position in relation to the various obstructions, and where you want to go when you leave. Except on a shoreline eddy, if there are no obstructions below you and no overhanging tree limbs and the like blocking your path, the easiest way to leave an eddy is just to float out the downstream end of it. Sideslips are effective in slow currents with little current differential. As the current increases and the eddy line becomes sharper, you should shift over to ferries or eddy turns and peel offs. In fast currents with a sharp eddy line, eddy turns and peel offs are the best methods to use.

Temper your method with the conditions. With a sideslip you can go straight in or out (although you'll probably find it easier to have your upstream end pointing slightly in the direction you want to go); ferries let you do this too if the current is not so great that it overpowers your efforts. For eddy turns and peel offs you will need a little more than a canoe length, *provided* you can do them correctly and precisely. Both eddy turns and peel offs, however, if done poorly may send you into some obstruction below such as the tree in the illustration. When you have something like this downstream of you that you have to clear, a strong ferry may turn out to be the only answer.

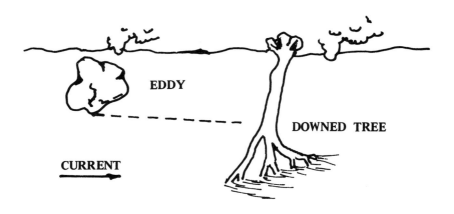

A place to be careful.

Leaving shore, even from a shoreline eddy, may require more drive than you think. When a canoe is parallel or almost parallel to the eddy line it will be "bumped" back into the eddy if you try to broadside across it. On a sharp eddy line it will even be pushed back into the eddy when the canoe is bow on to the line. The same thing can happen if you try to drift out of the eddy downstream and don't clear the eddy line before trying to cross it. You'll have to paddle on out the end of the eddy or cut the eddy line at an angle as in a ferry. In this case the upstream end should cross the line first.

A strong wind can certainly influence your decision on a landing place. In a hard breeze always try to go to shore downwind of an obstruction unless, of course, *downwind* happens to be *upstream*. In larger rivers where the wind has a broad sweep to push against, try not to approach the shore from upwind, particularly if there are waves. You'll find it much easier to shift over to the side of the river protected from the wind force by the bank or by vegetation.

The final consideration on going to and from shore or entering or leaving an eddy is where are you going when you leave? If necessary, position your canoe *before* you go to shore or cut into the eddy so you will be facing in the direction you want to go when you leave. This is generally applicable only where you can use a ferry and when one of your two ferry techniques is much better than the other and you would prefer to use your stronger one.

Overhanging Bushes and Limbs

Overhanging bushes and limbs can knock your paddle out of your hand, lean you backwards, or sweep you right out of the canoe, and it's very easy to run into them when you're preoccupied with maneuvering. These blows are often uncomfortable (if not downright hurtful) and can be serious if you're struck in the face or eye or skewered by a sharp branch. In addition, the frantic dodging that usually ensues can cause you to temporarily lose control of the canoe and lose sight of where you're going. If the bushes or limbs are thick enough or tough enough (and this also applies to former shoreline or island growing trees and saplings in the water in a flooded river), you may wind up broadsided and swamped.

And, one other word, dedicated to maintaining peaceful relations in a tandem crew. When a bowman pushes a springy limb out of his way he should try to remember there's a stern-man behind him who will probably strenuously object if that springy limb pops him in the face!

I've also mentioned that *grabbing* bushes, tree limbs, cables and the like while progressing down a river is a good way to exit your canoe. *Holding* on to bushes and such to keep your canoe in one place is fine. Just watch what you're grabbing as the bushes and tree limbs may also be good places to pick up a handful of wasps, hornets, stickers, snakes, or other things better left untouched.

271

Keep Your Canoe Dry

A little water in a canoe will go a long way toward sinking you. You should, therefore, try to keep it bailed out. Even a few inches of water spread over the bottom of your boat adds up to a lot of weight that makes the canoe hard to handle. Worse than the weight is the movement of this water. As it "sloshes" from side to side it unbalances the canoe first in one direction, then the other. It's hard to synchronize your leans and braces, and you may only aggravate the situation. Each "wave" is likely to increase in force and with much water in the canoe you may go over. About 6 inches of water in the boat makes it almost unmanageable, and a very delicate balance has to be maintained to be able to stay upright. In this situation steadiness and some careful bailing is called for. In a tandem canoe the bowman should make no effort to pivot around and help empty the boat; his efforts should be concentrated solely on keeping the canoe balanced with his braces and body weight while the sternman *very* carefully does the bailing.

A little water does go a long way. This started out with some standing wave splash--

272

--and ended with a change of clothes!

Losing Paddles

This is a "for-what-it's-worth" item that fits in well with going to shore. I've seen a lot of canoeists cruise up to the shore, lay their paddle across the gunwales, step out of the canoe (shaking it in the process), pull it up, tie it up, and go on with their business ashore, whatever it was. I've also seen them start hunting their paddles when a wave rocked the canoe and the paddle fell off in the river (that is, if it didn't fall in when they *left* the canoe).

The best way to *keep* your paddle is to lay it in the bottom of the hull when you're entering or leaving the canoe. At other times it's handier and easier to put the blade on the bottom with the shaft leaning on a thwart. *Don't* lay it across the gunwale unless you keep a hand on it. This includes the going-ashore case already mentioned, changing position in the canoe, lighting a cigarette, or just random eyeballing around the river.

Stirring Tea

A friend of mine used to tell canoeists who were not putting their all into their paddle strokes and maneuvers that they were just "stirring tea." This is a most fitting expression for using the paddle with less than the effort needed and does about that much good!

Get in the habit of making your maneuvering strokes quick, decisive, precise, and fully as strong as called for. In shoals and rapids, "strong" will usually mean full strength. When you want to pull the canoe to the side, hang out of the canoe, lean on your paddle, and *draw* as if your life depended on it; put every muscle you have into your backstroke; really haul on your pry; try to *bend* the paddle every time you do a maneuvering technique. Half-hearted paddle strokes give half-hearted results; half-hearted results sometimes lead to half a canoe!

WHITEWATER

Position in the Canoe

In a previous chapter, I talked about the trim of a canoe and the fact that a canoe hull tends to pivot around whatever part of it is deepest in the water. Thus in calm water on a windless day, the ideal trim would be dead level as the canoe is evenly supported. Choppy water, however, or standing waves, drops, ledges, or any uneven water surface, particularly when frothy, do *not* support the hull evenly, and the canoe will pitch, roll and yaw around its various axes as the support of its hull changes.

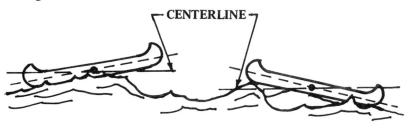

PITCH

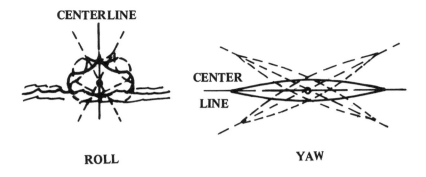

CENTERLINE

CENTER LINE

ROLL YAW

The movements of a canoe.

Too, in going over any kind of drop, ledge, or fall, the unsupported bow of the canoe will nose down and enter the water at an angle. The same thing applies in standing waves—the canoe drops into the trough and the bow digs into the waves. In both situations water is likely to pour in over the bow and swamp you.

Normal, calm-water tandem paddling position.

I've mentioned slowing down in such situations so you don't dig your bow in so much. In addition to slowing down you can redistribute the weight of the paddlers in the canoe. Moving the bowman back behind the front thwart lightens the bow, letting it ride up better in choppy water. This shift also makes the bow easier to move laterally from a weight standpoint and from relocating the deepest part of the hull (and thus the pivot point) toward the rear. At the same time it makes the bowman's job more awkward as he's now leaning over a broader part of the canoe and has lost some of his "forward-position" leverage. However, the advantage of a lighter bow usually more than offsets the increased awkwardness.

Calm-water demonstration of heavy-water technique of moving bowman toward the center of the canoe.

Moving both the bowman and the sternman toward the middle of the canoe lightens both ends of the canoe, reducing the amount of splash likely to come in at the ends. The canoe will pivot much more readily as its deepest point and longitudinal weight axis is now concentrated in the center of the hull. Once more this position increases paddling awkwardness, this time for both paddlers, but its advantages in heavier water

Lightening bow and stern—both paddlers have moved toward the center.

generally outweigh this.

Look Ahead, Scout Ahead, Plan Ahead

Don't paddle blindly down a river unless it's an old familiar river at a familiar water level. Don't tear off around a high water bend or let preoccupation with something else take your mind off what's ahead or what could be ahead. Listen for the sound of a change in the water, watch the terrain, and keep as long-range a view down the river as you can.

Approach a strange rapid cautiously, particularly if it is in a blind curve and you can hear it but can't see it. Stay in the slower water on the inside of the bend, and creep around until you can tell what's going on. On a straight stretch hug the shoreline unless you can easily back paddle faster than the current.

If the rapid is a new one to you or the water level in an old one is very different from what you're accustomed to in that particular place, you'll need to look it over before you plunge into it. If you can back paddle faster than the current (and you're really *sure* you can), you might coast up to the edge of the rapid and look at it as you ferry back and forth across the lip. Just watch out for a sudden chute that might overpower your back paddling. If there's an obvious relatively straight path or one requiring simple maneuvering, if you can see all the way to the bottom of the rapid and the run doesn't look rough enough to give you any doubts, then you might want to go ahead and run it. If all of these conditions are *not* present, then go to shore, get out, and scout the rapid on foot.

Scouting means just that. Examine the rapid from the top then walk down the shoreline beside it. Don't stop short. Go all the way to the end of the rapid or to the end of where you have any questions about the path and look back up it. Most of the time it will appear completely different, and paths and obstructions you didn't see from above may become immediately obvious.

Try to decide a complete course before you commit yourself. Don't blindly follow the first good slot you see without looking at where it's taking you. Even though you *are* threading through the obstacles *one* at a time, the idea is to get *all* the way to the bottom—upright!

Note the locations of eddies that you could use to duck into if the occasion arises. In noting these eddies to enter, bear in mind that you also have to get *out* of them so determine whether a back ferry or an eddy-turn entry would be better (if the water velocity gives.you any choice in the matter). Remember, too, that a run doesn't have to be one continuous ride. Some point in the rapid may demand that you pull into a nearby eddy and reposition your canoe for a different angle of attack on it. Or, using the eddy may just be an *easier* way to maneuver over to the next slot.

In the illustration you might pull into the eddy on the right, then drive across the main current and do your peel off in the left and better path. This at least gets you across into the chosen slot.

Scouting a rapid for a run means finding a *floatable* path down which you can maneuver. Watch the basic water flow, remember'the "filament" theory of water reading, and apply it. Use the "longest-outflow" method if you're in doubt. The "longest outflow" at least indicates that more water is coming out at that point at the bottom of a rapid than anywhere else. Visually work your way back up through the rapid from this outflow until you find a starting point at the top. This is also

278

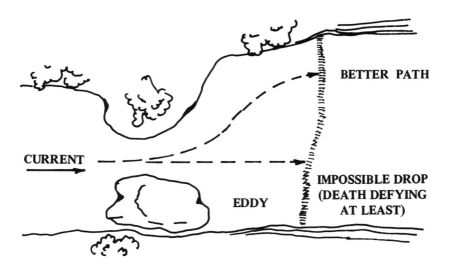

CURRENT

BETTER PATH

EDDY

IMPOSSIBLE DROP (DEATH DEFYING AT LEAST)

Using an eddy to reposition your canoe.

known as "reading the rapid from the bottom up."

You will certainly note any souse holes, hydraulics, and drops, and adjust your path accordingly to miss them if you can, or enter them at the most advantageous speed and angle if you can't. In sum, plan your run out as completely as you can before you start. Bear in mind that the view of the run from a standing position on shore bears little resemblance to the same view from a canoe. Many of those highly visible paths, eddies, drops and slots will become highly invisible once you're back down at water level. So, try to pick out landmarks that *will* be recognizable from canoe level, and then try to remember them so you can use them to guide your general path.

As in all the rest of canoeing there are some exceptions to the above. They apply strictly to water level. To repeat, you need check out a familiar rapid only if you're unused to its present water level or if the river has recently flooded. Flooded rivers move boulders and carry trees and logs that may get wedged in the path. The old slot may no longer be there or an approach may have a log across it. The first few runs after any period of high water should be scouted out. Sometimes a higher water level just blots out a rapid or simplifies it instead of making it tougher. Again, if it's familiar to you, you'll know at a glance if this is the case. If it's not—get out and look.

Although discretion is most emphatically the better part of valor in *any* obstructed water, most of the comments I've made don't apply too much to shoals in low, slow water. In many of them you can stop about anywhere you wish and reconsider your course or even get out and, dragging your canoe behind you, wade to a better slot. These are the places to practice; just watch out for those unexpected holes in the river bottom!

Ledges, Drops and Falls

Ledges, drops, and falls in a river mark elevation changes. They may be perpendicular to the water flow or angled to it at any angle. Being elevation changes, they usually offer increased current flow and shallower water, at least right on the ledge or at the edge of the drop or fall!

For a discussion of ledges, drops, and falls let's make an arbitrary distinction between the three. We'll say that a ledge is inclined. It's a loss of elevation, usually over some horizontal distance, but may include vertical drops up to about 2 feet high. Drops are straight down or nearly so, changes in elevation where your bow may descend abruptly. We'll cut "drops" off at about 4 feet high. Anything over that height with an angle from about 60 to 90 degrees on it we'll call a fall.

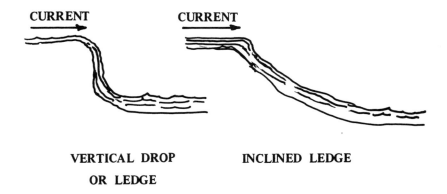

VERTICAL DROP   INCLINED LEDGE
OR LEDGE

Drops and ledges.

280

Let me hasten to add that the above is *not* an official designation; it's just something I dreamed up to help clarify matters a bit—I hope!

Another thing I'd like to add is that most of the comments on drops and ledges are interchangeable because, as pointed out, their differences are primarily only those of angle and height.

Ledges

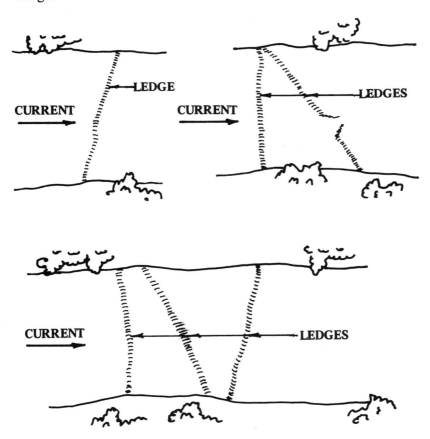

Various ledge configurations.

Ledges may be a single line of rock, multiple lines more or less parallel to each other and separated by "flat" areas, or multiple lines not parallel to each other, possibly connected in places and with "flats" in others. The elevation differences on a single ledge may vary abruptly (a drop), be inclined over some horizontal distance, or, most commonly, have both of these conditions, depending upon where you run it.

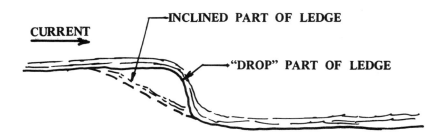

You'll often find that ledges are higher on one side of the river than the other or have a drop on one side and dwindle to nothing on the other. This seems to have no relation to the direction the shoreline is curving (or not curving) and, although I'm sure there is an excellent geological reason for each individual case, I'm no geologist. In canoeing terms, however, it just means that if you want to avoid a ledge (or find one) or go over the highest part of it (or the lowest), you can sometimes select what's more your choice by ferrying across the river and looking the ledge over before you start down.

A single ledge usually presents no problem in path finding in itself if you can find a chute or if there's enough water to run over the lip of it. Don't, however, devote all your attention to the *edge*—look below you and make sure you have enough water to drop into and that there is not an obstruction close downstream that you will have to try to dodge.

Multiple ledges, on the other hand, commonly present the necessity of dropping over the first ledge, then maneuvering back and fourth across the flats between the ledges to work your way down through them. Here it's best to try to follow the natural flow of the water along the shelves and down the chutes. Sometimes, this will take you right on through. These are also the places where the ability to ferry comes in very handy, particularly if the space from ledge to ledge is only slightly longer than your canoe or, as sometimes happens, slightly shorter. In the first instance, immediate back paddling is necessary. The instant the stern drops over and clears one ledge, the command "Back" is yelled out, the stern popped over in the right direction, and some furious back paddling started. In the second case, in which the ledge-to-ledge distance is *less* than canoe length and you have to ferry, you may have three choices, depending on the ledge: (a) find a chute or slot that you can drop down with the stern already angled in the direction you need to ferry, (b) go straight down, let the bow run on out over the second ledge, then assume your ferry angle and back paddle your way to the next slot, or (c) drop down with the *bow* pointing in the ferry direction, let the bow hang out over the next ledge, yank the stern around, and back paddle. Methods 2 and 3 are not recommended in any current that's very strong; you're likely to be unable to back off the next ledge and end up being swept right on over it.

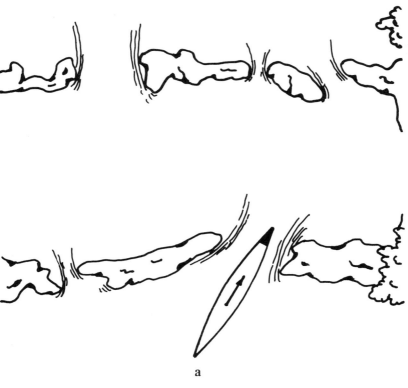

a

Ledge to ledge.

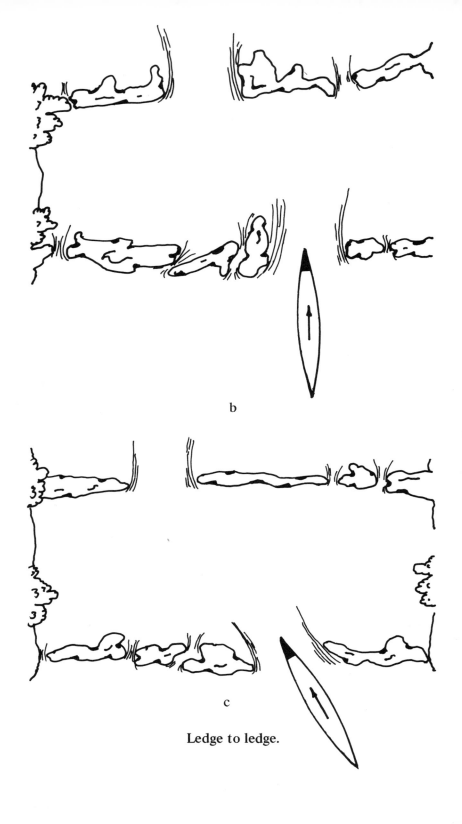

b

c

Ledge to ledge.

Many series of ledges offer an alternative to ferrying, or at least to constant, hard ferrying all the way across the flat between two ledges. Often you can use the eddies that form below a ledge to either ease your ferrying efforts or, if the eddy is pronounced enough, to turn broadside to the current flow and simply forward paddle over to the next path down. You will still have to ferry out of the chute or whatever that you used to clear the first ledge as there *will* be a steady current flowing down it. Once you clear this flow, however, you'll know by the feel of the water whether you can turn broadside or not. Normally you can tell visually before you ever go over the first ledge.

When crossing a shelf between two ledges by either ferrying or paddling parallel to the ledges, watch out for random tongues of fast water coming through chutes in the upstream ledge. You might drive across them if they're narrow, but it's a good idea to do some angle adjusting if they're wide or strong. If you're more or less parallel to the ledges, get some upstream angle on your canoe so you can ferry across the stronger area (unless you have some room to be swept downstream while you're powering across it); if you're already ferrying sharpen your angle. All angle adjustments should be done *just before* you enter the faster water.

The eddies often found below ledges and drops can also be used to pull your canoe back upstream or keep it from being swept downstream. Often you can run your bow or stern up to a low ledge upstream of you and just sit there and bump against it with your paddle in the canoe. Of course, don't try this if the upstream drop is higher than your bow or stern and the canoe can be pulled *under* the water flowing over the ledge; this leads to rapid swamping. Sometimes the backflow will also be strong enough to swing your canoe around sideways to the drop, which swamps you even faster.

Another situation in ledges is where the *current* actually turns, runs across the flats more or less parallel to the ledges, and turns again down another slot. In this case you have little to do except stay in the current and possibly help on the turns.

Series of ledges should be scouted before you start down. Ferry along the edge of the upper ledge if the current isn't too strong; otherwise, stop somewhere to go to shore. Follow all the scouting rules laid out before. Be cautious on any ledge that you can't see over from back up the river; reconnoiter it from a closer viewpoint to insure that you don't plunge over into some obstruction likely to do harm to boat or body!

A natural turn in the current.

Turning into the chute or slot on a ledge will often take some swift pivoting of the canoe. Simultaneous use of a draw by one paddler and a pry by the other will whip you right around, but make the strokes strong and decisive.

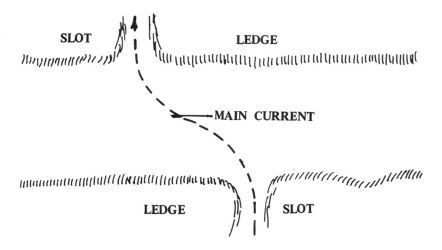

When pivoting like this, anticipate the turn; otherwise, you're likely to be swept sideways and go beyond the slot. Of course, you can always ferry back, but it's easier to just begin the maneuver at the right time. Don't forget that the bow may be entering the slot perfectly but the stern (and the largest part of the canoe) will still be exposed to any side current and could be rapidly swept around.

Some Specifics About Drops

Drops, at least by my definition under "Ledges," are more than 2 feet high and have a vertical or almost vertical descent. As with ledges, a drop or a fall may not extend all the way across a river or may change in height enough so you can find a usable lower point to run.

Running any drop presents the problem of nosing over as you float over the edge. The stern is still riding on the upper level, but at water speed the unsupported bow begins to drop as soon as slightly less than half the length of the hull (not even this if your bowman outweighs you) crosses the edge. This results in entering the water at an angle that varies with the height of the drop and your velocity off the edge.

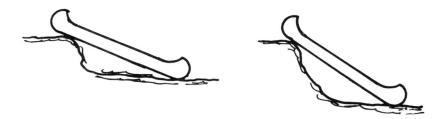

Angle and height of drop.

This brings us to two considerations. For one, you should always scout below a drop or fall to check for an unobstructed path at the point where you're planning to enter and *for enough water to take the dive* in. It's a tossup as to which is more disconcerting, dangerous, and damaging—hitting a rock above the water bow on, nose-diving into one just under the surface, or plowing head on into the bottom! All are, or can be, serious.

The other consideration is keeping your balance as you go over. You probably see more "gunwale grabbing" and air braces at a time like this than at any other. There will be a moment as you go over that you'll have practically nothing holding you upright *except* your balance. There's really nothing I can tell you about this except—stay steady!

Running a small drop. The sternman's paddle grip is *not* standard!

Drops up to about 3 feet high, even with a vertical descent, can be run by easing over them and letting your stern drop off after the bow is in the water or building up speed and "jumping" them. "Jumping" is probably the easiest way as it gives you less time to lose your balance and somewhat reduces the "bow-down" angle at which you initially hit the water. Above about 3 feet in an open canoe, particularly with a tandem crew, the best procedure will usually be to "jump" the ledge if you have enough room to build up speed. On all drops you might move your bowman back to relieve the weight on the bow and the tendency of the canoe to dive. Finally—don't forget to watch out for hydraulics below these drops.

A Word About Waterfalls

Waterfalls can be run. Some amazing heights have been tried by solo canoeists, and some of them have been successfully run. But I said—by *solo* canoeists. I don't recommend that a tandem crew run any *vertical* drop over about 4 feet high. As the angle lessens, the height can increase; it's as simple as that.

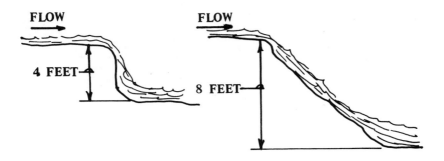

Falls—relationship of angle and height.

Running a vertical or an inclined fall is a "get-in-it-and-go" type of canoeing for it's certain that you're not going to intentionally stop halfway down. So be sure you scout first, get properly lined up with the slot, and keep your paddle out ready for use at the bottom. And don't forget what I said about having enough water at the bottom to canoe into!

Running Standing Waves

You have two basic choices of path in standing waves— right down through the middle of them or, if you can, skirting their edge. Either course is safe from an obstruction standpoint. Down through the middle is more fun if the waves are not too big to take in an open canoe. Shifting your bowman toward the

289

middle of the canoe and back paddling to slow down before you enter the first waves will help your bow ride up on the crest instead of nosing into the waves and either swamping or taking in so much water that the canoe becomes unmanageable. In heavier water both of you might move toward the middle. If you elect to (or can) take the edge route you could pick up water over the gunwale. You might also be kicked off course or broached by the wave force concentrated on one side of the hull, so run ready to brace and/or recover if you need to.

Running standing waves.

Hit standing waves *straight*. Running into one at an angle is an almost sure way to flip. You *might* be able to brace and recover, but you'll more probably sink. Keep straight down through a series of standing waves. Coming at an angle off one wave will mean the next one catches you crooked and will probably roll you. If you do broach down into a trough without swamping and the trough is big enough, you may be able to escape it by leaning and bracing downstream; the trough should kick you on out the end.

Running Souse Holes

Souse holes are rough on an open canoe, and the deeper they are, the rougher they get. You'll probably swamp in many of them no matter what you do. As souse holes are usually the beginning of a series of standing waves, the procedure of lightening the ends by having the paddlers move toward the center of the canoe should be followed. Depending upon the depth of the hole, your speed, and the angle at which you enter the hole, your canoe may bridge the souse hole completely or at least enough so you'll only take in a little splash over the bow and sides. Sometimes you can "charge" a souse hole that's not too wide and build up enough speed so that the bow, instead of immediately dropping into the hole, will run out farther before it falls and hopefully catch on the standing wave below it. Don't do this if it's obvious you can't bridge it and are going to dive in. All speed will do for you then is to bury your bow in the side of the downstream wave. When the souse hole is too big to bridge, follow your standing-wave procedures, and slow down before you enter it. Try to ease into it without digging your bow in.

Heading for a souse hole.

Always enter a souse hole head on. Any angle on the canoe relative to the current will almost surely flip and roll you into the hole. When you paddle into a souse hole try to maintain your no-angle position and paddle over the next crest. Even if you do swamp you'll be swept on out of it downstream.

Underwater Openings

Underwater openings in rock faces, tunnels that go all the way through the stone, or underwater ledges with open areas below them are not too common in rivers, but they do exist. Or perhaps I should say they may be common but are usually only found when a canoeist gets swept through one and emerges downstream to tell about it. Fortunately this doesn't happen too often, and even more fortunately most canoeists *do* live to tell about it. Still some don't, and drownings have occurred from a canoeist being pinned against the opening and held there by the pressure of the water flowing through it, from being swept into the opening and wedged, or from being held under too long while being carried through.

Openings partially under water are worse than those totally submerged because you're more likely to be swept into them. On the other hand, you *can* see them and take precautions to avoid their opening. Manned canoes are rarely pulled into one of these openings; it's the swamped canoe and the swimming canoeist that are caught, generally immediately after a spill when the paddler is still disoriented and hasn't achieved his rapids-running floating position.

There's really nothing you can do if pulled into one of these holes except pray that you don't get pinned in it and can hold your breath long enough to reach the surface downstream. Attempting to fight the current is impossible; total relaxation and letting the water carry you on through is your best chance.

On whitewater rivers that are new to you, ask about these holes and keep your eyes open for them. Local canoeists familiar with the river will probably be able to tell you about them if there are any.

Canyons

Canyons can offer particularly dangerous situations to

canoeists. Steep or sheer walls, possible lack of beach and portage areas, and lack of access into and out of the gorge may present impossible or very difficult situations for both self rescue and rescue by others. Scouting from the rim above may not be possible, and even if it is, it may prove impractical and of little use if the canyon is very deep. Bends may not have any usable eddies to scout from or to halt in, and even if they do you may find yourself faced with an impossible situation and no way to get back up the river. If rapids continue around a bend, scouting may be out of the question.

Not all canyons, of course, will present all of these situations. Many will have adequate shoreline and present no more problems than any other whitewater river. Until you *know* this, however, be wary of them. Canyons are one of the places where you should do all the information gathering you can and all the scouting you can *before* the trip arrives.

Broken Dams and the Like

Broken or partially destroyed structures in the water such as old dams, bridge foundations, and fish traps are often seen on rivers. They frequently have a chute or chutes through or around any parts still above the water and a rapid or shoal below them where some of the material has fallen in downstream of the break.

When running through such places watch for reinforcing rods, bolts, nails, and similar fastenings that may be protruding from the remains of the structure. They may be stuck out above the water and be relatively visible if you look closely enough, but they may also be just under the surface ready to catch your canoe hull or paddle blade. Watch, too, for ragged protrusions of whatever the structure was made of. Be especially careful if you're running such places through a narrow gap. If rods, bolts, and ragged places are present you may not be able to avoid being swept into them.

Chutes in such places may look inviting to swim through in the summer. Check them out first for those same rods, nails, and other fasteners. I know of a stretch on one river that is a favorite inner-tube ride. A little way down it there's just *one* log left of an old wooden dam. This log is barely under water during the summer and despite the length of time it's been there is still studded with sharp little nails. Many an inner tube has perished there, and many an inner tuber walked out with badly scratched legs and other parts as a memento of his failure to see it in time.

Logs in the River

Logs are an easy subject, but I've seen canoes dented, punctured, flipped and bent to a "U" shape either on or because of logs in the river. For those of you who have never seen a log in a river, they usually appear end-on to your canoe or crossways or somewhere in between, stuck up out of the water, nearly submerged, or just under the surface. End-on logs either stop you dead in your tracks (with accompanying dents and scrapes of a severity dependent on your speed and angle and the amount of log above the surface) *or* quietly flip your canoe over *or* tilt it alarmingly as you ride up on it. Crossways logs (and other angles) either flip you, roll you, stop you when you ride upon them, or broadside you against them with a consequent roll and possible swamping.

In case you're wondering where the "bent to a U shape" comes in, a ride up an angled, inclined log can turn you broadside to the current. If you're then swept down on something in this position and pinned on it in a good current, your canoe can rapidly assume this shape.

Although logs really are something else to watch out for, they can also represent any number of other things in the river. They serve primarily to illustrate that you should keep your eyes open, particularly when approaching a rapid or an obstruction. Don't get so engrossed in dodging the big problems that you stumble over the little ones!

Paddling Upstream

Most river canoe trips are downstream for the simple reason that it's a lot of work to paddle upstream. But occasionally you may want or need to go back up the river. A lot of this may turn out to be plain old back-breaking, arm-wearying labor, but there are a few things you may be able to do to help yourself.

Chief of these is use any eddies you can. The name for this is "eddy hopping." You paddle up as far as you can in one eddy and drive or "S" out or over or both to another one, crossing the river if necessary. If no obstruction eddies are present you can hug the shoreline eddy if the shoreline is clear enough to allow this.

Very small hydraulics and the eddies below ledges can often be useful to you, too. They'll give you a little extra push when you're trying to paddle back upstream over very low drops. Charge into one, let it grip the hull of your canoe, and paddle furiously (or, if the water is shallow enough, use your paddle for a pole).

And finally, when the situation calls for it, you'll find that wading and dragging are not frowned on and are, indeed, used in the very best canoeing circles.

TECHNIQUES OF A SORT!

Rock, Air, Tree, Bottom, Hand, and Foot Braces

These facetiously named techniques are not "standard" braces; at least you won't find them described as valid techniques in any canoeing book, but, valid or not, they are used (or tried) by us all at one time or another when desperation, shallow water, urgency, or instinct cries "do something" and we react to the cry!

All of these techniques are dedicated to holding up the canoe or fending it off some obstruction, and most are techniques of confusion. That is, they shouldn't be done but frequently are because you get confused and don't know what else to do! I feel sure that they will never be a part of *your* technique, but I present them so that you may identify them when you see all those *other* confused canoeists doing them!

Hand and foot braces need little explanation—a canoeist sticks out a hand or a foot to halt some impending impact or turnover. They're good ways to break arms, legs, ankles, and wrists. The canoeist may also substitute his paddle for the arm or leg, which is better and safer and only breaks paddles. Caution is advised in these "paddle-poke" techniques. Should you be tempted to try them, keep the length of the paddle at a flat angle with your chest; otherwise, the paddle blade striking an immovable object may result in the grip striking you in the chest.

Rock, tree, and bottom braces may also be executed with the hands and feet but usually fall into the "use-the-paddle" category. They refer, of course, to the specific item against which you are pushing or bracing (rock, tree, bottom of the river, or whatever). To insert one *real* bit of information here, however, rock and bottom braces *are* perfectly good techniques. You have learned the braces as used in *water*, but if a rock happens to be under your paddle or the shoal is very shallow and your blade rests on the bottom, so what? Brace on it anyway; it will hold you up and that's the idea.

An air brace is a bit back to the facetious again. It's the most simple of all. I'm sure all of you have seen (or will see) a paddle being waved frantically in the air as a canoe starts to turn over or the startled look on a canoeist's face when a high brace misses the water or doesn't support him and he goes plunging in. An air brace does no good at all, but you at least have the satisfaction of knowing you tried!

Gunwale Grabbing

I've mentioned this earlier in the book. It's a sight often seen on the river. When a canoe begins to roll, pitch, or yaw; starts over a drop; rides up on a rock; or does anything else involving much motion out of the ordinary, level, paddling plane, the novice canoeist often drops his paddle in the canoe, grabs the gunwales, and rides it out, grimly determined to balance his craft by body weight. In this case, however, determination, no matter how grim, can more often be translated as "vainly trying." Even experienced canoeists engage in gunwale grabbing occasionally as the solid bulk of the canoe (read as gunwale) *does* seem to offer more of a sense of security than the relative flimsiness of the paddle. *But* it's still the wrong thing to do.

Your braces are intended to steady and support you, but braces require a blade *in* the water. Neither will the paddle over-balance you; you can preserve your equilibrium quite as well holding it poised and ready to use as you can without it. So keep your paddle gripped in both hands and ready for action, not laid casually across the gunwales, gripped tightly to them by your hands, or tossed in the bottom of the canoe. *Use* your paddle effectively if you can; barring that, *try* to use it effectively, and, if nothing else, *look* like you're going to use it effectively!

CANOES AND EQUIPMENT YOU FIND IN THE RIVER

In whitewater sections of rivers you are likely to find all kinds of free-floating or beached equipment. Some may be in perfect shape, or at least perfectly usable, and some may be totally destroyed, but the question often arises as to what to do with it. Personally, I always retrieve the equipment, and *if* there's no identification on it, I haven't passed a spilled canoe somewhere up the river whose occupants may have lost the equipment, and it's not a valuable item, I keep it. In either of these last two cases, however, I *do* make an effort to identify the owner and return the items. More valuable goods such as cameras and packs (yes, these *have* found forgotten on bank and rock) are another matter. If you find them on shore, then whoever left them is downriver from you (or was—it may have been sitting there for a while). Ask any canoeists you pass if they have lost something up the river. I wouldn't get too specific about what *you* found until they identify what *they* lost. If your trip ends at, or you pass by, some point commonly used as a takeout, you should inquire of any canoeists there, too. If there's some sort of permanently occupied structure there such as a house, restaurant, canoe-rental place, or the like (that contains trustworthy folks), leave the item there. Whoever left it is likely to come back after it later.

Canoes found in the river are usually in poor shape. On the other hand, you sometimes find one that's not. Loose canoes are normally the result of a spill, and the canoe has been swept on down the river. The owners may be upstream hunting for it, may intend to get it later, or may have abandoned it completely. The problem is that you don't *know*, and yet you hate to leave a canoe to the clutches of some less-honest person! I would recommend that you leave a note with your name and address on it, possibly stuck on a stick. Take the canoe with you. This, plus leaving your name and address at the nearest local service station or store or whatever, should help the owner track you down if he does come back looking for his canoe.

IN CONCLUSION

I sincerely hope that your river-running knowledge has now been broadened a bit. There are a lot more things that could have been said, but most of them are the subtleties, things that are best left up to you to discover and to solve by applying your own paddling style and techniques.

As I said before, rivers are funny things, and you won't ever find the exactly identical situation or solution two times in any number of rivers or trips. Each situation is different, just as all canoeists are a little different in their ways of handling the situation. Learn from them and from each new trip. Accept those new things you see that you like or can use, and reject those that don't seem to work for you (but *do* give all of them a fair chance). Above all—keep paddling!

PART III
Safety, Rescue, Repair, And Logistics

Freddie Foolish
A Tale of Inexperience!

Freddie Foolish went a-floating/and he didn't
      take a friend,
No one knew where he was headed,/where he'd
      start or hoped to end.
Didn't take a life preserver,/had no paddle for a
      spare—
And the river, it was flooded,/but Freddie didn't
      care!

He launched himself into the flood/one early
      springtime day,
The current grabbed his boat at once/and
      swept him on his way,
What lay around the bends beyond/was far from
      Freddie's mind,
Though he'd never seen this run before,/he was
      not the cautious kind.

His boating skill soon proved to be/unequal
      to his need,
And doubts crept into Freddie's mind/as the
      river gathered speed,
Then he heard his paddle breaking/and the
      boat turned broadside to,
And Freddie gripped the gunwales tight,/knowing
      nothing else to do.

As the current swept more strongly/
      Freddie heard an awesome sound,
A rumbling of the water that seemed to echo
      all around,
And he saw the waves rise 'round him,/saw the drop
      that lay before—
But Freddie lacked the knowhow/to get himself
      to shore.

Somewhere on the river there are pieces of a boat,
There are items of equipment that slowly, softly
    float.
And somewhere too, poor Freddie lies,/but he really
    doesn't care
As he tumbles in the rapids/that he didn't know were
    there.

CHAPTER 12
VARIOUS SAFETY ITEMS WORTHY OF MENTION

Mishaps on a river can occur for many reasons. Some are created by basic inexperience and lack of canoeing knowledge. Others result from a simple lack of planning, such as too long a trip for the time you have. Still others are caused by unpredictable things such as bee stings, snake bites, and sudden storms. The list of what *could* happen is endless. Fortunately, mishaps of any serious nature are relatively few in occurrence considering the number of canoes on today's rivers. This is good, for obviously the canoeist attempting to ward off all the perils that *could* befall him on the river would be better off never leaving home as his trip would be no more than a torturous journey of anticipated disaster. However, there *are* many likely mishaps that can either be avoided or their probabilities lessened by the practice of some of the elementary precautions of basic safety.

There is no way to logically separate the practical aspects of canoeing safety from the practical mechanics of canoeing itself. Because of this you will have found (and will continue to find) many safety facts, applications, and rules scattered throughout the various other chapters of this book. This chapter discusses some of the items that are either not covered elsewhere or are only mentioned in passing. As I'm somewhat fanatical about safety, I also refer back to a few of the things that *are* discussed elsewhere.

LET SOMEONE KNOW OF YOUR TRIP

Don't just hop in the river and take off. Let someone know where you're going and that you've gone. Include in this information your put-in, your take-out, and your estimated time of arrival at the take-out. This way if you do get in trouble, at least everybody knows when to start worrying, and, if you haven't had a last-minute change of plans, the searchers know the general area in which to start looking.

ALLOW ENOUGH TIME

Allow enough time for travel to the put-in and for shuttling plus enough (and a little more) for the trip. Start early and don't get caught out on the river with darkness closing in unless you're intending to camp anyway. If you do get caught by darkness, don't try to pick your way down the river by guess, flashlight, or listening, just pull to the shore *before* dark and take off for the nearest road if there's one close enough. If not, settle down for the night. Here's where a map of the area would come in handy.

BE PREPARED FOR A FEW EMERGENCIES

Carry along a throw rope and a basic personal first-aid kit. Learn the fundamental first-aid measures for such things as shock, severe cuts, heat exhaustion, and sun stroke. Waterproof matches may be handy anytime and are vital in cold weather. In winter have an extra set of clothes, something that will quickly start a fire, and a knowledge of hypothermia.

LIFE JACKETS

This has been covered already but is vital—one jacket for each person in the boat, *always* worn if you can't swim or are in high water or cold water, and always put on at the hint of any situation that might demand its use. Life jackets do no good loosely draped over your body. If you think you'll need it then have it zipped, tied, or whatever, but have it firmly secured. In summer's hot weather, you may loosen it at times for the sake of coolness, but don't *forget* that it's loose and if it is, correct this before you need it.

PADDLING ALONE ON A RIVER

Don't! Alone means either solo or tandem in one canoe. The recommended minimum number of canoes on a trip is three. While there is nothing *wrong* with lone canoe trips under certain circumstances, each trip should be considered in the light of conditions on and for the particular ride and in view of the experience of the paddler. The problem when you are a novice canoeist is that your knowledge and experience may be too limited to qualify you to correctly assess the various factors

304

that create these conditions. Your paddle skills are also likely to be wanting. The combination of these lacks can prove to be dangerous if you're alone. In addition are the non-paddling mishaps that *can* happen, maybe only once in a lifetime to *you*—but you never know when that once may be.

Of course, there are times when it's just tempting fate to go alone and it shouldn't be done at all. Don't go off down any unknown river alone unless you know from a good guidebook what to expect or know someone who is familiar with that stretch, and your information tells you it's peaceful and easy. Don't go alone down any river with anything on it greater than a Class I rapid, and don't do it then unless you're an experienced river canoeist and are thoroughly familiar with that stretch. Even then it's not a good idea. Don't go alone down any river in cold weather or when the river is high or flooded. (Of course, all canoeists should stay off flooded rivers anyway.) Don't go alone on any narrow, swift rivers.

You may have guessed by now that I'm against single canoe trips on anything except a broad, flat river with big, gentle bends and in the warmth of the summer. You're right. I've been accused of being too cautious, but let me quote you an example. I know of a chute on a mild river I've often used for training beginning canoeists. The chute has about a 24-inch-high drop and looks canoe width. It has a good approach and appears to be the perfect place to run the drop, and it is, at certain water levels. At *low* water—yes that's right, *low* water levels—it still looks perfect but will tilt, swamp, pull down, and wedge your canoe under a rock in the bottom of the chute long before you get through reading this sentence. Your boat is then firmly held in place by the water running in and over it. I have seen a tandem team whose canoe was thus wedged try in vain to even *move* their canoe. Aided by two husky men, they moved it, but that was all. I have *never* seen a canoe come out of this mild-looking spot without *at least* six grown men *straining* to the point of hernia to get it out. Incidentally, I consider myself experienced, but *my* canoe has been hung in the slot several times when I misjudged the water level. Luckily I had those five other guys with me.

The point is that a lone canoe, tandem or solo, even in low, mild water *can* be inextricably pinned. In such a case, you

305

abandon your canoe and walk out. The situation could easily be more serious. Don't canoe alone until you know enough *not* to canoe alone! When you reach that stage you're ready to try it occasionally.

FLOODED RIVERS

Stay off them. Not only does high water completely change the face of an otherwise familiar river but it sweeps along tree limbs, tree trunks, and whole trees that can smash or entangle your canoe and you! High water undercuts trees and creates hazards on the outside of bends in the form of standing waves and trees partially toppled in the river. Islands are no longer, only the tops of trees stuck out of the water to possibly catch you. The shoreline may be under water and, in some rivers, you may actually *lose* the river and find yourself swept into trees and bushes with no idea of which way to go to the main river bed.

On top of this is the sheer weight and power of fast-moving, high-volume water, power that can overcome your efforts to combat it as if you were doing nothing. Ferries are likely to no longer be to the side but in a long diagonal downstream, and *any* maneuver needs to be started well ahead of time and timed perfectly. All of this is dangerous enough in a wide river with relatively low banks. Combine it with a narrow, twisting river and sheer banks and you've multiplied the danger tremendously.

OVERCONFIDENCE

This is the downfall of many novice canoeists. Canoeing looks so simple and easy when someone knowledgeable is paddling along, but then so does ski-jumping, surfing, and handling live rattlesnakes. Probably the worst thing that can happen to a brand new, totally unskilled canoeist is to actually luck his way down through some rough rapids his first time out. The bad part is that he usually begins to think he's invincible and continues on in this foolhardy manner until one day when his luck deserts him and only the skills that he never bothered to learn can save him. Not that I want any canoeist hurt or his canoe destroyed, but a good scare and a few bad dents and small holes go a long way toward demolishing the idea of super paddler!

OUTSIDE BENDS, LOGJAMS, TREES ACROSS THE RIVER

Any obstacle such as a tree or a logjam lying in or just above the river and through or under which water is flowing presents one of the biggest dangers in river canoeing. The danger lies in the fact that although the river water can still flow through (or under) these obstacles, your canoe cannot. A prime example is a fallen tree. Downed trees usually occur on the outside of bends where the current has undercut the bank. Often the main part of the tree has fallen in, but the roots have stayed attached to the bank. Because the outside of a bend is where the current will try to take your canoe, you should be cautious in all bends in a narrow river. The same thing applies to branches and limbs overhanging the river and less than canoe height above the water.

Two places to be cautious. The water can go through, but your canoe may easily be caught.

Logjams may occur beside islands, out from the bank, at bridge piers, on underwater rocks, or almost anywhere that one log or branch gets hung on something and then proceeds to catch more sticks, logs, and branches. The danger is the same; usually the jam will not be solid enough to deflect the water and provide a cushion, and the current could carry you up against it.

A sure place to broadside and sink if the current is strong.

What happens in either of these cases is that your bow strikes the obstacle, the current is too swift for you to back off it, and after a period of struggle your stern swings around. Once the canoe broadsides on the obstacle, the current will roll the upstream gunwale under the water and you with it. Should you be caught by some of the underwater limbs you're likely to drown. If you're not actually caught you may be held pressed against the obstacle by the force of the water and be unable to back off enough to get to the surface. The canoe will almost certainly be caught. This situation presents a very tricky and dangerous rescue problem, particularly if the canoe is held under water.

WEIGHT AND POWER OF WATER

Never underestimate the sheer weight and power of moving water. This is yet another common and extremely dangerous fault of novice canoeists. While dry facts and figures usually fail to impress anyone, consider that water does weigh about 8.3 pounds per gallon, and one cubic foot of water contains 7.48 gallons. In river terms that means that every 3 cubic feet of the river weigh about 186 pounds, as much or more than the average good-sized man. How many cubic feet are there in even a small canoeing stream?

Add movement to this weight, and you have an extremely powerful force pushing on your body. This force can not only move you down the river but also plaster you up against something and hold you there. Standing up in moving water only knee deep gets progressively more difficult as the current increases, despite the small area of your legs that this force has to work against. Sit down (or fall down) in this same current, and the force now pushing against the greater area of your torso becomes irresistible at anything beyond a comparatively low flow. This can be related to being rolled out of your canoe when it broadsides on some obstruction such as a logjam. Even if you are not actually caught and entangled by something under water, you may be pinned against it by the force of water and unable to overcome this pressure enough to free yourself. This is particularly true if your chest or stomach is against something but your legs are dangling free under it. Not only are you likely to be pulled further under the obstruction, but you can't use the power of your legs to help free your body. Even worse is if you're under an overhang and have to try to go back upstream to get out from under it. In this last case, with a swift current and no foot purchase to help you (and quite possibly even *with* a foot purchase), you are almost surely dead.

Throughout this book are various warnings to get on the upstream end of your swamped canoe. Remember the 3 cubic feet of water outweighing most men? How many cubic feet are there in your swamped canoe? A very rough calculation will quickly show you that a 17-foot canoe will hold at least 1,650 pounds of water when swamped. That's nearly a ton. Just this weight alone could crush you, but think about it moving 4 or 5 miles an hour down the river and catching you between its bow and a rock. All this concentrated force could nearly cut you in two and, at best, severely injure you. Only once do you have to be floating helplessly in a swift river and see a swamped canoe bearing down on you before you realize the wisdom of the "get upstream" rule.

I have been in numerous situations that illustrate this amazing and unthought-of power of water. I've seen canoes pinned in 18 inches of moving water *and less* when it took six grown men, all experienced canoeists, to get them loose. In faster current, I've seen a canoe pinned in about 14 inches of water when it took six men in the water and six more on each shore hauling on ropes to break it free. Moving water *is* powerful; unfortunately, few believe it until they've felt that power.

WINTER CANOEING

Rewards and Rigors

Cold-weather canoeing offers its own special rewards to those willing to undergo its rigors. Actually, with proper equipment and planning and an awareness of winter's particular hazards, the rigors need normally extend no farther than the agony of leaving a warm bed for a cold dawn.

Once on a winter river, the water is usually higher and the trip, up to a point, easier. The river presents a picture totally different from its summer-time aspect. The canoeist gets better,

A cold river—rewards and rigors in about equal doses.

less obstructed views of the bank and what's beyond, often discovering things he never saw on the green shrouded shoreline of warmer weather. Too, there is the reward of the winter's own particular brand of beauty—the icicles and frozen glitter of waterfalls and wet cliff faces and bushes, the white of frost or snow covering the trees and remaining underbrush, and the somber browns and grays and blacks of all of a cold world.

The river is often relatively deserted, so the twin benefits of solitude and enjoyment of its unique winter face are reserved for you and your chosen companions. It's a different and a rewarding facet of canoeing. But the rewards are not free. The winter canoeist needs a greater degree of fortitude to merely get out at all, and he needs more preparation and more equipment to enjoy the outing. Most importantly perhaps, he needs an awareness of the hazards of cold-weather river running, what causes them, and the effects these hazards can have on him.

Basics

Basically, the discomfort-producing factors of winter canoeing are wind, wet, and low temperatures, all of which the canoeist is freely exposed to. These can lead to mild or severe discomfort, colds, sinus problems, and various upper respiratory

311

ailments. They can also produce frostbite, hypothermia, and death. Most canoeists use caution and dress protectively enough if the temperature is really low. The point that is important is that the temperature itself doesn't really have be very low to be dangerous. A wet body, a strong wind, and 50 degrees can kill you. Lower temperatures just do it faster.

Cold and Its Effects

Cold is the absence of heat. This may sound obvious, but "cold" is not just what the thermometer reads. Cold is what the canoeist feels when he's tired and wet and the wind is blowing but the thermometer says a "safe" 50 degrees. He's cold because his wet clothes and the wind blowing across them are sucking the heat away from his body as fast or faster than his body can produce it. The problem is aggravated by weariness because his energy reserves have been lowered by day-long exertion and his body is incapable of producing the heat it could when it was fresh.

Your body is like a furnace whose fuel is energy. A certain amount of this energy is consumed just keeping you living. More is used up by activity and still more is given off as heat. When this energy reserve is lowered because of fatigue or hunger, its heat-producing capability is consequently reduced. Obviously, exposure, wetness, wind, insufficient insulating qualities of your winter wear, or any combinations of these can contribute to this reduction by forcing the body to produce heat to try to keep you warm. When the body's energy reserve becomes so reduced that it can no longer keep all your body warm, then it begins to work to conserve the heat of the trunk of the body and thus to maintain the normal temperature of your vital organs. To do this it uses an automatic process called vaso-constriction to cut down the blood supply to the skin surface and to all of the extremities except the head. This explains why your hands and your feet feel cold first and why you lose the ability to use your limbs when you are very cold.

Keep Your Extremities Covered

A common error is to dress warmly and effectively all over

your body then leave your head and hands bare. As pointed out above, the head is not affected by the automatic process of heat conservation. It continues to receive a full blood flow and consequently radiates a tremendous amount of heat. In fact, when uncovered, your head can lose up to nearly 50 percent of your body's heat at a temperature of 40 degrees. It loses even more as the temperature drops. Your hands also are great heat losers if left uncovered.

The first result of these uncovered extremities is that you may not *feel* cold, but you're forcing your body to work harder to keep you warm. This uses up energy, and that energy, remember, is your furnace's fuel. Cover your neck, head, and hands. The old saw about put on a hat to warm your feet is quite true!

Loss of Heat

Preservation of the body-produced heat, then, is the clue to warmth on the winter river. Several factors have a bearing on the ability to do this. Obviously, dressing warmly is one of these, and this has been discussed under Clothing in Chapter 4. You do lose heat through exposure. Bare skin or clothing with little or no insulation value lets the heat escape to the air. Wetness increases this loss by decreasing insulation (except in a wet suit) and by the cooling effect of evaporation if a wind is blowing. Heat always flows from a warmer to a colder surface. The cold-weather paddler must try to hold this heat loss to within comfortable limits.

Chill Factor

One of the biggest contributors to the *feeling* of cold is the cooling effect of the wind blowing on your body. The wind drives cold air into and through your clothing and whips heat off of bare or inadequately insulated skin. This effect is called chill factor. It's a measure of the effect on your body of a certain temperature combined with a certain velocity wind. It's expressed in an equivalent, always lower, temperature that would have the *same* effect on your body if no wind at all were blowing. The chart offers some examples. As you can see,

313

WIND CHILL CHART

Wind Speed	Actual Air Temperature						
(mph)	30 deg.	20 deg.	10 deg.	0 deg.	-10 deg.	-20 deg.	-30 deg.
10	16	-2	-9	-22	-31	-45	-58
15	11	-6	-18	-33	-45	-60	-70
20	3	-9	-24	-40	-52	-68	-81
25	0	-15	-29	-45	-58	-75	-89
30	-4	-18	-33	-49	-63	-78	-94
35	-4	-20	-35	-52	-67	-83	-98
40	-4	-22	-36	-54	-69	-87	-101

paddling around on a relatively mild 40-degree day with a 10-mile-an-hour wind blowing is the same as being out on a still day when it's around 16 degrees. Look what happens if that same 10-mile-an-hour wind blows, but the air temperature is only 20 degrees. You're down to an equivalent temperature of below zero!

The chart is for the effect on a *dry* body. If you're *wet* from splash or rain or spill, then your clothing (once again, wet suit excepted) has lost much of its insulating value. Your body may be using up energy and generating heat to its limits, but it's not doing too much good because there's nothing holding it in and warming you. The wind is not only *blowing* the heat from your body but cooling it even further by evaporation of the water in your clothes. The effective temperature working to rob your body of heat is far below that on the chart.

SPILLS AND RESCUE IN COLD WATER

When you spill into cold water—even in a wet suit—most people encounter the heart-stopping, breathtaking shock of the initial plunge into that low temperature. This affects different people to a greater or lesser degree. For many it results in a momentary helplessness and an apparent inability to breathe. It generates a somewhat panicky feeling, but the symptoms will pass quickly. More serious is that *any* wetness of your clothing or skin increases heat loss. Immersion in cold water because of spills, wading out to rescue a boat or for whatever reason, tremendously increases this heat loss. The cold water saps your

314

strength rapidly by its own low temperature. Vaso-constriction begins, and you immediately get the sensation of "numb" hands and feet and begin to lose control of your limbs and hands. This makes it harder or impossible to hold onto a rescue rope, to pull yourself out of the water, or to do anything useful to you or anyone else. Your trunk is swiftly robbed of its warmth, and hypothermia begins to set in. When this happens you are not only incapable of helping yourself but also of even *knowing* that you need help. You may drown or you may die of hypothermia. One is as fatal as the other!

All of this is not instantaneous, of course, but it does point out the necessity of getting out of cold water or a cold situation when you *feel* it as rapidly as possible. Depending upon the water temperature and your susceptibility to cold, you have a varying amount of time. The chart gives an idea of these times for a person not in a wet suit. Bear in mind that the figures are for *life*—you will be incapable of self-help long before these times elapse.

After you get out of the water you are doubly prone to chill factor and may be on your way into hypothermia.

CHART OF EXPOSURE TIMES IN COLD WATER

Water Temperature:	"Safe" Exposure Time:
40 deg. or under	Less than 10 minutes
40–50 deg.	5–20 minutes
50–60 deg.	15–40 minutes
60 deg. or above	1 hour or more

HYPOTHERMIA

Hypothermia is a condition in which the core temperature of your body—your normal temperature—begins to drop and your body cannot halt the process. The body loses heat faster than it can produce it, and in so doing uses up its energy reserves. When this reserve is exhausted, hypothermia begins, the core temperature continues down until you lose consciousness,

315

go into coma, and die. Hypothermia is a direct result of exposure to wind, wet, and cold and is one of the biggest hazards of winter canoeing. Its greatest dangers are that more cases of hypothermia occur in the relatively warm temperatures between 30 and 50 degrees when no one expects it than they do in really cold weather and that by the time *you* are in the first stages of hypothermia, you are too far gone to realize it.

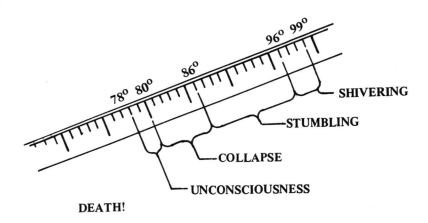

The degrees of hypothermia.

The first symptoms of hypothermia occur with the first few degrees of core temperature drop from about 99 degrees to 96 degrees; uncontrollable shivering, slurred speech, incoherence, and loss of reasoning power. At about 90 to 86 degrees, loss of control of the hands, stumbling, lurching, and a general slowing down and weakness occur. By now the shivering has usually vanished. To this point the victim is still conscious but is very confused. The final stages are inability to walk, falling down, collapse, a great sleepiness, and, somewhere around 80 to 78 degrees, unconsciousness. Extreme skin coldness, a faint pulse, and barely detectible or very shallow breathing are the main symptoms at this stage. Beyond this point (below about 78 degrees) lies death.

If for no other reason, the threat of hypothermia should convince you not to canoe alone in the winter. You are helpless once it strikes you, and your only hope is to forestall it by being aware of it and trying to keep out of situations likely to incur it.

As the body is no longer capable of furnishing its own heat, aid for victims of hypothermia consists of furnishing heat to the body. Recommended treatment is first to remove the victim from the hypothermia-inducing environment—put him out of the wind and rain and inside, if possible, in a tent, cabin, or whatever is handy. Build a fire, remove his clothes if they are wet, and get him into dry clothes and something warm like blankets or a sleeping bag. Give him warm drinks and possibly apply warmed canteens, towels, and the like to his body.

If the victim is nearly unconscious, try to keep him awake and give him warm drinks. Don't strangle him by forcing warm drinks down him, but do try to get him to drink them. Leave him naked and put him into a sleeping bag or blankets with another naked person. If you can, sandwich him between two naked people. This may sound strange, but the skin-to-skin contact is recommended as the most effective treatment.

If your victim is in this last stage of unconsciousness, you should try to get medical help if it's within reach. In the meantime, however, pursue the aid outlined above as far as possible. It could mean the difference between life and death.

FROSTBITE

Frostbite is indicated by a numb sensation and by a grayish-white appearance of the affected part—usually fingers, toes, nose, ears, or cheeks. If not caught soon enough it can mean freezing and permanent damage or loss of the frostbitten part.

Treatment is to thaw the frozen part—but not by rubbing it with snow or anything else. Rubbing will do more damage than good. Warm the part by having the person cover it with an ungloved hand or, if it's a hand that is frostbitten, by putting it under his armpit after removing the glove. Get him inside or at least out of the wind, and give him something warm to drink. If the part is wet, get it dry. If the skin doesn't respond to the hand warming, hold the part in lukewarm water, if possible, or wrap it in something like warmed blankets or towels.

SOME WAYS TO HELP KEEP WARM

Clothes of wool or better yet, a wet suit—both complete with gloves, head covering, and foot covering—serve for insulation in the winter. Reduce chill-factor effect by covering the wet suit or clothes with a windproof jumpsuit or at least a windproof jacket. A lot of canoeists put on their rainsuit tops or the whole rainsuit in cold, windy weather, preferring the condensation inside to the wind chill outside.

Eat often, don't get hungry. Your body's heat factory needs fuel and that means food, so nibble along all day. When you stop to eat take the time to fix something hot to eat or drink and to build a fire. Get out of the wind, rain, snow, or whatever the weather is.

Don't overtire yourself. Tiredness means you've used up your energy, and that means your body is low on the ability to produce heat. Stop early, don't push on to exhaustion.

SOME RULES FOR WINTER

Never boat alone in cold weather, and be sure your canoeing partners know what hypothermia is, what the symptoms are, and what to do about it.

Dress for the expected weather, but don't discount unexpected weather; wind and wetness are more to be guarded against than cold, so take your rainsuit and wear or take a windproof shell over your clothing. Wear a wet suit if you're likely to get splashed or spilled, if the temperature calls for it, or if you're particularly susceptible to cold. Wear a hat and gloves with whatever clothing you have on.

Carry waterproof matches and something to start a fire with. A pint or even a half-pint container of camp-stove fuel or kerosene will help get one going in a hurry. Don't rely on non-waterproof matches even in a watertight container. A short exposure to rain, the humidity of a raw day, or trying to strike them on a wet surface can cause them to crumble. Put a striker *in* your match case, under the cap for example, and then load the waterproof matches in this case with heads away from the striker.

Always carry a complete change of clothes in something

318

waterproof and a pocket or sheath knife. If your clothing, matches, and the like are tied in something (as they should be), you may not be able to untie the knots if your hands are cold or the knots are frozen. With a knife you can cut them loose. It's a good idea to carry a towel, too. Just drying your body off will help your comfort a lot. You might also consider carrying *another* complete change of clothing to leave in your vehicle; you could go in twice.

NATURAL HAZARDS

Hornet and Wasp Stings

Maybe these devilish insects are no problem in your part of the country, but they certainly are in some. Their propensity for building their paper houses on high limbs overhanging the water can be ignored if you don't stir them up by adventurously hitting the house with your paddle as you go by. Often, however, you'll find a big nest right at face level as you paddle along. If you don't see it in time you'll be instantly, furiously, and painfully attacked. This is not the least bit funny at any time, and should you be particularly allergic to their stings, a concentrated attack could easily kill you.

The only defense you have is to abandon the boat, preferably flipping it over upside down as you do so. Go under water then come up under the overturned canoe. There's plenty of air there, and even if there are a few trapped hornets there will be fewer than are waiting for you on the other side of the hull. You can then work yourself and your canoe away from the area. When you get clear the pain of the bites can be helped by dabbing them with ammonia, which should be in your first-aid kit if you're in hornet country.

Snake Bites

The United States has only a few varieties of poisonous snakes; however, one or more of these four types are generally found somewhere all around the country, so reasonable caution should be used. Personally, I have never known of anyone who was struck by any kind of snake on a canoe trip. But as canoeists and snakes are both out more in the summer, both like the cool shade along the bank, and the usual attire of warm-weather paddlers offers little protection against a strike, it could happen.

The best thing for a snake bite is not to get bitten, and caution is the great preventive here. Generally a snake will get out of your way if he knows you're coming and if he has a chance. The normal noises of an approaching canoe will usually assure this, if you don't just suddenly appear before he can retreat. Examination of wherever you're about to step or grab, combined with some judicious poking around with your paddle will usually ensure a clear path. While you're paddling keep your eyes open for snakes lying on limbs and in bushes over-hanging the river. Occasionally they'll flop right in the canoe!

The exception to these comments is the water moccasin or cottonmouth. Fat-bodied, heavy, and sluggish, the moccasin is belligerent, short-tempered, disinclined to get out of your way, and the most likely to strike without any provocation other than the proximity of a warm body. Unfortunately, he is the most likely poisonous snake to be along a water course; fortun-ately, he is not distributed throughout the country, being more a southern snake.

Should you be struck, bear in mind that the snake may not be poisonous even though the bite of a non-poisonous snake can make you sick and cause disturbing symptoms. The point is that in the confusion of the fear and shock attending a strike, it's easy to think the snake is poisonous when it isn't. The snake also may not have injected any venom (this happens about 25 percent of the time). However, don't take chances. If you can't identify the snake, then assume he's poisonous, kill him if pos-sible, and take him along with you for positive identification. In the appendix are instructions for what is currently the recom-mended treatment for snake bite. I hope you never have to use them.

Lightning

Get out of the water. The bigger the body of water the more danger you're in if a lightning storm begins. Paddle to shore, put your canoe up, get away from it if it's metal, and get off the bank. Do *not* get under the biggest tree you can find, and avoid the high points anywhere: they are where the lightning will most likely strike. Don't stand in water if you can help it. Try to find some dry ground or a dry log or rock to get on. Shelter yourself in some low spot that has noting prominent to attract the lightning to it. Should you be in a flat, open area, lie down on the ground or in a depression in the ground, if you can find one; otherwise, *you* may become the high point. Stay away from wire fences, the outside of metal buildings, metal pipelines, or any mass of metal. Should someone be struck, send for help, give him artificial respiration, and treat him for shock by elevating his feet and preventing his getting cold.

CHAPTER 13
SALVATION—THE RESCUE OF PEOPLE

There will most probably come a time when you or your boat, or both, will either have to be rescued or you will be called upon to help rescue others and their boats. The one sure way to avoid these situations is never to get in a canoe. Barring this somewhat drastic measure, the suggestions and techniques in this and the next chapter should prove helpful when the day comes to use them. However, as in everything else canoe related, do *not* wait to practice such things as rope throwing, rapids swimming, and canoe-over-canoe rescue until the time does come to use them. Practice first when errors will exact no penalty!

THE BIG RULE

Always concentrate on saving people first, then the equipment. Equipment is the least important and though it may be financially straining to lose it, it *can* be replaced—people cannot.

No matter how much equipment goes drifting off down the river on its own, most or all of it will be recovered. If you've followed the basic safety rules, someone will be there to catch it, and it will all be returned at the bottom of the rapid. If some *is* missed the chances are good that it will be found washed up on the bank, caught on a low bush, or bobbing in an eddy somewhere downstream. So worry about the people and rescue them—the equipment can come later.

LIFE JACKETS

All of the self-rescue techniques assume that you are wearing your life jacket. If you have put yourself into a situation that requires rescue and you do *not* have your life jacket on, then I suggest that once you extricate yourself from the situation you retire from river canoeing *voluntarily* as you're likely to be retired *involuntarily* if you continue defying the fundamental safety rules.

SELF SALVATION

Spills

Canoe spills may look slow and graceful to someone standing on the shore, but they happen awfully rapidly out in the boat. Reactions are usually zero until you've hit and sputtered to the surface. Then it's time to think about your next move. There are several DO'S, DON'T'S, and DANGERS to bear in mind when you find yourself in this situation.

Find the Canoe

If you're in no immediate danger, then first of all locate your canoe. When you spill in current your boat may prove to be very helpful in floating you to safety, or it may turn out to be your greatest danger. It all depends on circumstance and your location relative to the boat.

Once you've found your canoe, make sure you're clear of it. This is usually no problem as you'll probably be *thrown* clear anyway. Getting clear does not mean swimming away and abandoning the canoe, although there are conditions where this is the best course. Just make sure you're out of its way and not entangled or about to be entangled in its painters. The only thing you want connecting you to your boat is your *voluntary* grip on gunwale or painter.

Get Upstream of the Canoe

This is a fundamental rule in moving water. You don't want to be hit by or pinned against something by your boat, whether it's swamped or empty. Either way hurts, and if your boat is swamped, it could crush you. The common river name for this being caught between canoe and an immovable obstruction is "bear trap," a most descriptive term. It means an uncomfortable squeeze at best, trapped and drowned at worst. The weight of the empty, moving canoe hitting you is bad enough; if it's swamped, all that water weight combined with the velocity of the current makes it a tremendous battering ram that can crush any part of your body that's caught between it and anything solid and fixed. Broken bones are almost a certainty if you're hit with any force at all. Even when empty, the canoe could sweep you against something and, as it stops moving, turn on its side and expose its hull to the current, very effectively pinning you. Whether the canoe is keel upstream or open top upstream makes little difference in this situation. Even if the tremendous pressure alone does you no damage you'll be thoroughly trapped because you'll rarely be able to move the canoe yourself. *Avoid this situation.* You never know where an empty or swamped canoe is going or which way it will swing. Nothing controls it except the whims of the water and what obstruction it may strike. In addition, *you're* not too maneuverable while floating in the water either. So get *upstream* of it. If you're away from it you can do some backstrokes with your hands and kicking with your feet to slow down your progress and let it float on below you. If you're going to hang on to it, don't try to swim upstream, just grab the gunwale and pull yourself up hand over hand to the upstream end as fast as possible.

Use the Canoe

Your canoe can serve two useful purposes when you've spilled. First, even if it's totally swamped it has flotation in it

Rescue of a swimmer using the canoe. Note that the swimmer is in the approved floating position.

and will float. It's like a giant life preserver and will provide a lot better support for you than your life jacket (however, *wear* your life jacket; it's hard to don a canoe!). You can hang onto the upstream end of it and let it carry you on down the river if this course seems best. It is essential for your safety that you float with your feet downstream, knees slightly bent and your feet and body as near the surface of the water as you can manage. You can hold on with one or both hands and, I repeat, do all this on the *upstream* end.

The canoe can also serve as a shield between you and whatever obstructions may be in the water. It can stand the shock of hitting a rock a lot better than your body so use it if that seems the safest way.

Hanging On

Hanging on to the upstream end of a canoe means just that—*way* up near the end and to the side of the boat. Being halfway down the side of a canoe can put you in a bad position if the downstream end hangs or strikes and the boat suddenly swings around toward your side. If you're close enough to the end you can probably either get clear or quickly switch sides.

Hang on rather firmly to a thwart, to the gunwale, or even to the painter. You don't want to unwillingly lose your grip and your contact with the boat. Usually there will be some pull on your body because it offers more resistance to the water than the boat does. If you have a grip on the painter, don't loop it around your hand or any other part of your body. It could be painful—even fatal—if the canoe hung solidly and you were swept by or under it, then caught by the painter. The water pressure could make it difficult or impossible to slack off the rope enough to get free.

You'll find a few canoes around with sharp edges where the metal has been rolled under to form a part. If you have one of these, then, if possible, be selective of where you grip the boat. If the canoe strikes something it could halt abruptly and your "holding-on" hand go sliding down the boat, getting cut as it travels.

Straddling the upstream end of a boat with one leg down each side is not a good idea at all. It may seem like a great way to go, but the fun will probably vanish immediately if the downstream end suddenly stops dead on an obstruction!

When the Boat is Sideways

Often a swamped canoe will be swept down the river sideways or nearly so. Pick out what appears to be the most upstream end (if that end is clear and not the one about to hit a rock), and grab it. A little kicking or one-handed back paddling will probably let the other end swing on down. Pulling the boat into this position is safest even if the river looks clear. The boat could still hit something just under the water and having it parallel to the current reduces this chance.

It's a bad idea to hang on to the middle of the *side* of a boat being swept sideways. The danger here is that if the boat does broadside on something, the upstream gunwale (to which you are clinging) will probably roll under, carrying you with it and possibly rolling the boat on over until it hits you. This could really be dangerous if the boat catches on bushes, logs, tree limbs in the water, or anything similar through which the current can pass but the boat can't. If you're rolled under here you could be entangled under water by some of these limbs. If you're held by them you could quickly be dead.

Abandon the Boat

Sometimes it's the best course to abandon the boat and get yourself to safety. No one likes to lose a canoe, but a canoe *can* be replaced—you can't. The boat has a fair chance of surviving a solo trip down the river anyway.

If the boat is pulling you into a mass of limbs, a logjam, toward a waterfall, a souse hole, undercut, into even more turbulent water or into any situation that looks worse than the one you're in, *and you can improve your chances by doing so, don't hesitate to abandon the boat and strike out on your own.* The main idea of the moment is self-preservation; the *secondary* consideration is your boat and equipment.

If the water and air are very cold, forget the canoe, and get yourself to shore as soon as possible. Cold water will sap your strength quickly, and you don't need to waste what you have struggling with the boat.

Floating

Position

Whether you're hanging on to your boat or going it alone, you should try to position your body for maximum safety. The recommended posture is to face downstream, get your legs and feet in front of you and both legs and body up as near the surface of the water as possible, keep your knees bent, and paddle with your hands to maintain this position.

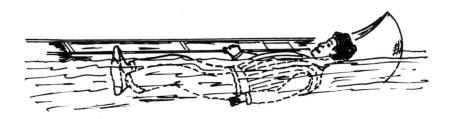

Using the swamped canoe for flotation.

Each of these items has a purpose. First of all, the position places you so you can see where you're going and possibly exercise some control over your course. If you can't control your direction you can at least be prepared for a possible impact. Impact is the reason for the bent knees and one of the reasons for the extended feet and legs. Your leg muscles are a lot stronger than those of your arms and give you a better chance of fending yourself off an obstacle. If nothing else, they'll cushion the impact and protect your torso. Impact on straight-out legs with locked knees is going to hurt or break a leg, but keeping the knees bent will give you some "spring" to absorb a blow.

327

Dangling Feet

The other reason for keeping your feet up is that you're less likely to hit an underwater obstacle. Apart from the fact that this hurts, these dangling feet can also get you into other, more serious problems. Tumbling is one. If your legs or feet strike something below the surface the current could start you tumbling end over end. Even if your feet don't hit anything, the current below the surface is slower than that at the surface, and this differential in speed could also start you tumbling. Either way you lose any control you may have had, lose sight of where you're going, lose the "cushion" of your legs, and expose your torso and back to damage as well as possibly winding up going backward down the river.

Even more serious—and potentially deadly—is getting a foot *caught* in something under water: a crack in a rock or a fork in a limb, for example. If this happens, the current could hold you so that you can't take the pressure off the caught foot and free yourself, particularly if you're completely out of position and are on your back facing *upstream*. In this position you're virtually helpless if you get a foot caught.

Get In An Eddy

A lot of times you may be able to work yourself into an eddy by ferrying with your body. Even if you're not near the shoreline, you will be out of the current and able to rest and think. Possibly you can climb out of the water onto whatever is creating the eddy. If there's someone on the shore with a rescue rope, then you're almost as good as safe.

There are two considerations about working your way into an eddy. First, if the water is very cold, there's no one on shore to help you, and you can't climb out of the water on what is creating the eddy—or you know you'll have to go right back in to reach the shore—then use the eddy only briefly. Don't float there until you succumb to hypothermia. Second, be careful of eddies where water is running over the *top* of the rock or whatever. A small amount of down-falling water is safe, but larger flows could be creating a hydraulic in that haven you're trying to reach.

Nearing Shore

There is usually an eddy of sorts right at the shoreline. The water will at least be moving slightly slower than out in the middle of the river, so you won't have to struggle so hard. The exception is that if you're on the outside edge of a bend it will be swifter. As you approach the shoreline, be wary of any bushes and limbs hanging over the water, lying in it, and possibly under it. Keep those feet up; don't ride through a rapid only to drown 2 feet from safety!

Don't Be Rule Bound

You're not in a great position to do too much when drifting in your life jacket in the water. Your field of view is limited, you may be being tossed around and up and down, and everything usually is happening fast.

Be flexible. Adjust your actions to the circumstances. If the day is warm and you're in no danger, then grab the upstream end of the boat and enjoy the ride. If the situation is different, then do something different. Let the temperature of air and water, the presence or absence of companions, the turbulence of the river, the amount and proximity of obstructions, what lies ahead and, of course, the amount of time you have, determine what you do.

THE RESCUE OF OTHERS

Generally a canoeist can rescue himself, but there are times when he will need help to get himself out of the water. Such exceptions to self-rescue could be in extremely turbulent, swift, or powerful water where he is either being tossed so that he can't control his direction or will be swept far down the river before he can work his way to shore. Other situations could be where he is being swept into or toward a worse condition such as a waterfall, if he is caught in a hydraulic, or is trapped in an eddy or on a rock with a strong, swift current between him and the shore. These are only examples for there are other likely situations where a canoeist may find himself in need of a helping hand. The point is that a good canoeist should know how to save others as well as himself.

Safety Lines

In rescuing others, you will have two situations, one in which the distressed person is conscious and can, to some degree, avail himself of the efforts being made to rescue him. The second situation is when the person is unconscious and all rescue efforts are up to you. In this last situation, when it becomes necessary for you to wade or swim out from the shore, *never* attempt the rescue without a safety line tied around your waist unless the water is warm and calm and the current slow. Commonly a throw rope is used for this safety line.

In cold water, no matter how slow moving, or in swift, strong, or turbulent water, do not go out without the safety line tied around your waist and controlled on the shore end by a good belay and/or several pairs of strong and willing hands. At your end, the rope should be tied in a bowline or some similar non-slipping knot, and the loop around your waist should be large enough for you to slip out of if you need to but small enough so that you don't slip out accidentally. Don't rely on your grip on the rope—tie it around your waist. The tying of a bowline is covered in the chapter on knots. Never attempt *any* rescue involving swimming without your life jacket.

The Throw Rope

The first and foremost method of rescue of others in river canoeing is by use of the rescue rope—specifically by throwing it to the person in the water. The effective use of a rescue rope (or throw rope as it's often called) takes some practice, and the art of throwing one has a few knacks about it that need some study. Rope throwing is so important that it is covered as a single subject in another chapter.

Wading Out

Extreme caution should be used in wading out for rescue purposes. You could lose your footing, get a foot caught in something on the bottom, or be swept under an undercut and

330

wind up in a worse situation than the fellow you went out to rescue. Use the safety rope, and never tie the shore end to a tree or rock unless you're really in a desperate situation and that is the last resort. You may find your strength less or the current greater than you thought and end up dangling on the end of the rope unable to pull yourself back to the shore against the current or to swing in to the shore beside you.

Swimming Out

If you're attempting to reach someone on a rock or in an eddy or in some similar situation where he is surrounded by swift current, it will usually be impossible for you to swim straight out to him as the current will sweep you down the river past him. In this case you'll need to enter the water upstream so that you can approach him on a diagonal course, swimming out as the current pushes you down. How far upstream you enter is a matter of the swiftness of the water, the distance you must cover, and your own swimming strength. Of course, once you reach him you'll probably swim into the eddy below where he is (if one exists) and climb out of the water there (if you can).

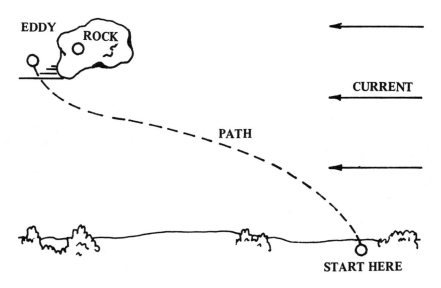

Approaching a stranded canoeist by swimming.

Hydraulics

If someone is caught in a hydraulic, then rely on your throw rope to get him out. If he's unconscious or beyond helping himself and you *must* go in after him, go in *only* with the rope around your waist and someone handling the shore end. In this situation *never*, even as a last resort, tie the rope to the shore. There is too great a likelihood that there will then be *two* of you caught in the hydraulic.

Using Your Canoe

Helping a swimmer while you remain in your canoe is rarely done in a rapid. You're busy maneuvering, and it's quite possible that your canoe will present more of a danger than a help. In swift, unobstructed current, however, you can paddle up to him and either let him hang onto the upstream end while you take him to shore, an eddy, or some other point of safety, or let him climb in your canoe while you or your partner leans and braces. When doing this, it's best to present the side of your canoe to the swimmer rather than the bow or stern. In this way you can reach them to help them in if they need it. If the water and air are cold, of course, get them in the boat rather than dragging them along in the water.

Re-entering a canoe from the water.

Should the person in the water be unconscious, you can either roll him into your canoe while your partner braces or hold onto him while your partner paddles to shore. You might also jump in the water to help get the victim in while your partner helps from in the canoe.

Helping an unconscious person that you can't get in the canoe.

Getting the dead weight of an unconscious person into your boat is tricky even with a tandem crew. If you're solo and in moving water, it's so difficult and likely to upset you that you will probably be better off just to get the victim's hands in the boat, tie them under a thwart, and then paddle to shore.

The rescue of someone stranded on a rock in the river is usually pretty simple. Just ferry out into the eddy below him, pick him up, and ferry back in.

CHAPTER 14
MORE SALVATION—THE RESCUE OF CANOES

Quite often canoes need no rescuing. They'll frequently battle their own way down through a rapids, finally floating clear, and either be retrieved by someone downstream or drift into an eddy somewhere. Usually they are swamped, and their rescue is simply a matter of catching them and emptying them of water. This is the first common condition of canoe rescue—a swamped boat but one that is floating free. The second common condition is when a canoe is hung or pinned on some obstruction. This latter situation requires more effort and thought.

EMPTYING A SWAMPED CANOE

First off, any swamped canoe is easier to empty if the current isn't tugging at it or sweeping at your legs while you're balanced on an underwater rock. So if you can, always hang on to its upstream end, work it into an eddy, *then* start emptying it. Second, forget all that stuff you may have read or seen about splashing or rocking or sloshing the water out of a swamped canoe. This is applicable if you're alone in the middle of a deep lake or alone on a deep, very wide and calm river while basking in warm weather and warm water. It's normally not necessary in river canoeing and could be fatal in winter. However, if you *do* want to learn to do these slow and laborious processes (which I can't say may *not* be useful sometimes) the Red Cross canoeing book will show you how.

In river canoeing you can almost always work your canoe to shore or to an island or else find a shallow place or rock to stand on in the river (preferably in an eddy). Then it's a matter of dragging one end of the canoe up the bank (or lifting it up) and letting the water run out the side or rolling the boat over, picking it up, and letting the remaining water run out all over you. This last maneuver is easier, of course, for a tandem crew.

If another canoe is along there's another simple way to empty a swamped canoe—canoe-over-canoe rescue.

Emptying a canoe by the "find-a-shallow-place" method.

Canoe-Over-Canoe Rescue

Under ideal conditions, using the canoe-over-canoe rescue method, a swamped canoe can be emptied, re-righted, and have its paddlers back in the boat in less than 20 seconds. Unfortunately for timing purposes, a river rarely produces ideal conditions. Nonetheless this method is probably the fastest and easiest way to get a swamped canoe back into action. A tandem crew in the rescue boat and cooperation from the rescuees in the water help the efficiency of the operation, but it *can* be handled (carefully) by a solo paddler with no assistance at all from the boat's former occupants.

A canoe-over-canoe rescue is simple if certain conditions are met. First, either get both canoes into an eddy or out in an unobstructed stretch of the river. Don't try it in shoals or rapids or where you're being swept down onto something. Straighten up the swamped canoe parallel to the current and, if you can, work it through or around the obstructions. Don't get your

335

canoe downstream of it. If necessary let the swamped boat go its own way rather than drag yours into trouble. As in all rescues, first of all see to the safety of the swimmers. Ignore the floating equipment unless it's within immediate reach; someone else will get it or you can pick it up later. If in cold water get the swimmers in your canoe, to shore, or somewhere out of the water immediately. If you're in rapids see that they are out of harm's way of their own canoe and yours.

Once into unobstructed water, work the swamped boat parallel to the current or into an eddy, and position your own canoe upstream and perpendicular to it. In a tandem boat put the bow of the swamped boat just aft of the center of yours or as near as possible to the broadest width of your canoe and still in reach of the sternman. For a solo rescue the swamped boat would be about even with the center of your canoe.

Canoe-over-canoe rescue.

A. Positioning the canoes.

If the rescuees are still in the water, have them position themselves on the upstream side and near the ends of your canoe and hold onto the gunwales to help balance your canoe. They get to this position by walking their hands along the gunwales of your canoe, not by swimming. This applies whether

336

you are solo or tandem. If tandem your bowman should also low brace or be ready to low brace on the downstream side.

Grab the bow of the swamped canoe and roll it over bottom up. You may find that some canoe books advocate pulling the boat up *then* rolling it. This *is* muscle straining. Lift up on the bow before it rolls completely over. This will prevent a vacuum from forming under the boat as you lift. If it does and you find it hard to pull the canoe out of the water, just tilt the hull slightly until one gunwale clears the surface and lets air in under the hull. Much of the water in the front of the canoe will now be poured out, and you'll be surprised how easy this is to do. Pull the bow up over your gunwale, and continue pulling until the now-empty canoe is resting across your gunwales upside down. Grab the rescued canoe's near gunwale, and roll it over open side up on your own gunwales, then slide it back in the water downstream of your canoe. Hang on to it until its paddlers "hand walk" the gunwales back to their canoe and re-enter it, then give them their paddles (or your spares), and *only then* release their boat.

B. Lifting the overturned canoe--

C. --across the rescued canoe.

D. The swamped canoe is now empty.

E. Turning the canoe upright.

F. Ready to go back into the water.

G. And back in it goes.

Canoe-over-canoe rescue is simple, fast, and easy. There is very little "muscle" required. Study the photos, then get out and try it a few times before you need it.

Canoe-Over-Canoe Rescue When Both Are Swamped

It's possible to use the fundamentals of canoe-over-canoe rescue to empty a canoe when there are *two* swamped canoes in the water and no other help is around. Position the canoes as for a standard rescue. Both canoes will be upside down unless one or both have a lot of extra flotation. If either does, let the highest-floating one stay right side up and use it for the "rescue" canoe.

Drag the "rescued" canoe up over the other canoe, and, when you get it more or less balanced (and empty), flip it over and slide it off the other canoe. The swimmers not actively engaged in the rescue will be holding the position of the rescue boat.

Although this method is a bit awkward and you won't get all the water out of the flipped canoe, it will get you back in a

340

canoe that's considerably drier than the one still in the water!

RE-ENTERING A CANOE

This can be done swiftly and easily, or you can swamp (or reswamp) the canoe. Boarding a canoe from the water depends more on your agility than your strength. The key is not to load all your weight on one gunwale and try to lift your body up. Canoes are stable but not *that* stable. Let the river support as much of your weight as it will for as long as it will, kick vigorously with your feet, and sort of pull the canoe in under you with your arms.

Obviously if one of a tandem team falls overboard, reboarding is much easier because the one remaining in the canoe can lean and low brace to one side while his partner gets in on the other side. If both are in the water, one should get on one side and balance the canoe while the other re-enters, and so on.

For solo re-entering, position yourself at the side of the canoe as near to its widest point as possible but where you can reach across the center thwart with one hand. Put the other hand on the near gunwale, get your feet up near the surface by kicking, and pull the canoe in under you, keeping pressure down on the hand farthest away from you. Keep kicking and work your body up over the gunwale until you're balanced on the gunwale, then swing your feet on in.

Possibly a better way, or at least easier for most, is to do approximately the same thing, except kick vigorously and just roll into the bottom of the canoe head first. This is not very graceful looking but *is* effective.

AND—IF YOU DON'T RE-ENTER

Your totally swamped canoe will support you and your partner while you are sitting in it. If necessary you can scramble back in it, sit on the bottom (*not* on the seats), and work it to shore by paddling with your hands (or your paddles if you have them). Do *not* try this in cold water unless you have on a wet suit—you shouldn't be out alone in cold weather anyway. Also, do *not* try it in any rapid or shoal or where obstructions exist that your canoe might hit. A swamped canoe will go where the current takes it, and there's little you can do "riding it out" except get yourself in more trouble. Better to abandon it completely or climb out, get on the upstream end, hang on, and float along beside it in the approved fashion.

PINNED AND HUNG CANOES

To my mind, a "hung" canoe is one that's simply caught on an obstruction, often by its keel, or by its hull if it has been ridden up on a shoal in water that proved too shallow. The canoe may or may not have some water in it but isn't usually swamped or being held tight by the force of the water running in it. The upstream gunwale has not gone under water, and basically only friction is holding it fast.

A pinned canoe, on the other hand, has usually broadsided on an obstruction, the upstream gunwale has gone down, and water is pouring in its open upstream face. It may be totally swamped or only partially filled with water but is being held firmly against (or bent around) the obstruction by the force and weight of the water pouring into it. Occasionally it may have its keel pointing upstream, but this is rare as most swamped canoes float right side up, and the instant the downstream gunwale stops moving (as when it hits a rock) the upstream gunwale sinks and the canoe winds up as already described.

Exiting from a Hung or Pinned Canoe

The cardinal rule (almost) of exiting from a hung or pinned canoe in current is to get out upstream of the canoe. Often a hung boat may be freed by simply taking some weight off of it. Sometimes that is just a matter of sticking one foot out and pressing down on the rock that's caught you. At other times one or both members of a tandem canoe may need to step out. Regardless of whether it's 1, 2, or 4 legs out, though, get them out upstream of the canoe. If the boat suddenly comes loose it could run right over you or roll over you or pin you, none of which is fun when the canoe is empty, and could be dangerous and deadly empty or swamped. This is the same situation as a "bear trap" where you are pinned between your canoe and an immovable obstruction. Avoid it by being cau-

342

A pinned canoe and unsafe rescue techniques. Note that the water is only knee deep.

tious—*and* getting out upstream!

Obviously there are going to be exceptions to this debarking upstream. If you've ridden up a rock that is stuck out of the water downstream and the water is deep upstream, you would naturally step out on the rock. In fact, the rock may be the only place you can get to free the boat. Nonetheless, as a general rule, do try to get out upstream. The idea is to position yourself so you're in a safe position when the canoe comes free and is once more being pushed by the current.

Hang on to the Canoe

Before you step out of a hung canoe, put your paddle in the bottom of the canoe; never just lay it across the gunwales. Then, when you do step out, maintain a firm grip on the canoe. As I said, sometimes the removal of just a little weight will free it. If you're in swift current when this happens the canoe may suddenly go on its way, leaving you stranded, or it could pivot around, slide, and get out of reach.

Don't Let "Hung" Become "Pinned"

The first thing to remember—and avoid—is that it's very easy for a "hung" canoe to become a "pinned" canoe. When you broadside on something the upstream gunwale will immedi-

343

ately begin to sink. If you can prevent the gunwale going down below the surface or get it back up before much water has come into it, then you may avoid a worse situation. Quick action is necessary, and there's no time to sit there gaping at the water. The action may be leaping out upstream and grabbing the gunwale or the end of the canoe to hold it up; or you might immediately throw all your weight to the downstream gunwale if you're up on a sloping rock that's out of the water and can act fast enough. Jumping out on the rock and sliding or lifting the whole canoe up on it also may save the day. The key is swift action to counteract as much as possible the water pressure and weight acting on the canoe.

Freeing a Hung Boat

I've already mentioned that one foot out or one or both crew members out is usually enough to free a canoe that has simply slid up on a rock or run into water that's too shallow. Many canoeists never step out in this situation but instead use their paddles to push off the bottom or nearby rocks. This is rough on paddles, particularly wooden ones. It's usually not only easier but also faster to just step out. (Wintertime provides a great reluctance to do so, however.)

If you're hung on a point or a line of rock under the hull, you can often free the canoe by shifting both crew members' weight to the end that has the longest length free. If this happens to be the downstream end, good. If it is the upstream end, be careful that you don't get swept right back on the point. This is another place where you see a lot of paddle prying going on.

Look Before You Leap

When you step out of a hung or pinned canoe, investigate where you're stepping *before* shifting your weight out of the canoe. The canoe may be hung on a rock, but where you step out may be over your head. It's a disconcerting feeling to put your weight down expecting a few inches' drop and to just keep going down. This is also obviously a good way to overturn your canoe.

Jiggling or Rocking

These are my own terms for what you see a lot of canoeists do when their canoe is hung. It's not an approved technique, and it's certainly rough on·the canoe, but it's done all the
time. In fact, I've seen canoeists do this for minutes on end
when they could have been free in a moment by simply stepping out of the canoe.

In this unorthodox method, the canoeist usually grasps the
gunwales or the thwart in front of him with both hands; then he
and his partner in a more or less coordinated movement hunch
forward and backward, thus gradually "rocking" and sliding the
canoe off whatever it's hung on. It's like "rocking" a car out of
a mudhole.

Running Backward

Frequently a canoe will hang on an obstruction near its
bow, the stern will be swept around, the bow will come loose,
and presto—you're out running a rapid backwards. Although
you may find a handy eddy to forward ferry into, you may also
have to do a reverse eddy turn into it, or you may find no haven
of calm water anywhere and simply have to run the whole thing
backwards. It's best to practice this before you need it, gradually improving your reverse techniques and skills in ever-
tougher rapids.

**A practice run backwards—something to practice before you
need it!**

PINNED CANOES

A pinned canoe is often not easy to unpin. It may be swamped or partially so with the weight of the water and force of the current holding it firmly against the obstruction. This is where the real damage is done to a canoe—an out-of-control swamped boat propelled by the current broadsides on a rock or tree. It smashes into it with all the considerable force that the water weight in it and its speed give it and often bends around the obstruction. Even with a foam-core ABS canoe, you're likely to have bent or broken gunwales and thwarts. A fiberglass canoe is likely to be snapped in two and an aluminum canoe bent or torn so badly as to require major repairs. It might also be ripped in two!

Analyze the Situation

Assuming that the paddlers are safe, looking over the situation is the first step toward freeing the canoe. If possible you want to make the water work for you; at worst you want to have it work against you as little as possible!

To this end look at the position of the canoe and try to determine where the water is exerting the least pressure or where you can get the most leverage. Most commonly you'll have one of the conditions shown in the sketches. In a, b, and c the canoe is facing open end upstream and is being held by the water running in its open, upstream face as in e and f. In d (and g) the canoe is keel upstream. In any of these cases the hull is probably bent and lodged on the rock by friction and by molding itself somewhat to the rock.

In sketch "a" most of the downstream end of the canoe is free, and the current is pushing at this end trying to dislodge it. All the pressure that is holding the canoe to the rock is up on a comparatively short section of the canoe. In this case you could utilize the current's help on the downstream end and try to work the canoe off in this direction by pulling out (upstream) on the caught end and gradually pivoting it around the rock or by lifting it as you pivot to reduce or stop the flow of water into the open top. The more you move it, the more the current on the downstream end will help you. Obviously your first at-

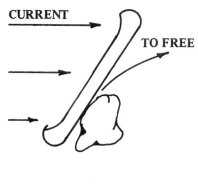

CURRENT

TO FREE

a

tempt would be to simply lift the short (upstream) end out of the water. If you succeed the boat is free anyway.

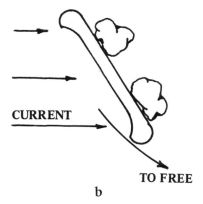

CURRENT

TO FREE

b

In sketch "b" the current helps push the canoe free if worked in the direction shown by pulling the upstream end a-round until the canoe is parallel to the current. Again, the near-er you approach parallel to the current, the more the current will help you pull the canoe free.

Sketches "c" and "d" show tougher problems. The boat is pretty well centered, so you have no "easy" end to work on. In sketch "c" the rescue is complicated by the canoe being bent around the rock. Here there is no simple way, and sheer muscle will have to do the work. If the canoe is pinned as in sketch "e" so not too much water is flowing in it, the easiest way (if you

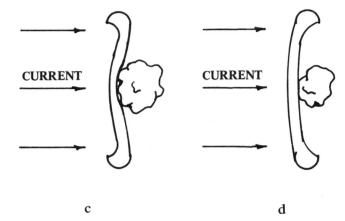

c   d

Some typical "pinned" situations.

can't lift it off) may be to roll it over as outlined below. If it's
down as in sketch "f" you probably won't be able to roll it. In
this situation lifting and pivoting the canoe toward one end will
probably prove easier, though not easy. If possible combine this
with a roll upstream (roll the lower gunwale downstream) to get
that gunwale free of the water pressure.

More typical "pins."

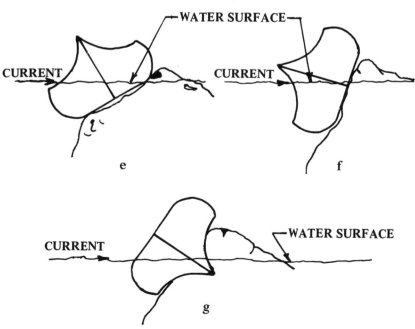

Roll the Canoe

Sometimes it may prove easier to roll the canoe to free it or to roll and lift or simply to lift it. Try to roll the *upstream* gunwale up and toward downstream so that the keel is facing upstream if the canoe is submerged or nearly so as in sketch "f." Roll the *downstream* gunwale up and toward upstream if it's not too submerged as in sketch "e." Combine this with a lift from the end or on the bottom so it doesn't just drop back in the water as you lift. Even if you end up with the canoe facing as in sketch "g," the bottom offers less resistance to the water than the open top, and you'll probably be able to lift it better or lift and roll the upper gunwale downstream.

Pinned by the End

Nine times out of ten, canoes get pinned in a broadside position. Sometimes, however, they will be pinned when they are parallel to the current. They may have one end wedged under a rock and water pouring in to the *top* of the canoe instead of over one gunwale. In this case your working leverage will be from the *free* end and it's this you'll probably have to lift and pull to get it loose. In fact, you may need to actually lift the boat completely end over end or at least raise it enough to take the water pressure off so you can pull the canoe loose. If the upstream end is caught you may have to flip it upstream to free it.

Use Leverage

Often the relieving or removal of pressure on a canoe has to be done in steps. Use a lot of effort to move the canoe a little, hold it in this position, possibly with the aid of ropes around the hull and snubbed to a rock or tree or held by other canoeists on shore, then renew your grip and move it a little more. Try to find the path of least resistance to your pull and one that will do the most good. The basic rule is to try to work the canoe into a position ever more parallel with the current and to get the upstream gunwale up out of the water. Once either of these goals is met your canoe is usually freed.

349

Use Manpower

Another basic rule—don't stint on the manpower if you've got it. Get as many out on the canoe as have room to work from the upstream side, and be very cautious as the boat could unexpectedly whip free. If the current is swift, use safety lines. Everyone should have on their life jackets.

Aid the efforts of those in the water by lines from shore or nearby firm footing and put more manpower on them. Don't tie directly to a thwart or seat; the chances are that they'll just bend, break, or rip out. Tie your hauling lines around the hull using a bowline or a slip knot. These ropes can be used to assist in the general effort, to snub or hold what gains have been made, and sometimes to do all the work. Obviously their efforts should be coordinated with the efforts of those in the water so that the rescue effort isn't working against itself.

Tie Up and Come Back Later

If the canoe is thoroughly pinned in a stream whose water level is likely to fall pretty rapidly and you can't work it loose, you might just tie it up to something and come back later when the water level has dropped. The only risk here is that someone else may come "rescue" it first unless it's attended during this time. I once freed my canoe with this method. Unable to move it, we tied it to an overhead bridge structure and left. When we returned we were amazed to find the canoe hanging by its ropes completely *out* of the water. Of course this made it simple to rescue it.

CHAPTER 15
ROPE THROWING AND RESCUE

The art of throwing a rope for rescue purposes requires practice. The rope does no good if it doesn't reach far enough, if it's long enough but misses the rescuee, if it's pulled out of your hands (or thrown out), if it's too small for the victim to hold, or if *you're* pulled into the water instead of pulling *him* out.

THE ROPE

A rescue rope should be strong, should float, and should be of some easily visible color such as white, yellow, or orange that will contrast with the water. Less than 1/2 inch in diameter will be hard for the victim to hold to, 5/8 inch would be better, and 3/4 inch really good. In sizing, however, you need to reach some happy medium between bulk, weight, and use. Most of the rescue ropes you'll see will fall in the 7/16- to 5/8-inch size.

There is no perfect rescue rope but, in my opinion, ropes of woven, hollow-core, polypropylene are as near as you'll come to one. They float, don't absorb water, are strong, and are readily available in easily seen colors. Their one disadvantage is their light weight, which makes them harder to throw accurately, especially in a wind. A nylon rope is heavier and throws well but lacks some of the other qualifications.

Whatever the material of your rope, the ends should be fixed so they won't fray or ravel. With polypropylene or nylon this is a simple matter of fusing the cut strands together with heat such as a match. In fact many stores selling such ropes by the foot have a machine that fuses the material as it cuts it.

The photos show how to work the ends of natural fiber ropes to stop their unraveling. A length of 50 to 60 feet has proven to be a practical compromise between what can be handled and what is most often needed.

"Frapping" the ends of a natural fiber rope.

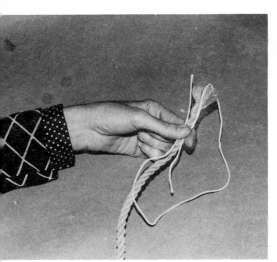 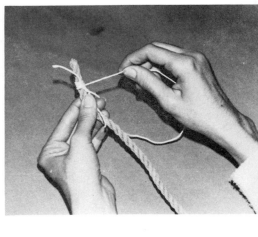

Left: Use a piece of cord or twine about 18 inches long. Make a loop so the ends of the twine are pointing in opposite directions. Right: Wrap until the whipping is as wide as the rope is thick.

 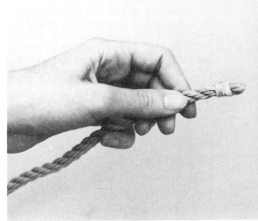

Left: Pull the loose ends until they tighten and cut off the left over whipping. Right: Trim the rope off near the whipping.

What happens if you *don't* fix the ends!

Knots, Knobs, and Floats

A rescue rope should have no knots or any "handy" balls, floats, loops or whatnots anywhere on it—including the "grabbing" end. Knots will weaken the rope but, more importantly, any protuberance that is intended to help the victim hold on better forces you to orient the rope when you're coiling it for throwing—a few more seconds that might make the difference in a successful throw or a miss. Of even greater importance is the likelihood of the protuberance or loop getting caught on an obstruction in the water, either preventing you from hauling the rope back in or forcing you to take valuable time trying to work it loose. Obviously if this happens you have already thrown at a victim and missed and are trying to get ready for another throw at someone else, or you have the victim clinging to the rope but have to let him work himself in—which may not be easy in swift current.

Availability

A rescue rope has to be along on a trip—it does no good stored at home. This is one of the reasons for the selection of size and length mentioned before. If a rescue rope is too big, bulky, and heavy, the tendency will be to leave it behind and

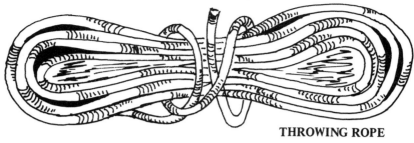

CLOVE HITCH

THROWING ROPE

Tying up the rescue rope.

hope you don't need it.

When the rope is in the canoe, carry it coiled and accessible, ready for use. You may not have time to straighten it out on the bank. A good method of coiling for carrying is shown in the photographs. Use one end of the rope to tie a clove hitch around the coils. Ropes will get twists worked into them in use and should be "shaken out" to remove these twists before they are coiled. To do this, throw the rope out full length and "whip" it up and down to straighten it out. Then, as you coil it up, let it slide through your pulling hand. You'll probably see the rope turning as the twists unwind.

The rope coiled for storage or carrying and tied with a clove hitch. An easy way to coil it is to loop it around the hand and elbow.

There are several opinions as to where a rope should be carried in a line of canoes—by the leader, by the sweep, or somewhere in between. All have their merits. The important thing is to have a rope along on a trip and to have someone and a rope (or several someones and ropes) along stationed below or at critical points on the shore by any place you think it might be needed—*before* the first boat goes down. This is easily done when you stop to scout the rapid.

Carrying the rescue rope in the canoe. Note the easily untied bowknot.

355

Care and Storage

Rescue ropes should be taken care of and reserved for this use only. Shake them out, coil them neatly, and store them in a cool, dry, dark area as constant exposure to sunlight, heat, and humidity can take their toll no matter what material the rope is made of. If they're dirty and muddy, hose them down and hang them up to dry before coiling.

THE MECHANICS

Two basic things are of great importance before throwing a rescue rope. First—don't throw it *away,* make sure that one end stays with you. Either hand the end to someone else and let him hold it, or drop one end on the ground and step on it. Make sure your footing is firm and that you're really standing on the *rope.* Sometimes it will drop down in a crevice or depression and your foot will be straddling it without actually having any pressure on the rope. Once you have a firm foothold, then don't forget and step off it. When you throw the rope, you should hang on to the last loop over your hand anyway, but you may forget this. Do *not tie* the rope to yourself or anyone else as you may be jerked into the water and take the rope with you (a good way to drown if it becomes entangled on something). Neither should you tie it to any fixed object such as a rock or tree as you may have to shift your location for an effective throw.

The second important thing before throwing is that the rope must be neatly coiled so that it will *uncoil* smoothly as it flies through the air. Granted, you may be in a hurry, but if the rope tangles it may not reach the victim. A sudden snarl at the end also prevents the flowing throw that is important for accurate aiming. In either case, the chances are that you have missed and might as well not have thrown at all.

Getting Ready

The following instructions are given for a right-handed person. Obviously you reverse them if you're left-handed. Shake the rope out, and let a foot or two lie on the ground by you. Plant your left foot solidly on this piece about 12 inches from the end. Hold your left hand palm up, then, pulling on the long end of the rope with your right hand, neatly loop the rope over your upturned left palm in side-by-side loops. You may need to give the rope a little twist with your right hand as you pull it in and lay it in your left hand. This will remove its tendency to cross loop. The direction and amount of your twist will depend on your rope, and only practice will show you this.

The throw.

A. Basic coiling of the rope in the hand.

The coils should be open and free hanging and of about equal length. The length should be 2 to about 3½ feet long, depending on your height and the throwing conditions. After some practice you'll find out what you can handle. When you get through coiling the *entire* length it should look similar to photograph "A." Obviously you have to make allowances for hand length—not everybody can hold 50 feet of coiled rope in one hand! The important—*very important*—point is that the coils not be crossed—they must be side by side. Crossed coils will cause tangles. Photograph "B" shows this crossing, so you'll know what to avoid.

B. Crossed coils—a sure way to a tangle.

Now, split the coils, putting half of them in your right hand and being careful not to cross coils in either hand doing this. Check to see that only a single smooth curve of rope runs between the coils in your two hands. Two loops means a cross somewhere.

You're now ready to throw, and everything should look something like that shown in photograph "C"—foot holding down one end of the rope, half the coils in each hand, all loops

C. The rope ready to throw.

over your hands side by side, and a single loop between the two sections of coils. All of this may sound lengthy and complicated, but once you do it a few times you'll find it's all very simple and will become an automatic procedure that takes only about 15 seconds.

The Throw

The actual throw is difficult to describe. It's a natural motion to some, while others find it very awkward and hard to grasp. Nonetheless, here's how it's done. It's basically a sideways or underhanded *slinging* motion in which the right hand does both the tossing and the aiming. The throw is made with a smooth, full swing of the right arm aided by a little simultaneous pivoting of the body. The coils in the right hand are released by opening the hand at the peak of the swing (or as determined by your aiming) and letting the entire group of coils slip smoothly out of your palm. These coils will begin opening up immediately, and their momentum will pull the coils on the left palm off loop at a time. Thus, the whole rope is tossed through the air, uncoiling itself as it stretches toward the target.

359

D. Throwing position.

Photographs "D" and "E" illustrate this. In "D" the rope is ready to be thrown. Note the twisted position of the thrower's body and the location of the hands and coils. There is no reason to look at the rope at this stage, so the thrower's eyes are fixed on the aiming point—the rescuee—in an actual rescue.

E. The throw.

Photograph "E" shows the rope just as it leaves the right hand. Again note the position of the body and arms—the result of a smooth, coordinated motion of the body and arms that will result in a good throw.

361

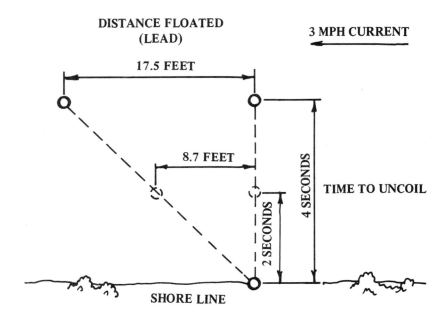

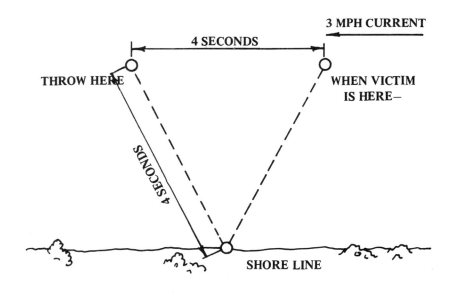

"Lead" in throwing a rescue rope.

Aiming

A throw, no matter how good, is useless unless it hits within reach of its target. Ideally, the rope should land right across the rescuee's chest—assuming that he's floating in the approved face-up, feet-downstream position. If he's in some fixed position such as stranded on a rock, then the rope should land by him or where he can catch or reach it.

Aiming at a stationary target is easy, but a moving one (such as a floating person) requires a little more thought. It takes a few seconds for the rescue rope to uncoil and reach its target. In that few seconds, a floating victim will have been swept downstream several feet or several yards, depending on the swiftness of the current. This movement may surprise you. In a 5-mph current, for example, if it takes the rope only 5 *seconds* to uncoil and land, the victim will have drifted downstream nearly 22 feet. Even in a 2-mph current, he will have traveled about 9 feet. Obviously then, you can't throw the rope directly at him because he just won't be there when it arrives.

To get the rope to the right place you have to "lead" the target, throw the rope at the downstream location where the victim will be when the rope lands. The amount of "lead" depends on the swiftness of the victim's movement and how far away he is, as you can tell from the examples given and the chart. The faster his movement and the longer the distance, the greater the "lead" must be. Obviously this is a matter of judgment and practice.

Belaying

Once a moving victim grabs the rope and the slack comes out of it, be prepared for a sudden jerk and a strong pull. If you're *not* ready you could easily be yanked right into the water. The easiest way to prevent this is to have several other well-braced people hanging on to *your* end of the rope with you. In the same vein, someone else can hold onto your waist, someone to his, etc. However, this is not as good a way since it's hard for people to stand close together on an uneven surface and all get braced together.

If it's up to you to take the shock, then do it mountain-climbing style with a belay. Hanging on to the rope with your left hand, loop *your* end of it around behind your back at or

363

F. The belay.

slightly below the belt line, and hold the part toward the victim in position with the right hand. Do this immediately after the rope is caught by the victim and before the rope is pulled tight. Now sit down (rapidly) and brace your feet (both if possible) against some strong protuberance such as a rock or tree root that you have selected *before* you threw the rope. Keep your knees flexed, your center of gravity low, and very important— brace with your body in as direct a line as possible with the rope and the pull. The strongest position will be with the rope run straight out between your knees. If the victim's pull is off at an angle to your belay, he may topple you over sideways and pull you in with him. Photograph "F" shows the belaying position.

Hauling Them In

It's tough to pull somebody in by hand-over-handing the rope in across the current, and it's almost impossible for the victim to pull himself in—he's hard put to just hang on against the pressure of the current. It's a strain on you and him. It's feasible, of course, to reel him in, and you may have to do it sometimes. But if you have a choice, it's a lot easier on both of you to just let the rope swing around in a big arc until the victim is in an eddy up against the shore, at the rescue boat, or wherever safety lies.

What To Expect If You're on the River End of the Rope

First of all, expect a big jerk (no pun intended) and next a plunge under the surface. You'll pop back up, but if you're floating on your stomach, you'll get a steady wave of water in your face until you reach an eddy. It's best to turn on your side, better to face slightly upward. Try to keep your feet up and just skid along the surface of the water. You'll find there is a lot of pressure on you trying to pull your grip loose. DON'T loop the rope around your wrist or hand even if you have time. The pressure will hurt—just get a good, firm grip with both hands and hang on.

OTHER USES

Rescue ropes are useful things to have on a trip. Although their primary purpose is to rescue people, they are often equally handy for helping to get pinned canoes off obstructions. Less dramatically, they hold up tarps and tents very well and have even been seen tied between two trees with a lot of river-wet clothes hanging on them!

FINALLY

All of this may sound complicated. It's not—but it will take practice to develop rope-throwing skills. The basic movements of coiling and throwing and aiming can well be practiced in your yard. You can even practice "leading" by having someone walk or trot across in front of you at a steady pace.

The river bank is an excellent place to practice if you can get some willing souls to volunteer to float down in their life jackets and be "rescued." On the river bank is *not* a good place to practice if the situation calls for a real rescue. Practice first where mistakes will exact no penalty.

CHAPTER 16
LOGISTICS—GETTING FROM HERE TO THERE
AND BACK AGAIN

The basic logistics of a canoe trip sometimes defeat the most logical mind. This is especially applicable to shuttles, which seem to totally baffle many novice canoeists. The shuttle, however, is only one of many things you should think of in planning a trip.

The following comments apply to *any* trip, whether there are a few canoes along or many. The larger the group, however, the more important some of the items.

PREPARATION AND TRIP PLANS

Any canoe trip deserves more or less. advance planning— less on easy, familiar rivers; more on those not so familiar; and a lot more on new and strange runs. Time spent in getting some basic background information and settling some of the practicalities of the trip will be repaid manyfold when the trip day comes. The more canoes in the group, the more important all this becomes. Not only will you look very foolish if you can't find the take-out road, for example, but hours spent searching for it (or the put-in, or portaging a long rapid, or any number of other things) can mean an unenjoyable race down the river to finish the trip before dark or even cancelling it completely. Obviously there will be more planning involved for a new trip, and this chapter is written with the idea that you are a novice river canoeist and nearly *all* trips are new.

You'll usually have one, two, or three basic sources of information for a new river. If you're lucky you'll have topo maps of the area, a description in a river guide book, and informative comments by fellow canoeists who have run the section before. Often you'll have only one or two of these, sometimes none, and sometimes what you will have will prove to err here and there. Two cardinal points, however, should always be observed: the less information you have, the more cautious you should be; and, a single canoe on a strange river is absolutely and totally unsafe and an open invitation to trouble.

Some good sources of information on canoeing.

BACKGROUND SOURCES

Maps

The very best general map you can get for a river trip is an up-to-date topographic map. Studying one of these that covers the river section you plan to run is a very good beginning.

For those of you unfamiliar with a topographic map, they are very accurate maps that show not only all the roads, houses, lakes, rivers, towns, power lines, etc., on a particular quadrangle (this is topo talk for a map covering a certain area) but also show the elevations and contours (more topo talk for height and shape) of the natural features of the land. Reading a topo takes a little practice and is out of the bounds of this book, but almost any good camping book will give you all the instruction you need.

The usefulness of a topo to a canoeist is manyfold. From a topo you can locate possible put-ins and take-outs, determine your proposed trip length, and spot man-made obstructions in the river such as dams (well, sometimes you can; they don't always show if the map is too old). Determining the difference between the elevation at the put-in and the take-out (given in feet) and dividing this by the number of river miles between these two points gives you the average fall of the river. This is a good indication of the swiftness of the water. A big elevation difference in a short, horizontal distance somewhere along the proposed run means a lot of drop and most probably a run of rapids or even a waterfall.

Contour lines on a topo map connect points with the same elevations. Commonly they are at 20-foot intervals, but this varies with the scale of the map and the range of elevation covered by it. A quadrangle in Florida, for example, might be drawn at 10-foot contours while one in Colorado might have intervals of 50 feet. The point is that the farther apart the contour lines are drawn on a map, the more level is the land. Conversely, as they begin to get closer and closer, the land gets steeper and steeper. The canoeist, by studying them, can determine if his trip will take him through flat, open land; in a valley between mountains; into a gorge or canyon; or anything in between. By combining this general view of the topography along the river with his calculated drop and looking at it in the light of experience, he can gain a pretty good idea of what the overall run is likely to be—rough, flat, and so on.

Topos have two drawbacks. They're not available for all areas, and they're invariably somewhat out of date because of the time it takes to produce one. However, recently released or revised maps will probably differ very little with what you'll find on the ground. About the only changes you're likely to find that affect your ride will be some rerouting of roads around the river. Older topos, however (and there are a lot of 20- to 40-year-old ones around that are still the latest available), may only barely resemble today's real world. You will find them useful for checking the general terrain and direction on the river, for rough mileages, and for river drop (provided no dams have been built), but you won't be able to rely on put-ins, take-outs, or much of anything else. Sometimes you'll even find that the river bed has changed here and there since the map was made, and of course, you may discover that part of your river is now a lake.

If topos are not available, there are many other map sources that you can search out. Some of these are listed in the back of this book. Forest Service maps are good, and so are some county maps. In many areas where the area itself or the local river is used extensively for recreation you'll find accurate, specialized maps available. Some of these will be nearly as useful as a topo except for determining the general topography and the fall of the river. The point is that a study of the best available map of the area may save you time, effort, and a frayed temper later.

Guide Books

Guide books to rivers are another source of information. You'll also find a list of some of these near the end of this book. Some river guide books are good, written for canoeing, and contain the information a canoeist needs. Others tell you little more than what you could learn from a map. A good one will tell you the location of put-ins and take-outs, what these points are like for entry into or exit from the river, and any difficulties likely to be encountered on the roads to them. They'll also tell you trip distance, note hazards in the river, describe what skill level is required for that run, and give you an idea of how to judge water level because shoals, rapids, and even navigability depend so much on this. A really good guide book will have maps of all or some of the rivers showing the natural and man-made obstructions or, barring a map of the whole run, will have sketches and explanations concerning the parts requiring more skill or having particular hazards.

Obviously river guide books are not available for every little stream everywhere. An amazing number of them are on the market, however, and there just might be one covering *your* particular river that will answer many of your questions.

Personal Information

Your final source of background information could be from others who have run the river. But— know your source and adjust what you hear accordingly. If you're a novice and an expert canoeist is describing a run to you, bear in mind that classes of rapids, heights of drops, and general difficulty tend to decrease as experience increases. What may be very simple to him may prove to be more than you're ready for just yet.

369

Remember, too, that new canoeists (and old ones) get their rivers mixed occasionally.

ANOTHER SOURCE OF RIVER INFORMATION
— BUT KNOW YOUR SOURCE!

Local sources, people who live on or near the river, are often the worst possible sources you can find. Many are familiar with the river only as far as they can see it from their porch or favorite fishing hole but, most of all, they don't look at it from a canoeing standpoint. As an example of this, I once inquired of a local fisherman if he had ever floated a particular stretch of river near his home. When he said he had, I asked if there were any drops or rough places in it. No, he replied, he often float-

370

fished it in a flat-bottomed boat, just drifting backwards down the river all day. Thus reassured, I went ahead and ran it. To this day I wonder how that man failed to notice the eight-foot waterfall that he drifted over backwards!

Personal Examination

This is the best way to check out a new run and settle which access points to use. It's better done before the actual trip. Gather up what information you can beforehand; then get out and drive the roads, locate the various put-ins and take-outs, examine the river from whatever access points are available, and determine for yourself the feasibility of a particular run. If you are to lead a group, spend whatever time is necessary to pre-run the actual river trip.

PUT-INS AND TAKE-OUTS

All put-ins and take-outs are not created equal. An ideal one will have wide paved roads to it with a lot of good paved parking area big enough to turn around in and a gentle, sloping paved access to the water. You'll rarely find even *one* of these, and if you should locate both a put-in and take-out on the same trip that answers this description, you can count yourself as twice blessed.

At the other end of the scale the access road will be some narrow, twisting, steep, muddy, and rutted road deep in the woods. The actual access point will have room to cram in about half the vehicles present, about 2 feet extra to turn your vehicle in, and a steep, slippery, overgrown, and *long* bank to fight your way up and down. For the sake of the continuance of canoeing, it's fortunate that many access points fall somewhere in between the best and the worst!

Many put-ins and take-outs will be at some public access point such as a bridge over the river. Parking is often a problem at these places as the shoulder may narrow as it approaches the bridge. Steepness of access to the water may also dictate a change of location. You should try to adjust your ride length to fit the best possible access points. Sometimes this is just a mat-ter of moving up or down the river one bridge or road to gain at least one good access point; sometimes it's impossible to adjust, and you will have to live with what you have.

You're always going to be faced with some runs that are tough at one or both ends and just can't be practically worked out any other way. However, if you do have a choice of which end of a trip to make the good access, choose the take-out. A bad one at the end of a long trip when you're tired is a terrible thing to face.

A typical put-in road. In fact, a lot better than some.

372

Road Conditions

The road in to your chosen put-in and take-out may affect your use of these access points. One of your sources of information should give you an idea of what these roads are like. Unless this source is really up-to-date, however, you may find the roads different from your sources' description. Dirt roads may have become gravel, have been paved, or become overgrown and abandoned, or rerouted; property may have been fenced off, bridges may have fallen down, and all kinds of changes may have been made.

Ruts, steepness, and narrowness and the effect of rain, ice or snow, particularly on dirt roads, should all be considered. Could a passenger car make it? Would it take a pick-up truck, or could only a four-wheel drive vehicle get in and out? If it *does* rain, could you drive back out at the end of the day? If you're running a group ride this becomes particularly important because of the different types of vehicles involved.

Parking, Unloading, and Turn-around Space

Put-ins and take-outs need some parking space because you'll have to leave vehicles at both ends for your shuttle. The number of cars left at which end and the mechanics of your shuttle will have to be adjusted by the parking space available at these two points. Adequate parking and unloading space also helps ease the job of loading and unloading canoes and equipment.

Whenever you park don't forget the twin considerations of safety and common courtesy. Obey whatever parking signs are around. Parking on the shoulder near a bridge may be illegal where you are, for example. If you do park on a shoulder, pull as far off the road as you can; if you park on a little-used road out in the woods, don't block it or park *in* it unless you're at its very end. Leave room for other people to pull in and turn around. When unloading on the shoulder of a highway watch out for traffic on the road. Remember, you're as much of a hazard to them as they are to you.

Driving in and out from a river access point is much simpler if you can just drive on around any other vehicles after you've loaded or unloaded. This is no problem with a through road such as at a bridge, but on a dead end access it can really create a jam if there is limited space at the end of the road. Always try to pull over and park out of the way enough so that whatever space is available for turn around can be used for this purpose.

Some access points will have none of this turn-around space, and you'll have to back out the way you came in or else back in to start with. This is all right if only one or two cars are involved or even with a large group that is arriving and leaving together, although the group situation will require a little patience as those who parked first will have to wait until later arrivals move in order to get out. The drawback to an access point with no turn-around space is that one single vehicle not belonging to your ride can pull in while you're on your trip and block the access point completely.

Permission

Permission is very important from the aspect of being arrested for trespassing, and because of the bad impression of all canoeists given to landowners by canoeists who show lack of respect for their property. Public access points such as highways, bridges, and boat ramps are fine to use as long as you don't block them or create a traffic hazard while loading and unloading or while parked, and they don't usually require any permission or have any restrictions on their use. Private access points such as campgrounds may require a fee, but the fee is your permission.

Common sense should dictate when permission is needed. Obviously few canoeists will seek to find the owner of a patch of woods on a river located deep in a sparsely settled area. This is a matter where each situation demands its own solutions *unless* you have to drive through gates or fields or yards or cross new or good-condition fences to get to the remote spot. If so it would be best from both a legal and ethical standpoint either to find the owner or change your access point.

If you ask permission and don't get it, then remain polite and go elsewhere. After all, it is their property and *their* right to deny you access.

If you get permission to cross or use someone's land, be sure to stay in the designated path (if there is one), *securely*

close all gates behind you, stay out of cultivated fields, don't disturb the livestock by horn blowing or chasing them with your vehicle, keep the area free of litter, and make the whole thing as unobtrusive as possible. All of this plus a personal thank you or a thank-you letter to the property owner after the trip is good insurance that you'll be welcomed back.

Portages

Portaging around dams and obstructions in rivers will occasionally get you into the trespassing area. Do it as quickly and quietly as possible. If it's across a landscaped area or a lawn

Portaging around the end of a dam. Note the "dragging" method of carry being used!

try to use an already established path, carry your canoe instead of dragging it, and try not to disturb anything. Obviously if the owner or anyone is standing there watching you, ask their permission to portage first even though it's the only way to go. What you do if they deny you permission is up to you. However, to avoid possible arrest and legal entanglements, I would suggest that you retreat as gracefully as possible and avoid that stretch of river ever afterwards.

THE SHUTTLE

This is the great enigma to many. I have seen some almost unbelievable examples of confusion on shuttle runs. Hopefully this section will clear it all up for you if you don't already know how they work.

Why a Shuttle?

A canoe trip starts at one point (the put-in), and the canoes progress to another point some miles down the river (the take-out). If it were not for the shuttle the paddlers would find themselves at the end of the trip (the take-out) with canoes and equipment, miles away from their vehicles (which are parked at the put-in), and no way of getting back to them. This means hitchhiking back to the put-in (not too practical when you're off out in the woods somewhere), walking to it (may take hours), a long, hard portage with canoe and equipment (just a joke, I wouldn't even consider this one), or arranging for someone to pick you up at the take-out at a designated time.

Apart from the difficulty and trouble of transporting yourself back to the put-in, then driving back to the take-out for your canoe and gear is the question of what to do with your equipment while you're gone. With a group this would be no real problem, but it could be if this is a one- or two-canoe trip. Your companion(s) might be youngsters or women that you wouldn't want to leave alone, and hiding the canoe even if there is somewhere to hide it is not very good insurance that it will be there when you return.

Mechanics of a Shuttle

The answer to all this is to run a shuttle, and here's how it works. First off, a shuttle requires at least two vehicles, so even if you and a partner are going in one canoe you'll still both have to drive. Normally you'll have two shuttle conditions, one for a large group and another where only two or three vehicles and one, two, or three canoes are involved. The key factor is the number of canoes, because three is about the practical limit for one car to carry for any distance.

For this second condition it's usually easier for everyone to meet at the take-out, park and leave all but one vehicle, transfer all the canoes and equipment to that one, then drive it back to the put-in. At the end of the river trip one of the vehicles left parked at the take-out will carry this shuttle driver, his canoe, and his equipment back up to the car at the put-in.

For a large group involving a number of canoes and vehicles, everyone meets at the *put-in*, unloads canoes and equipment, and gets all ready to go down the river. At this point a decision is made based on relative available parking space at the put-in and take-out. If there is adequate parking at the take-out for the vehicles present (the usual case), then all of them are driven to the take-out. *Only the drivers* of these cars go—the rest of the group stays behind with the canoes. At the take-out most of the vehicles are parked and locked, all the drivers get in as few vehicles as possible, go back to the put-in, and start the trip.

If, as sometimes happens, there is a lot of parking space at the put-in but very little at the take-out, the procedure is changed slightly. This is a little more awkward shuttle but occasionally becomes necessary.

Once more everyone meets and unloads at the put-in, but in this case only a few cars are driven to the take-out. All you need to leave there are enough to be able to bring back from the end of the trip all those drivers (once more, drivers only) whose vehicles are being left at the put-in. One or two (or whatever extra vehicles) will have to follow this early shuttle to the take-out to bring the drivers back whose cars are being left at the take-out.

In determining the number of vehicles to be left at the take-out in this situation, bear in mind that those vehicles left there will probably be reloaded with canoe(s), gear, and companions at the end of the trip and thus may have reduced passenger room on the way back to the put-in. One other factor—always try to leave the vehicles with two-canoe racks at the take-out. It cuts down on the back and forth trips if you can load up someone's canoe and all of his gear and carry him back to the put-in. Otherwise, he'll have to drive back to the takeout.

SAFETY

Rules and Skill Levels

Whether your trip consists of one canoe or a flotilla of them, safety should govern every aspect of the ride. You should strictly observe paddler skill and water classification levels and make certain that you don't get overconfident of your ability and thus overmatch yourself. You'll find these various levels described in the appendix of this book. You'll also find the basic whitewater rules that you should believe in, obey, and enforce on all your rides.

Leader-Sweep System

Use the leader-sweep system if a group of canoes is making the trip. The leader leads the trip and is familiar with the river and the effects various water levels will have on it. He knows its hazards and should be a competent canoeist skilled in rescue work. The sweep (the man in the very rear of all the canoes who makes sure no one lags behind him) should be equally competent and skilled. Sweep is often a thankless and lonely task, but it's a vital one. The basic policy is that no one gets ahead of the leader or behind the sweep.

Equipment

Someone on every trip should have a first-aid kit and a throwing rope along. The rope may not be used for its original purpose but could prove to be handy for rescuing a pinned canoe. Life jackets for everyone are a necessity, as are wet suits or extra clothing for cold-weather trips. If an emergency should develop and it's necessary to leave the river, a map of the area could also be vital.

Going Alone

This is covered in another chapter. The novice canoeist shouldn't do it at all.

Support Groups

This is a subject more likely to be encountered in heavy whitewater, but for the novice "heavy" water may be in any Class 2 rapid. Put in its barest form it means don't get into something that you're likely not to be able to get out of by yourself—a situation where it's highly probable that you'll need that help. This, of course, immediately returns to "don't canoe alone" and "don't overestimate your ability." Members of a support group are there to rescue you. They should be skilled canoeists, competent and knowledgeable in rescue techniques and with adequate throw ropes and boats stationed where they can be of the most use to you.

New And Strange Rivers

Every river and section of river will be new to you the first time you run it. The best and safest way is always to make your first trip with someone who has run it before. If there is no one around or that you know of who has done this, however, and you're doing it yourself, then a few remarks might be in order.

First off, gather what background information you can, and examine the section of the river you're going to run from all the access points you can. Don't overrate your ability, and don't go alone. Strictly observe all the recommended safety precautions and rules (see the appendix). *Ease* around the inside of bends, and keep looking as far ahead as you can until you're around them. Check the river ahead and on the sides for sharp lines that might indicate a drop, and listen to the river for the noises of shoals and rapids ahead. Finally, don't run a river when it's flooded. In the winter be particularly aware of cold-water hazards and cautious of high, swift water, and be doubly safety conscious.

MECHANICS

Length of a Ride

Having to race down a river to finish a ride on time is no fun. Neither is being caught out on a river after dark and having to "listen" your way down through shoals. This latter course can also be hazardous and shouldn't be attempted anyway. Consideration of some of the things affecting the time it takes to run a given trip will help avoid these unpleasant events.

Several factors will influence this time and therefore the length of a ride. First and foremost is the amount of daylight you have to run it in—obviously less on a short winter day or where there is a long, time-consuming shuttle. Some of this can be offset by starting earlier, even running your shuttle before dawn, but you still only have so many hours of light left.

Another factor is the type of water, its speed, and its obstructions. Fast, open water makes a fast trip and slow, open water a slow one. Shallow water may be fast or slow but if full of shoals, bars, and rapids may require a lot of path-finding that uses up time. A tough trip, one with a lot of rapids even with (or because of) high water volume, may be slow due to having to scout rapids or rescue boats. A trip requiring a lot of maneuvering and exertion may seem to go fast but also tires you faster and might well be shortened. Trips with rapids, shoals, and other obstructions may have bottlenecks through which only one or a few canoes can go at a time. With a large group this can be a very slow process.

The final major factors are the number of people on a ride, their skill level, and their endurance level. To some canoeists a 12-mile trip on flat water is like paddling the Atlantic; others can clip off 20 miles a day and think little of it. Some people who own canoes will be unable to negotiate the most elementary shoal without hanging on every rock in it, and some will grind along and get there but at an impossibly slow pace for the time you have for the trip. The larger the group the more varied will be the paddlers and (usually) the slower the overall trip.

All of this has to be considered in ride length. If everyone along is equally skilled (a rare occurrence), a big group will still be somewhat slower than a ride with only a few canoes.

Lunch Spots and Stops

Lunch spots are covered pretty well under the "Trip Leader's Guide" in the appendix, but I want to point out that in addition to being a refueling station for tired canoeists, they also serve other purposes. Chief of these is the adjustment of a time schedule—if you're running late, lunch may be short; if you're ahead of time, then a leisurely lunch can be enjoyed. Lunch spots are good places to just sit and talk and watch the river flow by. In the summer the selection of a good swimming area will add to the enjoyment.

One sometimes-overlooked factor on lunch stops, particularly on group rides, is that they usually *don't* occur at the halfway point of the trip unless you eat a late lunch. Normally by the time a shuttle has been run in the morning and you've paddled about two-fifths of the trip, your stomach and your watch will begin to tell you it's lunchtime. So more than half the trip is usually paddled after lunch.

381

Another idea for a lunch stop.

Toilet Facilities

On a mixed ride the standard canoeing rule is that women go upstream, men go downstream. The only explanation I have ever heard for this is that any ferocious beasts on the upstream shore have been scared away by the approach of the canoes. The women, therefore, get to go in this safe direction while the male canoeists must chance being torn, mutilated, and possibly devoured by whatever lurks in the bushes downstream.

If there happens to be only one possible direction in which to go, then all will have to take turns. This normally never creates any privacy problem if you keep your eyes open as to who's in the bushes and who isn't!

Toilet visits on canoe rides are generally made at the lunch stop, and the "toilet" usually consists of whatever trees or bushes are nearby. Obviously then, a lunch stop on a barren plain is ill advised if it's at all avoidable. Standard camping sanitation rules should always be followed, and if you don't know what they are, then I suggest you get a good backpacking book and learn. Chief rule—leave no evidence of your visit. To do so is not only thoroughly unhygienic but thoroughly disgusting and a perfect sign of the character of the offender.

VANDALISM

Unfortunately I have no helpful advice on this subject. In some areas it's likely to be a problem, and in others it's not. There is a steady debate over whether to park your vehicle in public view or to try to hide it. The first situation attracts attention to the car, but being in the view of passing traffic it may be less likely to be vandalized. In the other situation it is less likely to be noticed, but if it is you've successfully hidden the vandals at work. I don't know which is better. Probably your best protection is that a potential vandal doesn't know where you are or when you might reappear, but then it doesn't take long to strip a vehicle either!

Don't ask for trouble by leaving anything valuable lying in sight within your vehicle. Take your canoe racks off, and lock them in your trunk or elsewhere inside and, of course, don't forget to lock the whole vehicle up tight.

COURTESY

Canoeing courtesy has many aspects and applies equally to the shore and on the river. One facet is respect for private property and those who pass down the river trails behind you. If a few canoeists litter, fail to get permission to use private property, insult property owners, antagonize local residents, bother fishermen, and the like, then it's not going to be long before all canoeists are unwelcome in the vicinity. This can lead to vandalism of parked shuttle vehicles and unpleasant confrontations with local folks. It is a purely selfish attitude to think that your trip is fine—let the next guy worry about his! We're all canoeists or kayakers together—lumped into one big basket as far as the public is concerned. Remember, you may suffer from the attitude and actions of the group that preceded *you* down the river, too!

Another factor is the image any canoeist gives of *all* canoeists. Often it takes only one thoughtless or malicious action to give a bad general impression of any sport.

Still another aspect is courtesy on a group shuttle—specifically the returning of the shuttle drivers, their boats, and their equipment to the put-in after the ride. These drivers, remember,

383

are the ones who, at the morning shuttle to the take-out, pile everybody in their car and take them back to the put-in, which means that at the end of the ride *their* cars are still miles away up the river. It's disconcerting to these folks to have to run around and beg a ride. So in this case, it's the nice thing to do to hunt them up and ask if you can take them back to their cars. Some people do this anyway, but I've seen and heard of numerous cases where the shuttle driver got a brusque "NO" when he asked for a ride back. This usually has the effect that on the next ride, this particular guy won't even consider bringing a carload of people back to the put-in. So even if you're not asked for a ride but are going back to the put-in or to the campground anyway, yell out and ask if anyone needs a ride. Once more, remember that you may be out hunting one yourself on some future trip.

Another form of discourtesy is crowding on a river, cutting in front of someone or forcing them out of their path because they have to dodge you. The "one in a rapid" rule should always be observed to avoid incidents where another canoeist just can't wait and goes busting down through a shoal or rapid when another boat is still in it. This is not bad if there are two separate paths; it's when there is only one path that trouble can happen, especially if the second boat overtakes the first one. The first boat may be concentrating on what he's doing and not realize another boat is there until it looms up beside him or, worse, hits him. The same thing applies at the head of a rapid. The river isn't going to get up and move, so there's no big hurry and therefore no necessity for a traffic jam at the top. Yet you see it sometimes. Why not drop back and let somebody else go first?

If you're practicing a maneuver, wait until the area is clear of boats before you start. And—from the opposite point of view, don't get in the way of someone who is obviously working at some maneuver or technique. After you make an eddy turn, move over (if there's room) so someone else can turn in. On peel offs, be sure the river is clear before you start—don't pull out in front of an oncoming boat.

These are just a few examples of courtesy, but the idea is there. Basically, just remember that there are usually other folks and boats on the river, and they have as much right to be there as do you. They may not be gentlemanly in their behavior, but you don't have to compound the injury. After all, we all know that we're the nice guys—it's those nuts in the other boats we have to watch out for!

LITTER

Don't bury it, don't hide it, don't leave any traces at all of your having been on the river or the bank. If anything, leave it cleaner than when you came. Remember that cigarette filters, aluminum foil or cans, plastic, and glass just stay there for who knows how long. Tin cans *will* eventually rust but are unsightly on shore and dangerous on the bottom of the river. If you burn your trash or build a fire to warm up by on a winter trip, then observe all the safety precautions with your fire, make sure it's dead out before you leave, and eradicate all signs of its having been there. Take a plastic garbage bag and tie along on your trip with you, and carry out all trash and garbage or, if you build a fire, everything that doesn't burn completely.

TRIP LEADER'S GUIDE

The comments in this chapter have been explanations of some of the intricacies involved in a canoe trip. As I've mentioned before, the larger the group, the more complicated a trip becomes and the more important loom the logistics of a ride.

In the appendix of this book you'll find a "Trip Leader's Guide." This guide was issued to all leaders of trips in a large southern canoe club. Although it was written as a reference for large groups, much of what it outlines is just as applicable to small groups of a few canoes. It incorporates basic safety and preparation and transforms much of what this chapter talks about into the realities of a trip. It is, I think, a very good and concise outline to use for any trip.

CHAPTER 17
THE BASIC HOW-TO OF CANOE REPAIR

Sooner or later every river runner comes back from a trip facing the prospect of repairs to his boat. Most of these repairs are relatively simple and inexpensive if you do them yourself. Here are some tips on "do-it-yourself" repairs for the "did-it-yourself" damage. The hopefully helpful information covers aluminum, fiberglass, and ABS materials.

ALUMINUM

Damage to aluminum hulls usually consists of dents, leaks, holes, and bent or broken parts. All of these are minor unless your bent or broken part is a badly kinked keel or gunwale.

Dents

Dents and leaks are very common. Dents are easily fixed if the metal isn't creased. Many can be popped out with the hand or foot, a rubber mallet, or a soft-faced hammer. If the metal is creased or badly stretched, then the hull may still be disfigured after this "popping," but repairing stretched metal is usually more trouble than it's worth.

For creases you should back up (buck) the metal with something such as an automotive body repair dolly in an appropriate size and shape. This is a heavy piece of metal with a smooth face. The face comes in various shapes to fit the curvature of the surface that you're working. In use the dolly is held on the concave side of the dent and the metal tapped with a hammer from the convex side until it fits smoothly against the dolly. If you have no dolly, then any smooth piece of metal or wood can be used. An ax or hatchet head is good or a 2-by-4 block. The block can be roughly shaped for a better job.

When hammering on aluminum with a metal face, don't hit it so hard that you dent and stretch the metal the *other* way. Be careful, too, not to *thin* the aluminum by over-enthusiastic pounding if you're backing it with something. All you'll have is a weakened stretched area that still has a dent in it.

For large dents use a large striking face to distribute the force of the blow. Again, a rubber mallet or a shaped 2-by-4 is good. You can back up these large dents with the ground by laying the canoe over until the outside edges of the dent are resting on the earth.

To sum up, the important things on dent repair are don't stretch the metal more than it already is, and don't make a bump out of a dent by hitting too hard. Take it easy and work the dent out gradually with as little force as possible, using as large a striking face as practical.

Leaks

Small leaks are usually caused by loose or missing rivets. You can tighten loose rivets by bucking the shank (inside the boat) and hitting the head end (outside the boat) with a hammer. This sounds backwards, but it's the right way—more often you'll probably buck the head and beat on the shank.

Replace the rivet if the head is ground down. Drill a hole the same size as the rivet down through the head into the shank of the rivet and pop the head off. Tap the rivet out if it doesn't fall out. Be careful to drill straight and stay inside the metal of the rivet to avoid enlarging the rivet hole.

Rivets

New rivets can be solid aluminum or the waterproof "pop" type. Get rivets the same length as the original ones and, assuming that the hole is not enlarged, the same diameter. Solid rivets can usually be obtained or ordered from your canoe dealer if you don't need oversize ones. You should also be able to buy either solid or pop rivets locally. Check the type of head on your original rivets, and get the same kind. Some boats have a brazier head (sort of a flattened-out roundhead), some a universal head, and some have 100-percent flush heads countersunk in the hull.

If the original rivet hole is wallowed out and the new rivet is a sloppy fit, then don't use it. Drill out for an oversize rivet. There is a specific bit size for a specific rivet size that insures a good fit (if your drill bit is sharp), but, in general, if you drill a

387

COUNTERSUNK   **BRAZIER**   **UNIVERSAL**

Types of standard rivets.

hole .002 to .003 inch larger than the rivet, you'll be close enough. Drill bits of this size are usually sold in *numbered* sizes, such as No. 21, not in decimals. For the correct length of a rivet, add one and one-half times the diameter of the rivet to the total thickness of the material you are riveting.

The head on an oversize rivet may be bigger than the original head. This is fine for any head except the flush kind. If flush, you will probably have to slightly and carefully enlarge the countersunk area to have the same smooth hull finish as before.

Solid rivets are inserted from the outside, bucked squarely from the inside, and pulled up tight by a rivet gun or hammer blows on the *head*.

Don't dimple the metal by inadequate bucking or over-zealous riveting. Just tighten up the rivet by the application of firm, sure pressure, squarely applied.

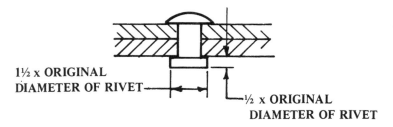

**1½ x ORIGINAL
DIAMETER OF RIVET**

**½ x ORIGINAL
DIAMETER OF RIVET**

The right way to pull up a rivet.

Pop or cherry blind rivets are put in with a "pop-rivet" gun available in cheap or expensive models. The cheap ones will usually do the job unless you have a lot of riveting to do. The

388

rivets are quick and easy to put in and pull up tightly. The gun does it all in one motion—no hammering or bucking. Get the "waterproof" kind (also called self-plugging), or you'll have an inconvenient drain hole in your boat.

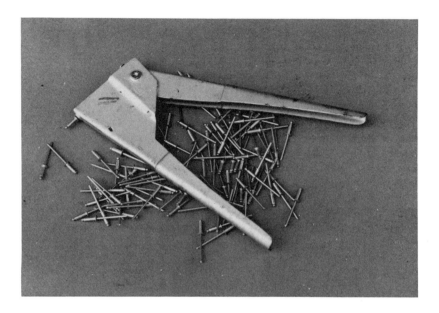

"Pop" or cherry rivets and a pop rivet gun.

Ideally a rivet gun with a head-fitting rivet set should be used. Most probably you'll buck with a hammer head and rivet with one, too. In riveting don't upset the rivet too much; a thin flange will be weak and more likely to work loose. Try for a shank looking like the sketch.

To sum up the riveting—get the right length, diameter, and alloy rivet and the correct head type. Put this in the correct size hole, head outside; buck it from the inside; and rivet from the outside. You should wind up with a pretty good riveting job.

Replacement of Simple Parts

Replacement of broken or bent nonstructural components such as seats and thwarts is simple and obvious. Remove the rivets or bolts holding them, and put the new piece in. If your gunwales are bent in or out, you may have to force them back into position before the new piece will fit.

Seats and thwarts can be bolted in instead of riveted, regardless of their original fastening. Use self-locking or elastic stop nuts on the bolts—they're better than lock washers. Use bolts—not machine screws. Bolts have an unthreaded shank where the load goes; machine screws are threaded all the way up and are therefore weaker. Allow one to two threads to protrude past the end of the nut when it's fully tightened. Be sure to get plated nuts and bolts or you'll quickly have rust stains everywhere you've used them.

Bent Gunwales and Keels

Mildly bent gunwales and keels are rather hard to fix, but the chore of straightening them out is nothing compared to replacing them, so you should make every effort to straighten those you have while still on the boat. Sheer brute strength will play a big part here as both members are designed to maintain the shape and rigidity of the hull and are therefore equally resistant to bending (or straightening).

Making a form out of a 2 by 4 or 2 by 6 shaped to fit the gunwale as it *should be* will pay off here. Use this form as a buck. On the other side use a large piece of heavy metal to distribute the load. If this metal is slightly curved to fit the gunwale, so much the better. Now by applying a big hammer to the metal form you should be able to bend the gunwale back into an approximation of its original shape. Another method of applying pressure is to use an auto jack, but you'll have to make a rig to hold the buck, the jack, and the canoe. If you do this, don't brace your rig on the *opposite* gunwale—you'll probably just bend *it* out of shape.

Keels usually bend up (into the boat). One way to force them back into shape is to make a rig as in the sketch and insert it above the bent place. The 2 by 4 should fit snugly against the hull and under the inboard flange of the gunwale.

The 2 by 4 or 2 by 2 pieces shown under the boat should fit closely along each side of the keel. Their job is to keep the keel an inch or so off the ground.

If your gunwales start bending up when you jack, then

clamp an additional 2 by 4 over the first one, tie around the boat with a strong rope, and tighten the rope by inserting a rod in a loop of it and twisting. You can reverse this whole process if your keel is bent out, but it will take more framing.

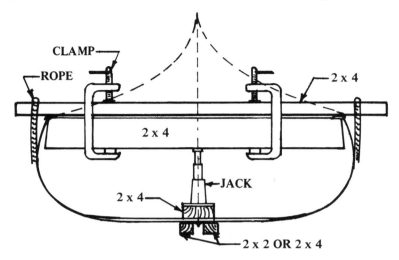

Homemade jig for straightening a keel on an aluminum canoe.

One way to brace a bucked keel.

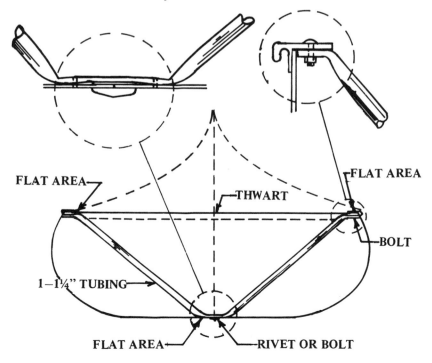

Sometimes the keel or the ribs supporting it are broken or weak, and the keel pops back up into the boat as soon as you put the boat in the water. The other sketch shows a simple way to fix this.

The support is 1- or 1¼-inch aluminum tubing, squeezed flat in the middle, and shaped to fit the keel and ribs. The ends are also squeezed flat. You can bolt or rivet to the gunwales and keel.

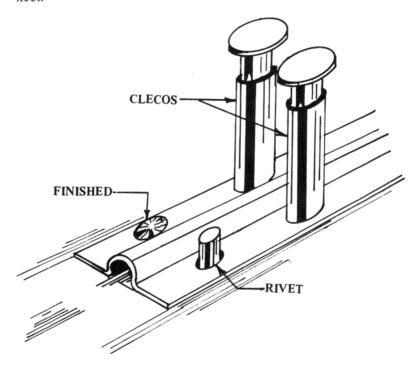

CLECOS

FINISHED

RIVET

The use of clecos.

Replacing Ribs

Replacing a broken rib is easy if the boat isn't bent. Unfortunately this rarely occurs, and you will almost always have difficulty lining up the new factory-drilled rib with the old rivet holes. If the new rib is not predrilled at the factory, it's an easy job. For a predrilled rib, remove the broken rib by drilling out the rivets. Lay the new rib in place, line up a few of the holes, and insert a handy little fastening device called a Cleco in these holes. Continue along until, by shoving and aligning, you have all of the old and new holes lined up and a Cleco in each hole. If you don't have, or can't borrow Clecos, then use nails, punches, or even loose rivets in the holes. The point is to get *all* the holes lined up *before* you start tightening down any rivets. Try not to wallow out the holes while you're doing all this fitting. Now, by substituting a pulled-down rivet one hole at a time for each Cleco, you won't find yourself getting down to the last few holes and finding they don't match.

If your new rib is not predrilled, line it up as evenly as possible with the old rivet holes. Holding it firmly in place, drill into the rib through a few of the old rivet holes just on each side of the keel line. Insert rivets, pull them up tight, and then work your way to each end of the rib by drilling and riveting on alternate sides of the keel.

Replacing Gunwales and Keels

Although this is a lot of work, these parts can be replaced. The use of the Clecos will simplify the job tremendously. I'd also suggest that you borrow or rent a rivet gun with the correct size head. Should you have to replace both keel and gunwales, I'd advise you to go shopping for a new canoe.

Holes

This is another fairly common repair. The basics are simple. Straighten out the area to its original shape as much as possible, use a file to round off any torn edges and sharp corners (these create stress points likely to be weak), and drill small (1/16-inch to 1/8-inch) holes at the end of each split to prevent it splitting further.

You can patch on the inside, outside, or both sides. The double patch will be stronger and is no more trouble except for cutting one extra piece of metal.

Get aluminum of the same alloy as your canoe, if you can. If not, get aluminum that is fairly easy to bend by hand and about the same thickness as that on your boat. DON'T use aluminum that is either extremely soft or brittle.

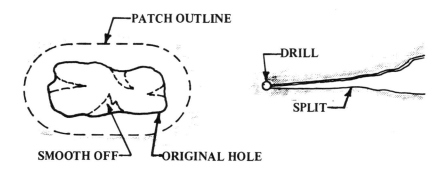

PATCH OUTLINE

DRILL

SPLIT

SMOOTH OFF

ORIGINAL HOLE

Repair of holes in aluminum canoes.

Trace the outline of the hole on the patch metal, and cut the patch about one inch bigger all around than the hole. It's neater looking, easier to install, and stronger if you make the patch some regular shape like a square or a circle. Round off all sharp corners. Use small regular or waterproof pop rivets (about 1/8-inch diameter) and space them about 1/2 inch apart and 1/4 inch in from the outside edge of the patch. It's a good idea, too, to rivet any "tongues" of metal out in the middle of the patch if you're putting on a one-side patch only. This isn't necessary if you're putting on a two-side patch.

Use a good, non-hardening sealer between the patch and the hull of the canoe. Smear it on liberally from the edge of the patch to about ½ inch beyond the rivet line. Wipe the surplus sealant off when the rivets are pulled down.

Position the patch, drill a few holes through the patch and hull, and either put pulled-down rivets or Clecos in as you go to hold it in place. Work regularly around the patch, watching to see that it doesn't start bulging somewhere. Don't let the patch flop loosely against the hull as you drill, or you may find you have some nonaligned holes. You may also wind up with a bulge. "Prefit, then drill" is the rule here for a good job.

Welding

Welding aluminum hulls is not recommended. Usually the welding will ruin the temper of the aluminum of the hull around the weld, and most of us don't have a tempering oven at all, much less one big enough for a canoe. One other factor here—aluminum welding tends toward the expensive, and not every welder can do a satisfactory job of it.

FIBERGLASS

General

Working with fiberglass is easy, and the repair of a fiber-glass boat is relatively simple. However, if you haven't done any fiberglass work before, it's likely to prove to be very messy. With polyester resin it's also rather smelly. Fiberglass work, then, is preferably an outside job or at least, not something to be done inside the house. A well-ventilated area where spills and drippings won't make any difference is best and safest. Ideally, fiberglass work should be done at about 70 degrees F, but adjustments can be made to allow for higher or lower temperatures. Don't work in the direct summer sun; if you're outside, get in the shade of a tree. The sun in conjunction with a hot day will heat up the area to be repaired so much that you'll find it almost impossible to get anything done before the resin gets hard. It's also best not to smoke or have open flames around the repair area. Finally, nothing will remove the resin from your hands once it has set up except scraping or boiling water, and boiling water is a little tough on the skin. Scraping *and* boiling water will remove it from metal tools; nothing removes it from clothes. The resin is also next to impossible to *wipe* off anything even before it sets up except with the aid of acetone or lacquer thinner.

"Fiberglass" work consists of saturating or "wetting down" a cloth-like material with catalyzed resin, removing the excess resin, and holding this wet material in the correct position until it hardens. A nice-looking repair job will also blend into the surrounding area. With care you can make a patch almost invisible.

The catalyst for resin is potent. A few drops does it. Stir the resin well to distribute the catalyst, and don't mix more than you can use immediately. The hotter the working surface, the faster it will set up; the colder it is, the longer it will take. So on cold days use more catalyst, on hot days use less. Don't fiberglass with working surface temperatures below about 50 degrees—your patch won't be as strong.

For any repairs to fiberglass, the area to be repaired should be dry. Remember it takes a while for all the little cracked places to lose their moisture, so don't get in a hurry.

Materials

Depending upon the amount of repair you're doing, you'll need to build up various thicknesses of material. You may use any or all of the following:

Cloth — A loosely woven, silvery material used for a finish coat and for building of thin sections.
Mat — A thicker, pressed-fiber, fuzzy material with no weave to it. Used to build up thickness faster than cloth.
Roving — A very thick, heavy material with coarse weave. Sometimes used for the inside layer of canoes.

Resin is the "glue" that holds fiberglass together. By itself it's a syrupy liquid but when you add catalyst to it, it hardens into a brittle, glassy-looking substance. In the process it also generates heat. Setting up to a hard state takes only about five minutes under ideal conditions, so you can see that it pays to hurry once you've added the catalyst.

Polyester and epoxy are the two basic types of resin. Each has its advantages and disadvantages, and each is available in "repair kit" form. The polyester resin is probably the more common of the two. Some people are allergic to one or both of them, so be cautious with it until you find out if *you* are. The odor of epoxy resin is not objectionable and won't permeate everything around; polyester resin is and will.

Tools

Other things you'll need are an old paint brush, a flexible squeegee of a width to suit your repair work needs (a putty knife or decal squeegee is fine), a can or jar full of acetone or lacquer thinner (to keep your tools in prior to final cleaning), an *old* pair of scissors (fiberglass cloth makes dull ones out of sharp ones very quickly), and a mixing stick or two. For mixing the resin and catalyst, use a wide-mouthed plastic jar or the cut-off bottom of a waxed milk carton. Don't use a glass jar. It's likely to break as the resin gets hot. Depending upon the repair, you may also need some thin cardboard and waxed paper. Finally—wear old clothes and shoes and, if you wish, thin rubber or plastic gloves.

Left: Basic materials for the repair of fiberglass. Right: Materials for aluminum patching.

Repair of Small Punctures

Small holes or gouges in a hull can be repaired by buying an automotive fiberglass repair kit. This is usually two tubes, one with resin and the other with catalyst, or it may be a small can of resin with a tube of catalyst. Bondo and White Knight are two trade names. It's often called "putty" and is actually a putty-like substance. I wouldn't recommend this for anything bigger than about ¼ inch in diameter and even then would suggest a layer of cloth on one or both sides of it. When using this putty, don't smooth out the hole in the hull. Leave it rough so the putty can grip. Do sand down and remove splinters and loose broken pieces on the outer and inner layers, however. To

397

use the putty, follow the directions that come with it to cata-lyze it, then force it into the hole or gouge until it is filled, and push the putty on until it comes out the other side if it's a hole. Back up the hole with your finger, and keep forcing putty in to make sure it's in all the little splintered edges of the break. Even up the putty with the rest of the hull, and let it harden.

When the putty has hardened and cooled, smooth it down and blend it in with the hull with 200-grit wet or dry sandpaper (used wet). Now paint to match your boat, and rub this down with automotive rubbing compound to blend the paint.

Repair of Larger Punctures

For larger holes up to about 1 inch in diameter, clean up the hole as mentioned before and cut up about twice enough small pieces of 7- to 10-ounce cloth to fill the hole. The pieces should be 1/4 inch or less and no particular shape—just scraps. You can also use shredded or chopped material. Thoroughly soak the scraps in just enough uncatalyzed resin to make a thick, gummy mass without any appreciable free resin. White cloth means it's not wet, so stir and mix until you don't see any white.

Use a good-quality auto-paste wax, and coat the outside and inside of the hull for an inch around the hole. You don't have to polish this—just coat it with wax. Tape a patch of waxed paper as tightly as you can over this and a layer of card-board over that. Try to get enough support directly over the hole so that the resin doesn't run out onto the hull. Turn the boat over on its side or in whatever position it needs to be to fill the hole, catalyze the mixture of chopped cloth or mat and resin (be sure to stir it well), and pack it thoroughly down in the hole. You may want to support the wax-paper, cardboard patch with your hand while doing this. Wipe off any surplus on the inside of the hull, and let the patch set up.

When it's hard, use coarse sandpaper (about 80 grit) to knock down any rough spots on the inside of the hull. Don't make it glassy smooth, just even it out with the hull. Remove the wax paper also. Any dribblings of resin outside the hole should pop off the waxed surface with a knife blade. Carefully knock off the rough spots here, too, and even up with the hull.

Remove the wax—make sure it's all off. Now fill in any low spots on either side with bits of catalyzed, resin-soaked cloth until the patch is flush with both sides of the hull.

Cut two neat-looking cloth (not mat or roving) patches about 1 inch bigger in all dimensions than the hole. Position the boat, and one side at a time lay the patch over the hole, paint it with catalyzed resin (use the old paint brush), squeegee it down firmly to the hull and the filled hole, wipe off any surplus resin around the edges of the patch, and let it set up to a "tacky" stage. Remember—wet the cloth down until you see no white spots, and be sure to remove the air bubbles. Repeat this process using a patch about 1 inch larger than the first one.

After it has all set up and cooled down, sand the cloth patches down lightly (about 100-grit wet and dry paper used wet), paint a light coat of catalyzed resin over them, and repeat this process using finer sandpaper each time until the patch is as slick as you want it. Be sure to blend (feather edge) the edges of the patch into the hull. When it suits you, paint and rub until the finish matches the rest of the boat.

Repair of Large Holes

Basically the same procedure is followed as for small holes, except start off by making the wax paper and cardboard backing and the oversize patch. If there's a large "flap" of broken-out material still hanging on, position it back in place. Then seal any holes and around the cracks by the procedures described here, in the preceding section, or under "Cracks" or "Broken Boats." Again wax the hull, but *start* about 1 inch out from the hole this time. Lay the cloth down on the wax paper, paint it with catalyzed resin, squeegee it, and center it over the hole. You have prepositioned the boat so that the patch is lying flat with the cardboard under it toward the ground. It makes no difference which side you patch first, but it will probably be better if you put the initial layer on the inside.

Hold the cloth layer in place until it sets up, then turn the boat over so the patch is flat and you're looking down on it from the top. Sand the edges of this patch down, and after removing the wax on the side of the hull, put two more layers on, each overlapping the preceding one by about one inch all around. Let them harden, then turn the boat over and cut mat (to build up quickly) or layers of cloth to fit inside the hole. Soak all of these in catalyzed resin, and lay them in all at once to flush with the outer hull. Squeegee them down to insure no air bubbles, good layer-to-layer contact, and the removal of excess resin. Let this set up at least to a tacky stage, fill in any depressions with cloth, and apply two layers on the outside— overlapping the hole and each other as did the inside layers.

After it has all set up and cooled, smooth and paint as before. Many canoes have an inside layer of roving, and if you wish you can start from the outside and make *your* final inside patch of this material. If you do this, however, I would cut the roving very carefully to fit the hole and make it flush with the hull instead of overlapping the hole.

Cracks

Pour catalyzed resin into the crack, force the edges back together, and secure them in place until the resin is set up. Then fill any holes with cloth and put a couple of layers of cloth on both sides, even if the crack is not all the way through.

Very Large Holes

Very large holes should have some kind of reinforcment built into the patch. Try to find out what is in the original boat, and use this or something similar. Cut the reinforcement into the solid part of the hull and fiberglass it in, then start building up. Overlap your patches about 2 inches all around when the hole gets bigger than about 6 to 8 inches in diameter.

Broken Boats

Position the pieces back in place, sticking them together with catalyzed resin and supporting them until all patching is done. Start off with an inside patch overlapping the crack about 3 inches, and build up to an overlap of about a foot. Four layers inside and two outside should do the trick; however, don't expect it to be as strong as the original boat unless the hull was very thin.

400

Replacement of Parts

The replacement of parts on a fiberglass boat is about the same as on an aluminum boat, except that you may have to remove some old fiberglass by cutting or grinding to get the old piece out and then to prepare new fiberglass to put the new piece in.

Finally

There are many other ways of repairing fiberglass boats. These outlined here should handle most of your needs. They may not be the best, but they do work. For particular problems or really big jobs, I suggest that you consult one of the several good fiberglass boat-building books around.

ABS

This material is very easy to repair. The repair techniques given are for the better type of construction in which the ABS forms the inner and outer sheathing of a foam core.

A heat gun (blower type) with a 300- to 500-degree range will remove dents. Apply the heat gradually to the area, and the dent will come out. Similarly, any deformed surface can be reshaped by heating it up to 300 degrees F. The only drawback is that if the skin of the material is split, it will tend to split more as the heat is applied.

For holes, cracks and cuts, clean the surface around the damage with a good detergent to remove wax, grease, and dirt. Uniroyal, Inc., the manufacturer of Royalex ABS (one of the best laminates available as of this writing) suggests a final rinse with prep-sol, xylol, or toluol. Now, using 60-80 grit abrasive, sand the area enough to remove all primer and any ragged edges back to the normal surface of the hull.

From here on it's very much like fiberglass work, except use epoxy resin instead of polyester resin. Follow the same procedures of shredded cloth mixed with catalyzed epoxy to fill large holes or gaps, and use fiberglass cloth to cover these holes or cracks or whatever. Uniroyal suggests coating the surface with the epoxy, then precoating the cloth with the epoxy also.

Be sure to roll or squeegee the patch down firmly for good contact between the layers. Finishing-out processes of sanding and painting are the same as for fiberglass.

RIVER REPAIRS

When a crackup occurs on a river you may be miles from your vehicle or any place to take-out, and necessity may force you to paddle on—cracks, holes and all. About the most useful thing you can have along is a small roll or at least a few yards of 2- or 3-inch-wide "duct" tape. This usually silvery-colored tape is used to seal joints in ductwork. It's very tough, very sticky, very useful, and can be found almost anywhere. For even a large crack or hole, just dry off the area where the repair is to be made, and start taping over the place. A single strip will cover a crack, and a small piece torn off will seal a hole. To span a larger hole just overlap the tape, and stick it to itself. It won't have much puncture resistance or mechanical strength, but it will surely leak less than the original place. Duct tape is also good for strengthening cracked paddles or thwarts, taping up torn clothes and shoes, radiator hoses, dislocated shoulders, broken collar bones, etc. It's really great stuff!

If you're without tape, try stuffing your undershirt or extra clothes in the hole, or whittle a wooden plug out of a stick. Even chewing gum will plug up a small hole.

Many bumps in an aluminum canoe can be "jumped" out by taking the boat ashore, positioning it so that it is braced by the ground, and "jumping" on the convex side of the dent with one or both feet (depending on the severity of the dent and the size of the feet).

Beyond this *I* will leave river repair up to your agile imagination. It's amazing what you can come up with when you have to!

CHAPTER 18
PLACES TO GO

At the beginning of this book I advised you to go out and paddle and practice and study. If you've heeded this advice, you should be a pretty fair canoeist by now. Whether you are or not, however, you'll probably be looking for new rivers to conquer anyway. So here's a list of some publications that will tell you "where," now that (hopefully) you know "how"!

The list is by no means complete, and new publications are coming out all the time. For local information I suggest that you consult with a local canoe club. They often know of sources of information that are not nationally published.

Most of the publications below can be bought from or ordered through camping and canoeing equipment dealers. If they're Library of Congress listed, then your local book store will have them listed in their "Books in Print" volumes unless they're brand new. If they are listed, the book store will be glad to order them for you. The American Canoe Association, 4260 E. Evans Ave., Denver, Colorado 80222, also maintains a book service from which you can order many of these publications.

Before embarking on this list and challenging whatever rivers they offer, let me add one final thought: have fun—but be careful. It's a lot nicer for *you* to tell the tales of your river adventures than it is for someone else to tell of the *last* time *they* saw *you*!

And now—happy paddling!

PUBLICATIONS

Adirondack Canoe Waters, Jamieson

Alabama Canoe Rides and Float Trips, Foshee
1,000 miles on Alabama whitewater and flatwater.

Appalachian Waters, Burmeister
Three volumes covering the Delaware, Hudson, and Susquehanna Rivers

Blue Ridge Voyages, Matt and Cecil
Shenandoah River and its South Fork

Blue River Voyages
Three volumes covering Washington, D.C., area in Maryland, Virginia, and West Virginia

Canadian Canoe Routes, Nickels

Canoe Trails of North Central Wisconsin

Canoe Trails of North Eastern Wisconsin

Canoe Trails Through Quetico, Denis

Canoeing in Louisiana

Canoeing Waters of California

Canoeing Whitewater River Guide
Covers Virginia, West Virginia, North Carolina, and Great Smoky Mountains area

Delaware River and Its Tributaries

Down the Wild Rivers, Harris
Various rivers including the West Coast

Exploring the Little Rivers of New Jersey, Cawley

Farmington River and Watershed Guide

Guide to Canoeing Streams of Kentucky
(State of Kentucky, Department of Public Information, Frankfort, Kentucky 40601)

Guide to the Wilderness Waters of the Everglades National Park

Illinois Canoeing Guide

Introduction to Water Trails in America, Colwell

Maryland/Pennsylvania Canoe Trails

Midwest Canoe Livery Guide
Covers midwestern states from Kentucky to Minnesota and
Ohio to Iowa

Missouri Ozark Waterways

New England Canoeing Guide

New England Whitewater River Guide, Gabler

No Horns Blowing
Rivers of Maine

Oregon River Tours, Garren

Portage into the Past, Bolz
The Minnesota-Ontario Boundary Waters Area

Sierra Whitewater
California Rivers

Texas Rivers and Rapids

The Weekender, Thomas
Maine Rivers

Water Trails of Washington

West Coast River Touring Guide, Schwind

West Water River Guides, Belknap
Five volumes covering Grand Canyon, Snake, Dinosaur, Can-
yonlands, and Desolation Canyon areas

Whitewater, Quietwater, Palzer
Rivers of Wisconsin, Upper Michigan, and Northeast Minnesota

Wild Rivers of North America, Jenkinson

Wildwater Touring, Arighi
Rivers of the Northwest

Wildwater West Virginia, Davidson and Burrell

Yukon River Trail Guide, Satterfield

MORE SOURCES

Federal

The U.S. Department of the Interior publishes a catalog called *Guides to Outdoor Recreation Areas and Facilities.* In this are listed many sources of canoeing information available from various agencies. The catalog is divided by geographic areas and by states. You can order it from the U.S. Department of the Interior, Bureau of Outdoor Recreation, Washington, D.C. 20204.

Also, there are regional offices of The Bureau of Outdoor Recreation which may have additional information. The Southeast Region office, for example, publishes *A Bibliography of Canoeing Information for the Southeastern United States.* This handy booklet, in addition to listing many sources not in the general "Guide," also contains a listing of canoe clubs in the Southeast. When you write for the "Guide" ask for the regional office addresses also.

State

Many states have information on their canoeing waters ranging from complete descriptions of their official canoe trails to one-page brochures. You never know until you write and ask! Try the state's Department of Publicity and Information or the nearest thing they have to it. This is usually located in the capital of the state.

Maps

Various kinds of maps are available, some of which you will probably find very useful. Wilderness Sports (Eagle Valley,

New York, 10974) stocks a tremendous supply of general and specific maps of use to the canoeist and outdoorsman. Write for their catalog as they have an unbelievable selection.

Forest Service Maps

These cover a specific national forest and show waterways, roads, and general geological features of that national forest. These are good for locating put-ins and take-outs and are available from the headquarters of the forest in which you're interested.

County Road Maps

These cover one county and show a lot of the little back roads and many of the streams. Sometimes they are very accurate, sometimes not, but they are useful for finding your way around the back roads. These maps are usually available free or for a small charge from the road department at the county seat of the particular county you want. If you have a choice of scales, I recommend 1/2 inch to the mile.

Topographic Maps
(Coast and Geodetic Survey)

These very accurate maps show elevations and features of the land, the waterways, and the roads. They are useful for locating put-ins and take-outs, calculating drop in the river and ride distances, and giving you a good idea of the terrain. These come in various scales, with the 7½-minute series most common. For coast and geodetic survey maps, write for an index of the state in which you're interested. If you live west of the Mississippi River write to Distribution Section, Geological Survey, Federal Center, Denver, Colorado 80225. If you live east of the Mississippi River write to Distribution Center, Geological Survey, 1200 South Eads Street, Arlington, Virginia 22202.

Many libraries have these maps and indexes, and you can use their collection to determine what you want to order. Some utility companies such as TVA also have these maps.

APPENDIX I
USEFUL INFORMATION

In this appendix you will find various pieces of information. Most of these guides and charts are referred to within the main body of the book and will serve to amplify or clarify points brought out in various chapters. As I said, the information is useful, but only if you read it, so don't stop when you get to this page!

Credit must be given to two well-known organizations for some of this information and for their permission to reprint it. The Water Difficulty and Paddler Skill guides are courtesy of The American Whitewater Association, and The Mouth to Mouth Method of Artificial Respiration technique is from the United States Coast Guard.

I. PADDLER SKILL AND WATER DIFFICULTY GUIDELINES

An honest evaluation of your paddling skills can go a long way toward making you a better paddler and keeping you out of trouble on the river. Overrating your skills can lead to dangerous mismatches of yourself and the waters you attempt. The two guides given below are here to help you avoid these mismatches. They were developed over the years by The American Whitewater Association and are generally accepted as the standard ratings for paddler skill and for water difficulty.

Obviously, the water classifications depend upon water level, water volume, your own educated opinion, and your experience, but they do form an excellent general guide. The water ratings given are for the eastern United States and stop at Class 6. In much of the western United States a 10-level system is used.

A. PADDLER SKILL LEVELS

Grade 1. A Beginner. Knows all basic strokes and can handle the boat competently in smooth water.

Grade 2. A Novice. Can use effectively all basic whitewater strokes in the kayak or in both bow and stern of the canoe. Can read water and negotiate rapids with assurance.

Grade 3. An Intermediate. Can negotiate rapids requiring complex sequential maneuvering. Can use eddy turns and basic bow-upstream techniques, is skillful in both bow and stern of double canoe, and single in canoe or kayak, in intermediate rapids.

Grade 4. An Expert. Has proven ability to run difficult rapids in both bow and stern of double canoe, and single in canoe or kayak. Has skill in heavy water and complex rapids.

Grade 5. A Senior Leader. In addition to expert canoeing skills, has wide experience and good judgment for leading trips on any river.

B. INTERNATIONAL SCALE FOR GRADING THE DIFFICULTY OF RIVER-CRUISING ROUTES

Rating	River or Individual Rapids Characteristic	Approx. Minimum Experience Req'd.
Smooth Water		
A	Pools, Lakes, Rivers with velocity under 2 miles per hour	Beginner
B	Rivers, velocity 2-4 mph	Beginner with River Instruction
C	Rivers, velocity above 5 mph (max. paddling speed), may have some sharp bends and/or obstructions.	Instructed and Practiced Beginner

White Water

I   Easy—Sand banks, bends without difficulty, occasional small rapids with waves regular and low. Correct course easy to find, but care is needed with minor obstacles like pebble banks, fallen trees, etc., especially on narrow rivers. River speed less than hard back-paddling speed.

Practiced Beginner

II Medium—Fairly frequent but unobstructed rapids, usually with regular waves, easy eddies, and easy bends. Course generally easy to recognize. River speeds occasionally exceeding hard back-paddling speed.

Intermediate

III Difficult—Maneuvering in rapids necessary. Small falls, large regular waves covering boat. Numerous rapids. Main current may swing under bushes, branches or overhangs. Course not always easily recognizable. Current speed usually less than fast forward-paddling speed.

Experienced

IV Very Difficult—Long, extended stretches of rapids, high, irregular waves with boulders directly in current.

Highly Skilled (several years' experience with organized group)

Difficult broken water, eddies, and abrupt bends. Course often difficult to recognize and inspection from the bank frequently necessary. Swift current. Rough water experience indispensable.

V	Exceedingly Difficult—Long rocky rapids with difficult and completely irregular broken water which must be run head on. Very fast eddies, abrupt bends, and vigorous cross currents. Difficult landings increase hazard. Frequent inspections necessary. Extensive experience necessary.	Team of Experts
VI	Limit of Navigability—All previously mentioned difficulties increased to the limit. Only negotiable at favorable water levels. Cannot be attempted without risk of life.	Team of Experts (taking every precaution)

II. SAFETY CODE

The safety code given below should be followed by *all* boaters on *all* trips. It was developed over a period of time by experts in the canoeing field from their own experiences and that of thousands of other canoeists. This code should become a habit with you, and you should make every effort to acquaint other canoeists with it.

A. PERSONAL PREPAREDNESS AND RESPONSIBILITY

1. NEVER BOAT ALONG. The preferred minimum is three craft.

2. BE A COMPETENT SWIMMER with ability to handle yourself underwater.

3. WEAR YOUR LIFE JACKET wherever upsets may occur. The life jacket must be capable of supporting you face up if you are unconscious. A crash helmet is recommended in rivers of Grade IV and over.

4. HAVE A FRANK KNOWLEDGE OF YOUR BOATING ABILITY, and don't attempt waters beyond this ability.

5. KNOW AND RESPECT RIVER CLASSIFICATION. (See section I of this appendix.)

6. BEWARE OF COLD WATER AND OF WEATHER EXTREMES: dress accordingly. Rubber wet suits or long woolen underwear may be essential for safety as well as comfort.

7. BE SUITABLY PREPARED AND EQUIPPED. Carry a knife, secure your glasses, and equip yourself with such special footgear, skin protection, raincoat, etc., as the situation requires.

8. BE PRACTICED in escape from spray cover, in rescue and self rescue, and in first aid.

9. SUPPORT YOUR LEADER and respect his authority.

B. BOAT PREPAREDNESS AND EQUIPMENT (changes or deletions at the discretion of the leader only)

1. TEST NEW AND UNFAMILIAR EQUIPMENT before undertaking hazardous situations.

2. BE SURE CRAFT IS IN GOOD REPAIR before starting a trip.

3. HAVE A SPARE PADDLE, affixed for immediate use.

4. INSTALL FLOTATION DEVICES, securely fixed and designed to displace from the craft as much water as possible. A minimum of 1 cubic foot at each end is recommended.

5. HAVE BOW AND STERN LINES, optional for kayaks depending on local club regulations. Use 1/4-inch or 3/8-inch diameter and 8- to 15-foot-long rope. Fasten securely to the boat at one end, and other end must release only if tugged. Floats and knots at the ends are not recommended.

6. USE SPRAY COVER WHEREVER REQUIRED. Cover release must be instant and foolproof.

7. CARRY REPAIR KIT, flashlight, map, and compass for wilderness trips; survival gear as necessary.

C. **GROUP EQUIPMENT (The leader may supplement this list at his discretion.)**

1. THROWING LINE, 50 feet to 100 feet of 7/16 inch to 5/8 inch.

2. FIRST-AID KIT with fresh and adequate supplies; waterproof matches.

D. **LEADER'S RESPONSIBILITY**

1. HE MUST HAVE FULL KNOWLEDGE OF THE RIVER. He determines the river classification on the spot and adapts plans to suit.

2. HE DOES NOT ALLOW ANYONE TO PARTICIPATE BEYOND HIS PROVEN ABILITY. Exceptions: (a)

when the trip is an adequately supported training trip, or (b) when difficult stretches can be portaged.

3. HE MUST KNOW WHAT CONDITIONS IN WEATHER, VISIBILITY, AND WATER TO EXPECT; he should instruct the group relative to these conditions and must make decisions on the basis of the related dangers.

4. HIS DECISIONS IN THE INTEREST OF SAFETY ARE FINAL.

5. HE DESIGNATES THE NECESSARY SUPPORT PERSONNEL, and, if appropriate, the order and spacing of boats.

E. ON THE RIVER

1. ALL MUST KNOW GROUP PLANS, ON-RIVER ORGANIZATION, HAZARDS EXPECTED, LOCATION OF SPECIAL EQUIPMENT, SIGNALS TO BE USED.

2. LEAD BOAT KNOWS THE RIVER, SETS THE COURSE, IS NEVER PASSED.

3. REAR-GUARD (SWEEP) IS EQUIPPED AND TRAINED FOR RESCUE, ALWAYS IN REAR.

4. EACH BOAT IS RESPONSIBLE FOR BOAT BEHIND; passes on signals, indicates obstacles, sees it through bad spots.

5. KEEP PARTY COMPACT. Divide into independent teams if party is too big.

F. ON LAKE OR OCEAN

1. DO NOT TRAVEL BEYOND A RETURNABLE DISTANCE FROM SHORE.

2. KNOW THE WEATHER. Conditions can change drastically within minutes. Beware of off-shore winds.

3. SECURE COMPLETE TIDE INFORMATION for trips involving tidal currents.

4. LEAD, REAR GUARD, AND SIDE GUARD BOATS ARE STRONGLY RECOMMENDED to prevent large groups from becoming dangerously spread out.

5. ESKIMO ROLL mastering should be seriously considered by kayakists on tidal or large lake waters. Canoeists should learn to right, empty of water, and board a swamped canoe.

G. IF YOU SPILL

1. BE AWARE OF YOUR RESPONSIBILITY TO ASSIST YOUR PARTNER.

2. HOLD ON TO YOUR BOAT; it has much flotation and is easy for rescuers to spot. Get to the upstream end so the boat cannot crush you on rocks. Follow rescuers' instructions.

3. LEAVE YOUR BOAT IF THIS IMPROVES YOUR SAFETY; your personal safety must come first. If rescue is not imminent and water is numbing cold or worse rapids follow, then strike for the nearest shore.

4. STAY ON THE UPSTREAM END OF YOUR BOAT; otherwise you risk being pinned against obstacles, or, in waves, may swallow water.

5. BE CALM, but don't be complacent.

H. IF OTHERS SPILL

GO AFTER THE BOATER; rescue his boat only if this can be done safely.

III. MOUTH-TO-MOUTH RESUSCITATION

This might prove to be a valuable technique. Like all such techniques it should be learned and practiced *before* the necessity arises for its use.

A. GENERAL

Mouth-to-mouth resuscitation depends solely on air being able to enter and exit from the victim's lungs. The clearing of the air passages (step number B2 below) is most important.

Be sure to move an apparently drowned person cautiously. He may be injured.

Loosen the victim's clothing, and keep him warm. Do not, however, allow this to interrupt the resuscitation efforts.

Start resuscitation immediately. Every moment of delay is serious. If possible, don't wait until you get him to shore: Start while you're towing him to safety if you can stand up in the water; as soon as you get him in the canoe if you're using that method of rescue. Continue resuscitation for at least four hours, until normal breathing is established, or until the victim is pronounced dead by a doctor.

Sometimes a victim will have a temporary recovery of respiration then stop breathing again. He must be watched, and if this does occur, the resuscitation must be resumed at once.

B. TREATMENT

1. Place the unconscious victim on his back, as you must be able to see his face.

2. If there is foreign matter visible at the mouth and throat, clean his mouth with your fingers or a piece of cloth. Check for chewing gum, tobacco, and mucous.

3. Place the victim's head as far back as possible in the "sniffing position" so that his neck is extended, and hold his lower jaw upward so that it juts out (it is most important that the jaw be held in this position).

4. Hold the jaw in this position with one hand and approach the victim's head from his left side.

5. Insert the thumb of your left hand between the victim's teeth, and grasp his lower jaw at the midline.

6. Lift the lower jaw forcefully upward so that the lower teeth are higher than the upper teeth.

7. Hold the jaw in this position as long as the victim is unconscious.

8. Close the victim's nose with your right hand.

9. After taking a deep breath, place your mouth over the victim's mouth, *with airtight contact*. Do not hold the victim's mouth open widely, as you must take the entire mouth of the victim inside your lips.

10. Blow into the victim's mouth, forcefully if an adult and gently if a child.

11. While blowing, watch the victim's chest. When the chest rises, stop blowing and quickly remove your mouth from the victim's mouth.

12. Let the victim exhale passively by the elasticity of his lungs and chest.

13. If the chest does not rise, improve the support of the air passageway, and blow more forcefully.

14. Repeat these inflations 12 to 20 times per minute. One method of timing is to mentally chant, "In goes the good air, out comes the bad air," in a regular rhythm.

IV. TREATMENT FOR SNAKE BITE

A. GENERAL

The basic idea in snake-bite treatment is to slow the spread of venom by retarding the flow of the blood. This is done best by cooling the area of the wound, applying constrictors, and keeping the victim as quiet and still as possible.

Do not use the old "cut and suck" method. In unpracticed hands, particularly in moments of stress, it could do more damage than the bite itself.

Do not use antivenin kits unless you are certain the victim is not allergic to the serum. There is a high incidence of reaction, and to some people the reaction can be worse than the effects of the venom.

Do not use a tourniquet; *do* use a constrictor. A tourniquet *stops* the flow of blood; a constrictor only retards the flow. Tourniquets are dangerous because over-long halting of the blood supply to a limb can do irreparable damage.

Keep the victim quiet and still. Treat him for shock by propping his feet slightly higher than his head (unless he's been struck in the face or neck) and preventing his becoming chilled. Keep the wound horizontal.

Go or send for medical help immediately. If the victim will be hard to get to, the medical help a long time in coming, or you have no suitable first aid for snake bite, take the victim to the medical aid rather than wait. Time may be a greater danger than the exercise.

B. TREATMENT

1. Apply a constrictor above and below the bite.

2. Pack the bitten member in ice or in the cold-pack part of your snake-bite kit. *DO NOT* spray the area or wound with a refrigerant—you could freeze and damage the limb. Do not let water run on the wound; put the ice in a waterproof bag, and put that on the wound.

3. Go or send for help immediately.

Obviously, you may not have any ice along on a canoe trip. If you don't, try to get some at the nearest house. This is a good reason for always knowing where you are on a river and the location of the nearest roads and towns.

APPENDIX II
TRIP LEADER'S GUIDE

GENERAL

For this trip *you*, the trip leader, are the representative and the authority figure of the Canoe Club to those on the ride. *You* are responsible for the safety of the group and for the success of the trip. You are also responsible for the impression that new members or guests get of the club and for the impression that property owners, fishermen, and anyone else not on the trip, but who may see you, get of your club in particular and canoeists in general.

For this reason always remember that, although *you* should enjoy the trip too, the trip leader's primary responsibility for this particular run is to the club and to those members who are on the trip. Your direct responsibility begins when you reach the river bank and ends when you reach the end of the trip and have assured yourself that everybody is capable of making his way back home or to the put-in.

Generally, you will have little trouble regarding the observance of rules on trips. However, enforce the rules on even the mildest of trips—this prepares everyone to automatically obey them when they are *really* required. Safety is the first consideration, behavior next. Read over the AWA whitewater rules. We all operate under the same rules, and any guests or new members on a trip know that the prerequisite for participation in a club function is a willingness to adhere to these rules.

The club's goal is uniformity in the mechanics of the trips. You will possibly have to bend the rules sometimes or circumstances may force a different way of doing things. However, in general try to follow the outlines given in this guide.

You should carry a throw rope (and know how to use it) and a first-aid kit.

MECHANICS OF THE TRIP

A. BEFORE THE TRIP

1. Prerun the trip *immediately before* the trip—preferably the weekend before—so that you are aware of the condi-

tion of the river. If you are thoroughly familiar with this stretch, you don't *have* to prerun it, but if you do not, be sure of your lunch spot, etc.

2. Select a lunch spot large enough for the anticipated group. Bear in mind that this need not be the halfway point of the trip as you usually only paddle two to three hours before noon. Try to select a spot that has easy landing; room to tie up the boats; is level; has easy access; is dry; and is not covered with mosquitos, ticks, and other things liable to detract from the enjoyment. You'll rarely find a place like this, but do the best you can. Try to avoid places where the public congregates.

3. Note any hazards, and be sure to note their approaches so that you'll recognize them on the group trip.

4. Bear in mind on meet, shuttle, and ride start times that it takes a while to get everything going in the morning and that with inexperienced people along it sometimes takes a long time to get them all down the river.

B. AT THE PUT-IN

1. Arrive early and get your own boat, etc., in the water, and get yourself ready to go. Then you can tend to getting everything else expedited.

2. As people arrive, see that they get unloaded and ready to go and move their vehicles out of the way immediately. You'll almost always have some last-minute arrivals, and getting all this done as the members arrive avoids a last-minute rush.

3. Lend a hand. Set a good example of helpfulness. Don't go off and start a conversation and ignore everything that is going on. To keep things moving you'll have to circulate and watch what is happening.

4. Start the shuttle ON TIME. Be sure everybody knows

the shuttle is leaving.

5.   Judge the way to run the shuttle by your knowledge of the put-in, take-out, and parking space. Vary your shuttle plan accordingly.

C. ON THE SHUTTLE

1.   To repeat—make sure everybody knows the shuttle is leaving.

2.   Be sure of the way. If parking permission is required, get it *before* the day of the trip. Be absolutely sure of this permission.

3.   Drive at a relatively slow pace; remember, the cars at the end may have a hard time keeping up.

4.   When you pass an intersection, take a fork at a "Y," stop at a stop sign, get into traffic, or anything else that may disrupt the shuttle line, slow down, watch your mirror, and make *sure* that everybody is there and knows which way to go. This is particularly important at a turn onto a small, relatively unnoticeable road. In other words—don't lose anybody. Remember that you may be the *only one* who knows the way to the take-out.

D. AT THE TAKE-OUT

1.   Make sure you don't block roads or accesses. Park all the vehicles compactly and out of the way.

2.   Make sure that nobody has left anything in his vehicle that he intended to take on the trip.

3.   Remind everyone to lock their vehicles, roll up their windows, and take their keys with them.

E. AT THE PUT-IN IMMEDIATELY BEFORE THE TRIP

1. Get everyone together, and make a short talk about the trip, covering points such as length of ride, type of water, particular hazards, etc.

2. Check to see that everyone has life jackets. Tell them whether or not to wear them.

3. Remind them to tie their equipment in, tie their glasses on if they wear glasses, take spare paddles, and put their wallets in something waterproof. If it is a winter trip, remind them of extra clothes in a waterproof container.

4. Explain the leader-sweep system. In any event, tell them not to precede you or lag behind the sweep and if they *have* to stop to tell the sweep.

5. Appoint a sweep—someone who knows what he is doing. He should have a throw rope, and so should you. Identify the sweep to everyone. Be particularly careful of whom you appoint as sweep if the ride has a lot of rapids. If it has, the sweep should be a good canoeist, experienced in rescue of boats and people.

F. ON THE TRIP

1. Set a pace that will get you down to the put-in in the time allotted, including the lunch stop.

2. Don't race, but don't poke along either. If you have a very quiet section but you know there is a place down the river that will be slow because of rapids, etc., then go a little faster in the easy part so you'll have more time at the harder places.

3. Keep watching behind you; the group will usually trail out a long way. If they trail out *too* far, you may be going too fast. On the other hand, you'll find there will usually be some members who will drag along no matter how slow a pace you set. Use your own judgment, but

don't run off and leave everybody.

4. Don't let people paddle on out in front of you even if they know the river. This sets a bad precedent for those trips when the trip leader knows of some hazard ahead but the others don't.

5. Don't let people paddle off to the side and stop or go off down channels around islands, etc., that put them out of your sight.

6. Generally, you will go through rapids first, then position yourself at the bottom for rescue if needed. Obviously, you only need to do this if you think there is a likelihood of rescue work. But again, remember that what may be easy for you may be very difficult for less-experienced people.

7. When selecting a path through rapids, if you have a choice of an easy and a hard path (or harder), always consider the overall experience of the group. Of course, everyone is free to select his own path, but most of them will probably follow you.

8. If you have time you might stop at a rapid and play in it.

9. If you have a spill in open water, consider using it as an opportunity to demonstrate canoe-over-canoe rescue. Be sure *you* know the *right* way to do it.

10. In rapids—strictly enforce *"one in a rapid at a time."* Point this out *before* you go through. Jamming boats into a rapid is an excellent way to mess up boats and people. Don't let it be done!

11. Use the lunch stop to even out your schedule. If you're ahead of time you might make it longer. If you're running behind you might cut it short—all depending on your knowledge of what lies down river, tempered by

consideration of the experience level of the members on the ride.

G. AT THE END OF THE TRIP

1. Be sure nobody has lost his keys or can't get his car started and that the shuttle people (those whose vehicles are at the put-in) have a way to get themselves, their boats, and equipment back to the put-in. Try to avoid anyone having to go to the put-in to get his car, then coming back to the take-out for his boat, etc.

2. Go home and relax—you've earned it!

APPENDIX III
GLOSSARY OF TERMS

ACCESS POINT — A place from which a river may be viewed or examined. Usually assumed to be one to which you can drive, such as a bridge or a road. An access point is not necessarily suitable for a put-in or take-out.

AFLOAT — The opposite condition to a-sunk. Just a little touch of humor.

BEAM — The width of a canoe measured at its widest point.

BILGE — The rounded section of the lower hull of a canoe extending roughly 6 inches above and below the water line.

BLADE — A part of a paddle. The wide, flat end that goes in the water.

BOW — The front of a canoe. Distinguished by the bow seat being farther from the bow than the stern seat is from the stern.

BRACE — A paddle technique used to steady or right the canoe and as a pivot point for some maneuvers. Low and high braces are the most common.

BROACH — To turn broadside to the current. Commonly used to mean being turned sideways in the trough of a wave so that the canoe is parallel to the waves.

CANOE — A boat intended to be propelled by paddles and of greater length than width, whose bow and stern are higher than the low point of the gunwales and with a relatively flat bottom that rounds into rounded sides. Commonly considered to be open topped and with symmetrical bow and stern.

C1 — A specialized form of totally decked canoe with a cockpit. Very similar in appearance to a kayak except that the bow and stern are higher than the cockpit. Paddled from a

428

kneeling position with a single-ended paddle. The paddler wears a spray skirt to cover and seal between his body and the cockpit edge. "C1" is a one-man version; "C2" is a two-man version with two separate cockpits.

CREST — The foamy, featherlike top part of a wave where it collapses under its own weight.

CROSS — A direction referring to a paddle technique done by crossing the paddle over the boat to the opposite side of that on which the paddler is paddling. Done without changing hand position or grip on the paddle.

CURRENT — The rate of flow of a body of water. Usually taken to mean velocity.

CURRENT DIFFERENTIAL — The difference in current between two parts of the same body of water as between the water just downstream from a rock and that in the main stream.

DEPTH — The minimum height of a canoe measured vertically from the top of the lowest point of the gunwale to the top of the keel inside the boat.

DRAFT — The distance from the water line down to the lowest point of the canoe. Usually considered to be when the canoe is normally loaded.

DRAW — A paddle technique used to pull the boat to the paddle side.

EDDY — Still or slowly moving water, usually behind an obstruction whose downriver velocity is low compared to the main current. Eddies may also have a slight upstream current.

EDDY LINE — The line dividing the main current from an eddy. Generally, the greater the current differential between the eddy and the main current, the more distinct or sharp this line will be. In slow current the line may be indefinite.

EDDY TURN — A maneuver for turning into an eddy from faster-moving water by taking advantage of the current differential.

FERRY — A maneuver for moving sideways across a current by taking advantage of the force of the current.

FERRY, BACK — A method of executing a ferry in which the bow faces downstream and the paddlers backpaddle.

FERRY, FORWARD — A method of executing a ferry in which the bow faces upstream and the paddlers paddle forward.

FREEBOARD — The distance between the lowest point of the gunwale (usually at the center of the canoe) and the water line.

GRIP — A part of a paddle. The end that is held by the upper hand and is opposite the blade end.

GUNWALE — The top part of the top edge of a canoe that extends the full length of the boat on both sides and meets at the bow and stern.

HEAVY (WATER) — A term used to describe large rapids with big waves and souse holes. Very turbulent water and very strong current. Approximately Class IV and above.

HYDRAULIC — A dangerous water condition in which an upstream surface current combines with a partially downstream underwater current to create a rolling force at the base of a fall or obstruction. This force will hold you in the same location and tumble you in its currents rather than letting you drift on out downstream.

KAYAK — A narrow, shallow, totally decked boat similar in appearance to a "C1" canoe (but usually shorter and narrower) and with the bow and stern lower than the cockpit. Paddled from a sitting position with a double-ended paddle. The paddler wears a spray skirt to cover and seal between his body and the cockpit edge. "K1" is a one-man version; "K2" is a two-man version with two separate cockpits.

KEEL — The structural member running down the bottom of the boat from end to end and usually down the center of the bottom. It protects the bottom and provides rigidity. Canoes commonly have lake, shoe (whitewater), or no keels.

KEEL LINE — On canoes with no keel, a reference line taken to be the same location as the location of the keel if the boat had one.

LIFE JACKET — A device that provides extra buoyancy for the swimmer wearing it. It encircles the neck and extends over the upper torso, either over the chest only (yoke type) or over both the chest and back (vest type).

LOWER HAND — The hand holding the throat or just above the throat of the paddle. The hand, therefore, normally closest to the water.

OFF-SIDE — A direction referring to a maneuver done toward the side opposite that on which the paddler is paddling. In off-side maneuvers, paddle sides and hand positions remain the same, but the techniques change.

ON-SIDE — A direction referring to a maneuver done toward the side on which the paddler is paddling.

PADDLE — A device with a flat blade at one end connected by a shaft to a grip at the other end and used to propel and maneuver a canoe. Intended to be held and controlled by the hands alone as opposed to oars which rest in oarlocks attached to the boat

431

PAINTERS — Short lengths of rope attached to the bow and stern of a canoe and normally used for tying it to the shore or down to a vehicle.

PEEL OFF — A maneuver for entering a swifter moving current from an eddy and in which the power of the swifter current is used to turn the canoe downstream.

PFD — Personal flotation device. Any form of device intended to add buoyancy to a floating person. For canoeists, only yoke or jacket types are suitable, although PFD includes seat cushions, life rings, and ski belts.

PORTAGE — A land path around a rapid, dam, fall, or some other obstruction in a river that cannot be run or that you do not wish to run. Also used to describe the act of carrying your canoe and equipment around this part of the river.

PRY — A paddle technique used to move a canoe to the side opposite that on which the paddler is paddling. Prys use the bilge and the side of the canoe as a fulcrum to increase the power of the stroke.

PUSH-AWAY — A paddle technique used for the same purpose as the pry, but in which both arms push the paddle, and the leverage of the side of the canoe is not used. Consequently, a weaker stroke.

PUT-IN — The place on a river where you put your canoe in the water at the beginning of a trip.

RIB — A structural member run laterally across the inside bottom of a canoe. Ribs may be "U"-shaped and run from gunwale to gunwale as in a wooden canoe, may be only across the bottom as in aluminum construction, or concealed in the hull bottom as in some fiberglass canoes.

ROCK GARDEN — A conglomerate of water (usually shallow) and rocks protruding above the surface in roughly equal parts. Used to refer to a place requiring a lot of maneuvering due to the many rock obstructions.

RUDDER (TO) — To trail the blade of the paddle behind and/or to the side of the canoe and use it as a rudder to steer the boat. Used by the stern. Not a river technique except on long, straight, relaxed stretches.

SEAT — A cross member in a canoe used to sit on or prop against while paddling. Most common-length canoes have two seats.

SHAFT — A part of a paddle. The long, slim, round, oval, or flat section connecting the blade and the grip.

SHEER — The amount of upward curve of a canoe's sides along its gunwales from the middle of the canoe to its ends.

SHEER LINE — A line following along the sheer of a canoe.

SHUTTLE — The process of arranging the parking of vehicles at put-ins and take-outs so that you have transportation a-waiting you at the end of a ride.

SOLO — One paddler in a canoe. Normally, the solo paddler sits near the center of the boat.

SOUSE HOLE — A trough or "hole" in the water just down-stream of an obstruction. Usually the first trough in a series of standing waves. Souse holes may hold you in high-volume water flows.

STANDING WAVE — A wave that does not flow and break as an ocean wave does. The water within a standing wave changes, but the wave's formation and location do not.

STEM — A part of a canoe. Often used to mean the bow of a canoe but actually the extreme end of either end where the hull comes together.

STERN — The back of a canoe. Distinguished by the stern seat being closer to the stern than the bow seat is to the bow.

SWEEP — The canoeist assigned to bring up the rear of a canoe ride and whose duty it is to see that all canoeists on that ride remain ahead of him.

TAKE-OUT — The place on a river where you take your canoe out of the water at the end of a trip.

TANDEM — Two paddlers (bow and stern) in one canoe who (hopefully) paddle together.

THROAT — A part of a paddle. The section where the shaft and blade join.

THWART — A lateral brace in a canoe running straight across from gunwale to gunwale.

TRACK — Two uses. One refers to the tendency of a canoe to maintain its initial course when paddled or when subjected to other influences such as wind and waves. Lake keel canoes track better than shoe or no-keel canoes. The other use refers to walking along the shore or wading in the water and towing a canoe up a rapid (or letting it down through one) by the use of ropes called "tracking" lines.

TRAIL — Refers to anything dragging along behind your canoe such as your painter. Also, commonly used to describe letting your paddle or blade ride along in the water either as a brace, as a rudder, or because you're tired!

TRIM — The degree of levelness with the water surface when a loaded canoe is in the water such as bow down or stern down. Trim is adjusted by shifting gear or paddlers.

TROUGH — The depression between two waves.

TUMBLE HOME — The curve of a canoe's sides from its broadest part inward toward the gunwale when viewed from the end. Not all canoes have tumble home.

UPPER HAND — The hand holding the grip of the paddle. The hand, therefore, normally farthest from the water.